CONCRETE CARNIVAL

CONCRETE CARNIVAL

DANNER DARCLEIGHT

THE PERMANENT PRESS
Sag Harbor, NY 11963

"Crewed Up" was first published in *The Kenyon Review*
"Getting Out: Notes from the Road" was first published in *Fourth City: Essays from the prison in America*

For information, address:
  The Permanent Press
  4170 Noyac Road
  Sag Harbor, NY 11963
  www.thepermanentpress.com

Library of Congress Cataloging-in-Publication Data

  Dercleight, Danner, author.
    Concrete carnival / Danner Dercleight.
      pages; cm
    Sag Harbor, NY : Permanent Press, [2016]
    ISBN 978-1-57962-437-8
      1. Dercleight, Danner. 2. Prisoners—United States—Biography.
    3. Authors, American—21st century—Biography. 4. Prisons—
    United States. 5. Prisoners' writings, American. I. Title.

  HV9468.D47 A3 2016
  365'.6092—dc23   2016002729

Printed in the United States of America

For my mom and dad, kind and gifted people.

Author's Note

I have changed names to protect the innocent, the not-so-innocent, and the bashful. I don't live in the land of the free, and prison officials have ways of silencing those who write about what goes on behind the wall.

But the larger reason is I've learned from reading the work of prison writers—contemporaries like Piper Kerman, going back to Jack Henry Abbott and Jean Genet, and further back to Dostoyevsky—and the prison experience is very much standardized across time and geography. There's a tendency to dismiss nefarious goings on as something isolated to one prison or one state—the work of a rogue crew of guards, poor managers, violent gangs, a deteriorating physical plant. The differences that exist are differences of degree, not kind. As Andy Dufresne learned in *The Shawshank Redemption,* the names change, but the rackets stay the same.

Sea to shining sea, prisons are ubiquitous in America. You drive past, giving the walls and razor wire on the horizon barely a thought. If those of us inside are thought of at all, it is as the Other, a homogeneous group lacking all the traces of humanity—fears, loves, disappointments, desires, talents—possessed by those in the world. My aim is to make specific the men and women our culture treats as indistinguishable. I am an American, a prisoner, one of millions, and I write about what it is like to be alive inside the criminal justice system.

The meaning of life must be conceived in terms of the specific meaning of a personal life in a given situation.

—Viktor Frankl

Buy the ticket, take the ride . . . and if it occasionally gets a little heavier than what you had in mind, well . . . maybe chalk it off to forced conscious expansion: Tune in, freak out, get beaten.

—Hunter S. Thompson

ONE

GETTING OUT: NOTES FROM THE ROAD

*What's your road, man?—holyboy road, madman road,
rainbow road, guppy road, any road.
It's an anywhere road for anybody anyhow.*

—JACK KEROUAC

The prison wall stretches like a dark gray band in the van's rearview mirror. As we speed away, the gray line tapers down—in under a minute it's gone, and I've covered more distance than I have in almost a decade.

This is the first time I've been outside of a prison wall in all those years. I'm relieved that the feel of driving hasn't made me throw up farina onto my shackles (a tale of car sickness that I've heard from peers who've gone on medical trips to area hospitals). My handcuffs are tethered to a waist chain (think praying, but at crotch level), the leg irons limit my gait to one-and-a-half foot baby steps. The van's windows are tinted and it's cozy.

The transport officers are a friendly sort, road guys, pros. Gunslingers. They get hazard pay and beaucoup overtime—and everyone likes leaving prison, even guards. Especially guards. The one riding shotgun, M, pushes aside the morning paper and turns to speak to me through the black metal cage. Chuckling, he says, "You really pissed someone off." He's fishing. Like most of the prison's population, he's been fed the tiniest morsels of my story, and is hungry with intrigue. M knows I didn't do anything wrong . . . aside from entering into a relationship with a prominent woman from the community. Something like this happens often enough for the Department to have an unofficial policy in place: flick the inmate to the far end of the state so fast his fucking head spins. Luckily, the powers that be didn't hang a bogus charge on me and ship me out via the Box.

Be that as it may, I'm not going to give either of them something that will anonymously appear in the local rag. It's time for this tale to disappear. I misdirect. "Get this," I tell him, "on my way out the door, I was told never to come back." The pair glance at little old me, shake their heads, and laugh at the absurdity of it all. Darkest pit in the state and I've been eighty-sixed, and barred from returning—admittedly, I'm wearing that with pride.

Two hours ago, I was in the mess hall when an odd hush fell over the place. A guard and a sergeant escorted me back to my cell, where I had forty minutes to pack everything I own—clothes, books, papers, toiletries, canned food, and assorted miscellany—into four duffels. I gave away practically half my cell in order to hew to the four-bag limit. Guards inventoried everything while I stayed moving in a thrumming frenzy of distraction. It's a good thing that Yas was at work—if he were around, we'd both be teary-eyed, brothers being separated. Whit, another close friend, carried the bags downstairs for me and put them in a cart. The effort left his flimsy white state undershirt absolutely drenched with sweat. This I learned when we hugged good-bye, natural, close. He drew the back of his hand across his forehead with a characteristic humble gesture, and fixed me in a melancholy gaze. We'll likely never see each other again—that's what this prison life is all about. Impermanence and loss are offered as a crash course. Walking out the door of the cellblock, I turned back. Oscar and Whit gave me sad waves. Under escort, I pushed the cart with my property through the halls, drinking in the scenery one last time, waving good-bye to confused friends. Passing more than one checkpoint, I overheard a guard pick up a phone and report that I'd just walked by.

The fact is, we're driving away from this beef at fifty miles an hour, blowing the speed limit so they can get me to a depot prison in time for a large transport bus. The trouble is behind me, and I feel good, better than I have in a week. I am on my way to a new home, and taking this show on the road.

The trip ahead of me promises to be sedate motoring through scenic countryside. There'll be a few stops as we spend the night at prisons along the circuitous route. Despite being shackled and under armed guard, I feel an exhilarating sense of freedom traveling through *the world,* sharing the road with citizens.

We crest a large hill and I'm greeted by the slow, waving arms of a cluster of wind turbines. How many times have I stared at the whitish blades from the distance of my window, the sun rising behind them as I sat in bed, penning quixotic paeans to their kinetic beauty. "Wonderful," I realize I just said aloud. P, behind the wheel, glances at me in the rearview. "The wind turbines," I say. "They're beautiful."

We make it to Prison B in just over an hour.[1] Since we're not allowed to travel with watches (or any personal effects), I catch the time where I can—the van's digital display, a hack's wrist as he removes my cuffs. It's just before noon. An inmate porter lugs my four heavy bags of property away to a staging area. I tell the transporters that it was a good ride, and then wish them both well. P tells me that he worked for a time at Prison F, where I'm headed, that it's a shit hole, but that I'm a "smart kid" and will be "fine." I thank him for saying that.

---

1. Allow me to letter the prisons for your convenience. The names would likely mean nothing to you anyway.

They help me out of the van, and flank me as I waddle indoors to the holding pens. Some forms are signed and custody of me is transferred to the locals.

The bull pen is the same one I sat in on my way upstate. Modern construction, heavy turquoise mesh instead of bars. Thick, blond wood benches which haven't been burnt or scratch tagged (we can do minimal damage when we're shackled and lacking toys). A black con with designer frames and a red kufi stands in a corner, speaking sheistily to a Hispanic with perfectly coiffed "waves." We don't acknowledge each other. I sit a few feet away from them. Straightening my back, I close my eyes and take good, deep breaths. Ever since *Silence of the Lambs*, the quiet white guy who doesn't seem to belong in prison can easily pass for someone who'll slip his cuffs and eat your fucking face off. I smile.

The gate opens and a couple more men shuffle in. One has a cast on his leg that goes up to the thigh; he's been shackled creatively to accommodate the crutches. The other is a slight Middle Easterner in his early forties with kind, dark eyes. He vibes "engineering student gone wrong," not "cabbie with a vehicular manslaughter." This man sits next to me and, after a time, asks what prison I've come from.

I've spent most of my time *inside* housed in the better areas of prison, working the better jobs, avoiding the riffraff. My instinct here is to play it cold and aloof. But on the road, we're all in it together, and life can get pretty boring when you give your peers the high hat.

With a smile, I tell him where I've been doing time, and inquire about him. We exchange names and abbreviated bios. Nassim was a med student who crashed and burned into the party scene in the early nineties. When he was twenty-three, I was thirteen, yet we partied at some of the same nightclubs.

Another man is brought into the pen. Small, mocha-skinned, in his late thirties. As soon as the guard walks away, he pulls out several cookies he managed to hide in his pocket.

Sitting alone in the corner, he eats. In my head, I name him "Dusty," because he reminds me of a Dusty I knew in county.

It dawns on me—mainly from seeing men shackled to each other in an adjacent pen—that I'm with the special cases. The Hispanic with the waves in his hair volunteers that he escaped from juvie decades ago. The dude with the crutches can't be shackled to someone because of his limited mobility. Nassim's on the mental health caseload. Who knows what Dusty's deal is. The black kid in the red kufi is a high-ranking member of the Bloods. In describing a ticket he caught last night for a stolen TV in his cell, he mentioned that the hacks doing the search could've written him up for his photos.[2] That and the fire-engine-red kufi badge him as a Blood, and high rank—call that my intuition after being around these guys for so long.

Nassim has the minimal affect of a medicated depressive. He's really pissed at himself for catching another dirty urine and getting kicked out of a medium-security prison. I just listen quietly, letting him work through things. Mainly, he says, he's missing his partner, a smart, compassionate chap named Tom. I first hear "partner" as running-, or crime-partner, a friend he was getting baked with, breaking bread with. And that's when Nassim begins making vague, low-intensity passes at me. I know I'm easy on the eyes, but we're shackled, in a bull pen with other men, destined for different parts of the state. What's he hoping for? I guess it's just flirting. So as to stop Nassim before he gets too hot and bothered, I drop a non sequitur: "Fuckin' crazy, man. Three days ago I was eating a fantastic meal over a table with my mates—Whit, Yas, and Doc. We had spaghetti with calamari in ink sauce. Normally, I'd bread and fry zucchini flowers, but they won't be ready till midsummer. So, I made this perfect, garlicky foccacia."

With a watering mouth, he asks what I did to get the boot from Prison A.

---

2. The only way you can get written up for the content of your pictures is if the subjects are throwing gang signs.

I mention Lily. It feels good to talk of her during this tumult—and lets Nassim know what team I play for. But now he's all abubble with questions. Rather than stopping his inquiry by saying something hurtful and permanent, I excuse myself, shuffle the few feet to the toilet, and have a piss.

When I return to my square of bench next to Nassim, I can tell he's about to resume his inquiry. "Hey, man," I say. "You were a med student, do an intake on me."

Immediately, his posture straightens, he's transported back to a time before everything went to shit. In this manner, he does a full workup: history, vital stats, chief complaint, symptoms.

This isn't entirely to misdirect Nas. I've been suffering from a bizarre food allergy for the past six months. The prison doctors haven't been any help. They ran blood and urine tests, tried different courses of powerful antibiotics, then threw up their hands: *The tests show nothing abnormal, come back in a few months if this is still bothering you.* By keeping a food journal, I learned that it was milk, whey, and lactic acid starter cultures (found in virtually all processed meats) that produced not a traditional, gassy lactose intolerance, but rather: debilitating lethargy, swollen tonsils, extreme mental fogginess, severe gut pain, and the entire spectrum of urinary problems (weak stream, dribbling, difficulty starting and stopping, frequent urination). After symptom shopping, the best I've been able to self-diagnose is that I'm suffering from some mutant nonbacterial prostatitis that has somehow commandeered my digestive tract from stem to stern. I'm thirty-three years old and this is hell. Is a life without pizza, cookies, and Nutella even worth living? I know my condition is going to complicate this trip. On the road we're fed cold cuts and cheese, neither of which I can eat. I'm going to get ravenously hungry, then end up eating something that makes me ill and poorly suited to handle the complications of the road.

Nassim—willing to spend the time, but lacking the tests and tools of the trade—says it sounds like I have, go figure, nonbacterial prostatitis along with a severe allergy to milk products. I thank him and say it was fun.

Meanwhile, my attention has shifted to the Blood, standing a few feet away, leaning against the thick turquoise mesh. He's about my age, boyish face, very nice skin except for a thick scar that runs from the corner of his mouth back to his ear—the *de rigueur* battle scar of gang life. He's telling the Puerto Rican with waves about all the "books" he's written. Writing, like several other creative endeavors, is a latent talent that often gets nurtured only after someone finds him or herself behind a wall. Guy like this probably reads and writes only when he's in the Box, his stretches in general population are spent (gang) politicking. It's a shame, because there's definitely some intelligence there. With proper mentoring, he could do something good. As creators, we are what we eat. He's consuming garbage, when he reads at all.

"Gentlemen, excuse me." They turn. I address myself to the Blood. "Are you getting your work out there?"

"How you mean?"

"Online." I talk of establishing an online presence, brand building with blogs and social networking sites, even mention a few sites that feature new talent. "You're a writer, man. You can't be creating in a vacuum. You need feedback."

He's accustomed to boasting about specifics, not discussing craft, and subjects me to the ending of what he's currently working on. It's *Le Femme Nikita* meets *Kill Bill,* Pam Grier times Halle Berry. The story culminates with the protagonist taking a hyperviolent and ironic revenge on the man who raped her in the beginning.

"OK," I say.

"Word. I always have some fucked-up hate sex in my shit."

"Sounds like good fun. Let the boys in marketing worry about it."

The gate opens and a beefy hack steps into the pen holding a garbage bag filled with our lunch. He drops the brown bags into our upturned hands, then leaves. I survey the contents:

cheese sandwich, bologna sandwich, two chocolate chip cookies, a juice (Little Hugs, which come in a cute, faux barrel). I can consume four slices of bread and sugar water—the rest will fuck me up. Nassim has miraculously gotten one sandwich with processed turkey, which he agrees to trade with me. I give him the cookies as a thank you.

When the gate opens next, the beefy hack calls us out, one at a time by our last names, in no apparent order. We drop our garbage in the larger bag from whence it came, and stand in front of a hack who's to apply our waist chains. My guy's all thumbs. Black, late thirties, wedding band, bad breath, glasses, uneven moustache. A newjack. He's doing it all wrong, but instead of being an asshole and yelling at me, he does this endearing, nerdy fumfurring: shifting his weight, shaking his head, furrowing his brow.

"It's OK, man," I whisper (we're less than a foot away from each other). "You'll get it." I make myself as pliant and unthreatening as possible. I feel for this guy, who probably takes shit from his wife, shit from his coworkers, and I can hear black inmates calling him a "lame" or a "bird-ass n'ga." Sweat begins to pock his brow. "It's all right to ask a coworker. It gives them a teaching moment with you, shows you're confident enough to ask for help." As I say this, I realize I've spoken way out of school, so I prepare to get put in my place.

Instead, he asks for help, a decent guard shows him how it's done, then steps off. Now that I'm chained properly, the newjack and I smile at each other. I decide against asking him to adjust my too-tight handcuffs, don't want him to think I had an ulterior motive all along.

At the next station, the trip sergeant asks my name and number, then confirms my mug against my mug shot. I get a guard to unfuck my cuffs so they're not cutting into my wrists, then waddle outdoors into the drizzling rain, and board the bus.

It's a Greyhound-type affair with a large state seal emblazoned along its exterior. A cage up front for the driver, sergeant, and hack, similar cage in the back. The walls of the toilet have been replaced with plexiglass and metal. The seats are hard plastic with a thin rubber pretense of padding. We're told where to sit. You don't have to worry about picking a riding partner—you're shackled to him. But not me and my band of special cases. We're boarded last, sit toward the front, and each has a bench to himself.

We get under way. The guy I named "Dusty" turns around and says I gave the Blood good advice on his writing back in the bull pen. He himself does some writing, illustrated books for his little girl.

I've heard of guys doing this, if you have a modicum of creativity, it's something nice you can do for your kid. I'm glad I don't have kids. All the storybooks and cards in the world can't make up for the fact that your child is growing up without a father on hand. "Keep on, man. Your kid must really appreciate it."

"Yeah," Dusty says wistfully.

The guard tells him to turn around.

As we leave the prison grounds and turn onto what passes for a major thoroughfare in this dusty patch of nowhere, the sergeant stands and addresses us from the other side of the cage. "OK, men, we're now on the road. That means there's no talking. We'll be arriving at (Prison C) in approximately an hour and twenty minutes." When he turns to sit back down, I see his sidearm. A chunky, brushed-silver revolver luxuriating in a black leather holster. A cannon in a corset.

I don't know why his announcing our ETA tickles me so. Almost like we're paying customers—yet our flight attendant is packing heat. I'm grateful for the imposed silence. In a previous life, there was little my brain appreciated more than long drives alone, on some of the same roads I'll be traversing in the coming days. Those were the licentious road trips of college, the felonious drive to and from home, my Jeep's cabin awash in purple haze and drum 'n' bass. But even now, shackled, I feel some of the same freedoms of the road. Until I touch down, all is possible. Better to travel than to arrive.

On the highway, we drive into a rainstorm. Yesterday (Monday morning) I was sitting in a dayroom in Prison A when the weather report came on. I put down the *New Yorker* and looked at the seven-day weather graphic. A bevy of smiling spring suns bifurcated by today's rain clouds. Through the tinted windows the sky looks almost light brown, a sienna-muddied yellow ochre. All that can be heard is the varying hum of wheels on the wet road. My eyelids grow heavy and I begin to hear music in the low vibrations, a song I shared with Lily. The reassuring electronic melody of Ladytron's "Blue Jeans" rocks me to sleep.

In Prison C's reception room we have our cuffs and shackles removed. A pair of nurses stands behind a cart on the way to the cellblock. One is dour, one sweet. "Name?"

I give my last name. The call and response of the initial touch point.

"Number?"

Rattle it off.

"Take any meds?"

"No." Then, the lie I formulated five minutes ago: "My TMJ problem is acting up and my head is killing me." With a handful of aspirin packets, I'm on my way. Planning ahead to the evening, when the lack of caffeine begins to crack my skull. We're not provided coffee on the road—hopefully the aspirin sees me through the day or two of caffeine-withdrawal headaches.

In case one couldn't navigate himself to the cellblock door fifty feet across the lot, there are yellow boot prints in a line across the black top. It's rather cute.

The cellblock is loud with the noise of hundreds of men, their TVs and radios, their taunts and tautologies. This is coming almost entirely from the three upper tiers, the guys who call this prison home. The ground floor (the "flats") is for transit. A guard is motioning to me from so far down the tier that he looks small. The far end, fifty cells away, is easily the length of a football field. Some time ago I made this slow walk past the scores of double-bunk cells—nothing's changed. It's all the same chilly dismal.

The guard radios to have the cell door closed after I step in. Quick scan of both bunks: there's only one blanket. I make the guard aware of this, then request another blanket from the inmate porter. My calculus is thus: the eventual bunkie will punch me in the face and take my blanket, or, perhaps worse, he'll meekly shiver and I'll feel like a warm, heartless bastard.

The sink works, the toilet flushes. We each have a "mattress" and a pillow. There are half a dozen individually wrapped pink-foam lollipops with "dentifrice," i.e., toothbrushes. A porter wheels a cart past and tosses in a sheet, pillowcase, small towel, and a tiny bar of soap. I plead with him for something, anything, to read. He says he'll see what he can do, then moves on. The fluorescent is angled low, the cell is dark and dank and damn chilly for late spring. Grotty from constant turnover, I'm careful not to touch any surface I don't have to. Washing up, I pay special attention to my bruised wrists that smell like dirty metal. Suck down some aspirin. Make up the bottom bunk, stretch out, and massage my temples. When I last passed through en route to Prison A, I spent six miserable, mind-numbingly boring days here—delayed because of Memorial Day. As part of a recent cost-containment initiative, the Department keeps the buses off the road on Wednesdays. We were told we'll be back on the road Thursday. That means I've got tonight and tomorrow night at the least, and can't say anything more with certainty.

There's a shouting match going on above me, on the second or third floor—not knowing the players, I can't tell whether this increasingly aggressive staccato is their routine mode of convo or the prelude to a fight. When I first came through here—a scared newjack on his way to the big leagues—there was a guy shouting across many cells to his friend, A-Train, who was getting released the next day. Don't be coming back, he said, stay away from those guns. Hell, yeah, A-Train yelled in reply, guns is played out, I'm'a stab me a muhfucker. He went on to describe hand-to-hand fighting with a knife, how intimate it is when you block a punch, stab your opponent through his rib cage, and hear him grunt and wheeze. He imitated such grunting, which made me envision the damage he'd caused during his bid, then A-Train laughed, almost boyishly. In those early days, when I was still so greedily examining everything that was taking place around me, it was unavoidable that he would make such a strong impression on me. That interchange was burned into my memory, coming as it did before I saw—or heard—people getting stabbed.

The sound of boots gets me to my feet. Outside the cell, flanked by a guard, is a black guy roughly my age. Wild hair sticking straight up like a youthful Don King. Eyes behind large glasses with thick, black frames stare back at me. The gate cracks, he steps in, it bangs closed, the guard walks away. "Waddup, kid?" I say.

"How you?"

These are vital moments—we're both sniffing each other out, assessing threat level. He just got out of the Box. "Lemme guess," I say. "For stabbing a bunkie who asked too many questions."

Awkward silence. Then he erupts in genuine belly laughter, and I know we'll be OK. I extend my hand and offer my name. We shake and he says, "JT." JT is quiet for a moment, then says, "Fuck it. I'm going home. My name's Paul."

Paul takes off his glasses, says they're just for show. They make him look like a geeky black kid to the guards and I can see why he'd want that. A porter comes by, tosses in a blanket, linens, and a book for me. A shitty murder mystery, dog-eared and greasy from countless readings, but I'm grateful to have something. Paul asks him if anyone's selling weed. The porter doesn't know.

"Have you tried to cop anything?" Paul asks me. "I've got stamps." (Translation: There are stamps snug in the finger of a latex glove secreted up his ass.)

"Nah." I'd smoke with him, but am not willing to do anything to make it happen.

After all that time in the Box, Paul is mad for conversation. He's a likable fellow, I oblige him. We each tell how we came to be on the road, where we've done time, volunteer very abridged versions of our lives prior to prison. He's shocked when I tell him I'm doing twenty-five-to-life for murder. I tell him, "That's called 'cognitive dissonance,' man. Don't worry, I'm a pussycat." The dissonance is also internal. I have a hard time reconciling the person I am with the creature I was for a couple years in my early twenties. The animal that visited death and destruction upon the lives of good, caring people— behavior that will forever haunt me, causing me to whimper and shake my head against the pillow. The past is the past, yet it often feels like present tense. But, as a psychiatrist once told me, there's no making sense of the senseless. Instead, I've begun to grapple with learning to forgive myself, questioning if that's even possible.

He fishes for details.

"Heroin. I freaked the fuck out. Let's move on."

On we move. Paul tells of a string of bank robberies, claims to've been on the show *America's Most Wanted*. He's now on his way to an immigration holding center. A Guyanese national here on a visa, Paul is being deported.

Still, the parole board hit him last week with two years. It's all a meaningless sham. When metrics of performance rest solely on the quantifiable, any bureaucracy will "juke the stats," as David Simon, creator of *The Wire,* termed it. I've seen this same scenario several times in the past few years. The board denies parole knowing full well there's an "immigration hold." Someone—you, your consulate, or a parole officer—contacts Homeland Security and the deportation process begins immediately. Parole keeps its numbers up, while Corrections saves over sixty thou' (the cost of housing an inmate for his two-year parole hit). Juking the stats . . . my country 'tis of thee, sweet land of chicanery.

Dinner arrives and the porter tells me it's around four thirty. Chow is turkey tetrazzini, so I wash the cream sauce off a few gnarly pieces of lung meat and make a sandwich. Standing over the sink with my back to him, I can feel Paul looking askance. After I explain my horrible food allergy, he gives me his peas.

Day Two. Wednesday. I wake as the food cart stops in front of the cell. The air is bracing. I take the trays, hand Paul's up to him on the top bunk. The orange juice I use on the cornflakes alerts me to my sore throat. This mental fog isn't all early morning haze—I consumed something that has made me sick. Ugh. Now I have this to deal with for the remainder of the trip. Headaches, lethargy, malaise and mental fogginess, urinary stream like a showerhead. Aspirin, and back to sleep.

It was belatedly that I came to appreciate the value of my bond with Whit, Yas, and Doc. There was a stretch of time when, even though we were in close proximity, I couldn't have been more emotionally distant, courtesy of my drug-seeking behavior. Thankfully, my last few years at Prison A were spent keeping company and spending quality time with the boys, letting them know how much I cared for them. The experience has taught me the value of cultivating friendships, even when it's temporary, like it is on the road. After lunch, I teach Paul Ghost, a word game my grandmother taught me. He immediately takes to it and almost beats me. Now it's his turn to choose a game. Paul calls for Box games, the drawn-out diversions of men who literally have nothing better to do. The most tedious is one in which the players agree on a category (animals, say), then take turns listing every example from each letter of the alphabet. After being in the Box for a year, Paul got used to the dark, and I led a vampiric life in college. We lie in our bunks with the light off, dreamily reciting the names of people, places, and things. I fall asleep often.

Day Three. Thursday. After breakfast, the porter tells us we'll be leaving shortly. In the darkened cell, Paul and I take turns washing up with the dribbled cold water. No matter, we're happy to be getting out of this dungeon, back on the road. I'm conscious of leaving the cell nicer than I found it. The blanket is folded, there's aspirin and something to read.

The sound of cells cracking open grows closer. Paul and I shake hands. I wish him luck with the business ventures he has planned for Guyana. He tells me everything's going to work out fine with me and Lily—a throwaway pronouncement from a near stranger in a dark prison cell. Yet it warms me, and I thank him.

Nassim sits next to me in the reception room's bull pen. Paul, destined for another part of the state, is in a different pen. It gets loud, the clock reads eight fifteen, and my head feels like paper cuts. As a group, we're particularly interested in each other during transit, there's always something to tell. *Where you coming from? Where you going? Do you know—? Did you hear about—?* Bull pens like this are key nodes on the prison grapevine's information superhighway. Nassim was bored shitless during our stopover because he didn't have a bunkie (almost definitely because *Homosexual* is indicated in his record). Several feet away sit fellow travelers Hoyt and Tattoo Lou, giggling to each other about how much fun they had during their stay. "Duuude," says Hoyt, a lazy eye fluttering in my direction.

"I know," says the heavily tattooed one. "We were blowin' it down the minute we locked in."

Blowing it down is the new slang for smoking pot; I've been hearing it a lot the past few days, as is the style with new slang. Two guesses as to coinage: "Blowing it up" becomes "down," like "beat up" morphs into "beat down"; or, it's named after the process of blowing a cloud of smoke down a flushing toilet to avoid detection.

"Blowing. It. Downnnnuh," echoes Hoyt.

There's something pathetic and desperate about it all. When I was drugging in Prison A with Ray and Tommy G., and referring to myself as Odi, did I really once sound like that? *Jerkoff.*

Nassim leans close: "You know, you're totally my type."

"You know, I'm totally straight."

He tells me about his last boyfriend, whom I resemble.

Out of the blue, I go into journalist mode and ask all manner of questions. *Isn't it really hard to be openly gay in prison? What's it like to get split up from your partner? How do you know whom to hit on? How'd you know I wouldn't freak out and hurt you for an unwanted advance?*

This last gets Nassim talking. Not only does he like a long, protracted challenge, but he'll choose a tough, unlikely mark, then spend months trying to get in his pants. This modus operandi has, admittedly, earned him a few beatings, which he chalks up to the cost of doing business.

"C'mon, man," I say. "You're a smart guy, a good person. You've only got a few years left, don't risk your safety. Stick with sure things . . . go for the low-hanging fruit."

Nassim stares at me for a second, then we both crack up. "I hope we're shackled together on the bus," he says.

As luck would have it, the ankle eighteen inches from mine belongs to a big, friendly seeming black kid. In the moments before we get under way, he and I exchange names. Like many guys from the South (his family moved from Alabama when he was five), he goes by the handle "Country," but says I can call him J. J's a good-natured type who giggles at almost everything I say.

We pull away from Prison C and quiet is enforced. For kicks, I nudge J, who's in the window seat, and motion to the car next to us at the stoplight. A pudding of a woman talks on the phone while her Lhasa apso frantically licks his balls in the passenger's seat. When J looks back at me, he sees my wildly contorted face, which sends him into a fit of snorting laughter. The guards look in our direction and we take it down to a mumbling titter. We'll be on the road until late afternoon. The sun is shining and I have good company.

After a couple hours, we pull off the highway and find ourselves rolling through a quaint little hamlet. Rather nice for a prison town. For prisoners, freedom appears somehow freer than actual freedom, as in, freer than the freedom that exists in the world. We don't equate freedom so much with nine-to-fives, mortgage payments, and mouths to feed, so much as we do with coming and going as we please, and eating and wearing whatever we want. This exaggerated and childish notion of freedom seems to be a natural by-product of living in a walled city; we're great dreamers.

My peers crane their necks wildly and make raucous comments about asses as we pass them by. *Run!* I want to scream to these small-town folk, who stroll on Main Street completely oblivious to the busload of murderers, rapists, thieves, and derelicts in their midst.

Inside the wall of Prison D is a parking lot that serves as a bus depot for a few hours during the day. Buses pull in from the numerous prisons in this part of the state, lose some passengers, take on some more, swap baggage from cargo holds, serve a bag lunch, then get back on the road. The guards and driver disembark and mingle with the other crews on the black top. Sweaty, they suck down cigarettes, consult clipboards, compare notes, laugh.

We watch from the air-conditioned interior. Hoyt, several rows in front of me, grins lickerishly, speaking in urgent, hushed tones to the Puerto Rican he double bunked with in Prison C. The nonverbal cues say it all: Hoyt's assuring this schmuck that he'll get paid for the drugs consumed over the last two days—and Hoyt's about to talk him out of some more.

I hear someone say, as if he's a paying customer, that the logistics of our trip "don't make no sense," because he's been taken completely out of the way on our roundabout journey. But it makes perfect sense if you view us as non-time-sensitive cargo. Pooling in centralized distribution hubs keeps transportation and labor costs down, while maintaining efficiency. UPS uses its Louisville operation to just such ends.

Pairs of men shuffle by to use the toilet. I tell J I have to take a leak, and we clumsily move down the aisle. J's back is to mine as I stand before the smelly chemical toilet. With great relief, I begin peeing. J kicks our leg chain, and giggles as I splatter the floor. "Nice, asshole."

J can't understand why I give him my cookies, meat, and cheese in return for two slices of his bread. As I scarf down the bread and chase it with red-tinted sugar water, I'm forced to tell yet another person about my mysterious allergy. Explaining the condition, answering the questions (almost always the same), and responding to the recommendations are almost as tiring as the symptoms themselves.

The bus quiets as we eat. My eyes drink in the red-brick buildings all around us. With a chuckle, I remember my "low-hanging fruit" double entendre from earlier. After a line like that, I can phone it in for the rest of the week.

J gets my attention by pulling on our leg chain. Apropos of nothing, he says, "You think everythin' happens for a reason?"

When I first *went away*, hearing evangelical inmates spout such sentiments angered me to no end. It implies that my victims were part of a divine plan, which I refuse to accept. Over the years of solitary meditation on this subject, I've cobbled together a *weltanschauung* akin to that of Seneca, Viktor Frankl, and Voltaire—a happy cocktail of stoicism, existentialism, and optimism.

I tell J that a year ago, I would've answered this question differently. (Alas, with Lily's miraculous appearance, I've grown somewhat Panglossian.) "I think *some* things may happen for a reason, even if we don't understand it at the time. So it's really on us to find the meaning in it, you know? To make the most of the path our life has taken."

J thinks about this for a moment, narrows his eyes, nods his head. "Mm-hmm, hell yeah. Thass deep, son."

"Eh," I say, "I read it on a Snapple bottle."

This earns J's hearty laughter. He leans over and we bump (cuffed) fists.

"Hey, look," Hoyt says to no one in particular. "Sergeant's getting his dick sucked by that dog."

And damned if a sergeant isn't leaning into the fence, a black tail wagging joyously from behind the white shirt. Everyone laughs. It dawns on me that Hoyt is one of those self-appointed jesters who seem to make it their duty to amuse their gloomy comrades. The sergeant turns to speak to a hack and we see that he's feeding the pooch not his dick, but the same sandwiches we just ate.

It's a handsome, happy, midsized dog, black with a splash of white on his chest, a year or two old whose home is a long patch of grass in between the prison wall and an inner fence. There's a brown doghouse and a smattering of toys. When I passed through here a decade ago, the dog was old and graying. Like the current iteration, it subsisted on bag lunches. The dog owes its existence to a tower guard's nostalgia, a remnant from the days before ground sensors and motion detectors made a guard dog obsolete. A guy says, "That dog ain't tough." A sociopath responds, "I'd kill that fuckin' dog if I had to."

The bus starts to back up, guards hop on, and we roll past the black dog smiling at us. "That's cruel and unusual," someone says. It's these types of moral sentiments from most of my peers that make me feel that, despite our horrible crimes, there is an underlying moral goodness and most, if not all, of us are capable of redemption. "Wah'did that dog do to deserve this?" says an old black man. "He in jail just like we is."

> I see trees of green,
> Red roses, too . . .
> And I think to myself—

Is a song I hear as the driver scans between country stations.

We're motoring through a beautiful part of the state. Vineyards are beginning to cover the slow hills in bluish green. Garage sales, farmers' markets, open-air cafés hiring for the summer. A roadside lemonade stand operated by a fair-skinned boy and girl, smiling, squinting above their freckles. Rockwell couldn't have painted it truer.

The bus rumbles low, downshifts as we descend into the river valley. J is sleeping peacefully. The wide river teems with pleasure craft—sail and power, a crew team, wave runners—like slow-moving moths against a dark-blue screen. As we speed along the bridge's expanse, J's head lolls onto my shoulder. With the river moving slowly below, and the false dauphins and scoundrels seated around me, I momentarily fancy myself Huckleberry Finn on an adventure with his good friend Jim (though if I try to jump from this raft I'll wind up with a bullet through my neck).

Over the river and through some woods . . . and the air pumped into the bus begins to smell different. Greener, cleaner, more familiar. Not counting the trip upstate a decade ago, I'm on roads that I haven't seen since my youth. Strings of memory are pulled taut, and clearly remembered scenes become bittersweet. The idyllic weekends spent with my brother at our grandparents' country house: swimming, eating, exploring the woods. The spastically horny summers at sleepaway camp: sailing, lying, exploring the girls. I recognize road signs for old diners, local institutions that now offer free Wi-Fi.

Nestled into blast-carved shale are a few old trailer homes. In front of a silver capsule, a trio of lowlifes sits in flimsy lawn chairs nursing a midday beer buzz. They immediately recognize the bus's markings, and acknowledge its shackled passengers with a show of solidarity, a solemn nod, a raised beer can, the (index finger and pinky) rock 'n' roll salute. I promise myself that I'll remember this tableau. *Good gentlemen, how long has it been since you've ridden in such fashion? Have you laid your heads in some of the cellblocks I've called "home"? Does the sight of us make you shudder and drink in your freedom all the more?*

A dull ruckus a few rows ahead draws the aggravated attention of the sergeant. "It's real simple guys. There's no talking. Keep it up and your property will never arrive." He fixes the guilty parties in a stare, then sits.

Absolute silence. The prospect of losing everything you own will have that effect. Flight attendants would be envious of the sergeant's ability to make that most credible threat.

At Prison E, J and I say good-bye as a guard removes our leg chain. He's led away, probably to disciplinary housing.

The bull pen—one of five—is very cold. The A/C is set as if the room were crammed tight with a hundred felons. Or, possibly, this pen is normally reserved for hard cases and the twenty or so of us are just unlucky. On the plus side, I now have a concrete example for the term "cooling my heels."

Opposite us, the pen is filled—easily seventy-five bodies, SRO—with guys who just got dropped off by the deputies from their county jails. Prison E is a Reception Center that processes roughly 7,000 men annually into the state prison system. Just like these men, I once had on the clothes from the day I was arrested (cargo pants and a ribbed sweater, musty from sitting in a property bag during my year in county), moving into the big leagues, I was scared and alone.

The managers of this human warehouse run a streamlined operation. These newjacks are about to get stripped of their clothes, assigned a number that will be their name for the remainder of the bid, marched naked into a cold shower for delousing, handed a small towel and boxers, put in a barber's chair and have their heads shaved, given three changes of clothes and a pair of boots, fingerprinted, photographed, fed, watered, and put to bed. The transformation from person to institutional property is then complete. In the coming weeks, they'll have their IQ tested, undergo a complete physical and psychological evaluation, and give up a vial of blood for the state's DNA databank (a privilege for which their inmate accounts will be encumbered to the tune of fifty dollars). If lucky, they'll be transferred within a couple months to a prison where they can put down roots, get a job, make some friends, find a groove in which to do their time. The smart money quickly learns to discard the pop-culture guidebook to prison. An inmate knows he's an inmate, an outcast, and he knows his place in relation to guards and society at large, but no prison number or state-issued clothing can make him forget that he's a human being.

The gate to our pen slides open, the guards call us out one at a time to remove our cuffs and waist chain. Nassim walks up to me and says, "God love you." I've never had anyone say that to me, let alone a gay Shiite Muslim convict. "Salaam," I say in response.

Prison E's cells are big and single occupancy and have hot water; trapezoidal with a window, a desk built into the wall. Over a stainless steel sink I bird bathe, lathering up my bruised wrists. It never occurred to me how filthy handcuffs are, but there's a good reason the guards wear latex gloves when removing them. Inmates do all the scut work in any prison, but would no sooner be allowed to disinfect a pair of cuffs than a guard's nightstick.

Enjoying the quiet, I lie in a clean bed staring out the window as the sun sets the sky ablaze. My thoughts quickly turn to Lily. Whatever ease and inner strength I'm feeling is all due to her love. I was away for ten years when she appeared in my life, bringing warmth to a harsh existence. Loving me has cost her dearly—her job, for one—yet she's still here. That's why I'm dealing so well with the road: she's my armor. Whenever I begin to worry that she'll leave me, I remind myself of what she said during our visit Monday, the day before I left; when I told her I'd be getting transferred to Prison F, she said, "My car can drive there."

For me, the sun rises and sets with Lily, my never-ending fount of happiness. Unlike the superficial relationships in my past, I have in Lily a partner, a companion. The love I feel for her registers as a fluttery warmth in my chest, or the involuntary smile that appears whenever I think of her. We're more than just the plot lines of a Lifetime movie. The bond we share continues to make each of us better, stronger people— the whole is truly greater than the sum of its parts. We are, in a word, happy.

To be sure, there are times when we feel the limitations of our relationship, the lack of physical contact, or even, like now, not having access to a phone. But whether it's phone or letters or solitary thinking, we can emulate proximity, and bring comfort. We've learned that what's necessary for making a relationship work isn't having money (though that certainly doesn't hurt), or children, or, as the simplistic advice of self-styled relationship gurus has it, going on date nights. It's being emotionally available for each other. Doing little kindnesses. She sends me pictures of puppies, and adorns her letters with glitter stickers; I draw for her, and pass along or summarize articles relevant to her interests. She and I part company with quick messages written on each other's arms.

That's the thing about us: we're willing to work on the relationship and keep working on it. Many of my married peers are the same way. We're grateful that someone sees us for the person we are, not simply as the criminal act we senselessly, regrettably committed five, ten, twenty-five years ago.

And like a dog rescued from the pound, we show our gratitude daily. You can usually tell when a guy in here is in a loving relationship: his head is out of prison, and he knows there are far more important things than the slights of guards and pettiness of peers. Having someone who actually wants to hear from you, and listens with compassion, does more to turn a life around than all rehabilitative programs combined. Being loved like that turns your life on.

Day Four. Friday. Voices and human activity directly outside my ground-floor window pull my eyes open in the dark predawn. Five o'clock? Six? These are the men from my house who are leaving today. I roll over and burrow under the pillow.

I'm surprised when my door clicks open after the morning count. I've never done transit at Prison E. As opposed to Prison C, I'll be walking to the mess hall for meals and there'll be some time out of the cell. And showers. And phone calls!

When we get back from breakfast, the twelve of us sit on plastic chairs in the bright dayroom and watch garbage TV. Designed for thirty-six, the house feels empty. I'm told it'll fill up by tonight, which makes sense. A transit house turns over its inventory like a produce jobber.

The house officer gets off the phone and reads a list of all the guys who'll be leaving later today: everyone but me and an old black Muslim called Shaheed. The prospect of spending the weekend here puts me at ease, it's a pleasurable delay of the inevitable—let's travel, and never arrive.

Turns out the high-ranking Blood with the red kufi and D&G frames goes by "LS." This he tells me after lunch as we talk through portals in our cell doors. He's baked and excited to be going back to the city for a bullshit court case. LS thanks me for the advice I gave him on his writing three days ago, says how his homies just tell him "the shit's good," without offering any real comments. He floats a business idea for when he gets released: baby-safety products. Some woman his lawyer knows wants to help him get on the straight and narrow. I talk fervently about brand building and leveraging free technology; suggest that he try to get a B-school marketing class to do some free work on his venture; stress the utility of exploiting the "bad kid gone good" story frame all the way to the bank. LS is sharp, he realizes I'm not full of shit. I think of my (dare I say?) lagniappe as community service—not so much for him as for the community he won't be terrorizing should he be successful in business. He wants to keep in touch, have me as a consultant. When he asks my name, I give a fake. LS gives me his "government" (the name on his birth certificate) and schools me on how to drop it if I ever get in trouble with his "people" (the Bloods). Though I'll probably never have to use it, I thank him for this underworld version of a Police Benevolent Association card.

His door opens and he comes over to shake hands. "Hold ya head, kid."

"You, too," I tell him. "Remember, he with the best narrative wins. Either you define yourself, or someone will come up with their own version of who you are."

It's now just Shaheed and I, so the guard deputizes us as porters for the house. The job is 20 percent work, 80 percent perk. In each cell we toss a roll of toilet paper, soap, toothbrush, toothpaste, and a set of linens.

The guard is youngish, cool, ex-military. "What now?" I ask him.

"Watch TV, relax."

"Can I use the phone?"

It's good to hear my brother's voice, a constant amidst the change in scenery. All these years, he's never abandoned me, even when I've given him reason to. Though he's three years younger, I look up to him as a role model, a true mensch. I bring him up to speed, assure him that I'm safe, ask that he relay all this to the family. Graciously, he texts Lily for me, and she and I have a quick, but emotional exchange.

Standing under the water of a hot shower is invigorating. It's my first since Monday night.

I lock in before the three o'clock shift change. It's been a productive day. I swept and mopped the cell's linoleum floor, so now I can walk around barefoot. On the desk are five sheets of paper, three envelopes, a pen, and T.C. Boyle's *Talk Talk*. The latter is a real gift from the gods. Behind the wall, schlock lit is the genre of choice, glossy covers featuring bloody weapons, foggy nights, or dragons. In transit houses especially, the Bible is wildly popular—its onion-skin pages can be used as rolling paper. Shaheed gladly handed me the novel from his cell, and I hid my enthusiasm at encountering a proper author.

My pen hits the paper and I'm home. Journal entries couched within letters to loved ones. Prison E allows us five free letters a week, which is really considerate.

In the evening, doors open and close, boots shuffle, and the house fills up a few guys at a time. Toilets flush (think: staging area for the unloading of hidden cargo), tobacco smoke wafts into my cell. For homophobes, they sure manage to cram a lot of stuff up their asses. It's known as "slamming" or "stuffing" or, the odd-sounding "boofing." To keep contents safe during shipping, the process entails using a latex glove, plastic bag, or condom. Tobacco, weed, dope, pills, stamps, matches, lighter, weapons; I've heard of guys slamming sensitive information on scraps of paper like spies in hostile territory. I'm really pleased with myself for giving up smoking two years ago. Otherwise, I'd be doing like the guys who didn't "pack" for their trip: frantically offering items from tomorrow's breakfast in return for a few measly shreds of loose tobacco and a match peeled in half. And for those who can't find matches, the "third rail" awaits: a paperclip stuck in an electric socket, brought into contact with pencil lead, will make enough sparks to light a cigarette (while giving you a jolt).

Day Five. Saturday. After breakfast is cell cleanup. As a porter, I bring around a broom and mop setup for the guys who want it (I also ferry tobacco, matches, stamps, and morsels of food from cell to cell like an incarcerated Hermes). In between this frenzy of activity, I duck into my cell, strip off all my underclothes, then get back into my shirt, pants, and boots. Taking advantage of the house's washing machine and dryer, I do a single load of whites.

After lunch, the guard reads off all the cells that will be leaving Monday. I'm one of several who will be staying. The rule is you can't use the phone once you're told you'll be leaving (on the grounds of security risk), so not only do I get on the phone first (another perk of portering), but because two-thirds of the house will be leaving, I won't have to worry about a long line of angry men behind me.

As the sun sets, I enjoy a session of yoga on the clean floor. Kick into a handstand supported by the cinder block wall—good for seeing life differently. This is who I've become: someone who checks his alignments, and works to see things from other perspectives. I do every restorative pose in the arsenal, easing away the aches that come from traveling in shackles, sitting on hard benches, and sleeping on pathetic mattresses. The two rolls of toilet paper liberated earlier from the supply closet, I now use as props under my sacrum. Seated on the floor, I work on my breathing.

On the little desk I do much writing, nearly exhausting my replenished supply of paper (while most everyone hustled for something to smoke, I finagled another fifteen blank sheets). For Saturday night entertainment, I consume more than half of *Talk Talk*, carefully allotting enough reading to last me a few more days. This has always been me, more ant than grasshopper.

Day Six. Sunday. Another gorgeous afternoon spent indoors, in front of a television (not like we have the choice to go outside). Almost the entire house sits quietly watching *The Little Rascals* (the movie version from the nineties). It's the wildest thing: thuggish gangsters with gold teeth, neck tats, and bullet scars not only watching this movie, but delivering certain lines along with the actors.

I take a seat in the back next to a forty-something white guy who has the look of Hunter S. Thompson, balding, wiry, bespectacled, and squirrelly looking. I introduce myself. "Steven," I whisper, "what do you make of this?"

He simply shrugs. But I think I get it. Yesterday, after everyone locked in, I sat alone in the dayroom watching the *Puppy Hour* on WE, absolutely captivated by those impossibly cute, wriggling little fur balls. These men are pouring some artificial sweetener onto a sour patch in their bid.

Day Seven. Monday. Hearing my cell number over the PA springs me out of bed. The sun hasn't yet risen. A disembodied female voice says all the cells just called will be leaving in ten minutes. Is this a mistake? No, I quickly decide. The house officer did me a good turn by not telling me on Saturday, so I could continue using the phone—the best of all possible worlds. I seal the envelopes and hurriedly address them. Brush my teeth while I pee. Get dressed. Instinctively scan for something I'm forgetting. The next occupant will think he's hit the jackpot: extra TP, two pillows, a match, a good book, paper, and pen. (Perhaps he too left his previous cell better than he found it and I'm an instrument of karma.)

My hair is wet, my brain still numb as I stand in company formation in the courtyard, breathing the brisk dawn air. The guards count heads and check names. On the walk to breakfast, we drop our mail in a box. There's yet another strip search. I've been through hundreds of them—you get used to it, but it's no less humiliating, peeling off one layer at a time, slowly. *Show your mouth . . . behind your ears . . . turn your socks inside out, don't shake 'em . . . drop your drawers . . . lift up . . . turn around . . . lift your left foot, right . . . bend over, spread . . . all right, get dressed.* It's nothing personal, which perhaps makes it all the more dehumanizing. Their bored and clinical gaze says they'd rather be anyplace else, too. More waiting in bull pens.

One of the trip officers starts at the back of the bus and walks forward, asking our names and filling in a seating card (if they need to lose someone's luggage, this is how they know who's who). Well built and friendly, he moves amongst us with an easy air, the ex-marine jokes with us and we respect him. Guards and cons alike call him Pooch, a shortening of his surname. He's in his mid-to-late forties, but hasn't aged much over the decade since I last left Prison E. At the front of the rows, he props himself up on the back of a bench and addresses us, his accent sounding like home. "Mornin', fellas. Youse know the drill: tawk, but keep it down. We'll be on the road a little maw than three ow-ahs. Questions?"

A joker says: "Yeah, Pooch. Where we stoppin' to eat?"

"My mothuh's house. Hope you got strong stomachs. Haven't seen 'er in a dawg's age, I'll cawl 'er right now."

This is the last leg of the trip. Cruising on the highway, I begin to feel anxious, uneasy. It's been awhile since I've had to establish myself in prison. The past seven or eight years have been spent in relative comfort, keeping time with great friends, working good jobs, involved in various programs and activities, like the writers' workshop, helmed by Jameson, that felt like home for over four years. I miss my friends: Yas, Whit, Doc, Renzo; Jameson, my mentor; my boss, Mr. Bernard. We can get in trouble for contacting each other third-party, but I plan on keeping in touch.

We blow past a billboard for a local tae kwon do dojo, a red and blue yin yang reminds me of a televised lecture I took in during my last weekend in Prison A. The talk was given by a professor of psychology whose name I instantly forgot, but the topic was embracing chaos. We suffer ennui, he said, when our lives are too ordered. Using a PowerPoint slide of a yin yang, he spoke of optimal experience. The dots within each paisley are to remind us that there is always a little chaos in order, and vice versa. Ideally, we should straddle each paisley: one foot in chaos, one in order. Hearing the lecture made me think back to my most stressful times over the preceding years, the cause of each instance was the fear of disruption to my established order. I was so content that I spent months at a time cringing, waiting for a shoe to drop.

The lecture also softened my mind. Life is change, I realized, and I need to get on with it. Attachment to places kills the soul as surely as attachment to things. I vowed to flow with the current as it takes me to someplace new, to open myself to the universe, and learn from it.

Looking around at the faces on the bus, I realize that I have more time in than many of them. I'm no newjack. I paid my dues in the yards, crewing up with heavy hitters, making the right moves, keeping my mouth shut when need be. I've met thousands of men, and helped many of them. I haven't an enemy in the state. My name, as they say, is golden.

As to navigating the local bureaucracy, the names will be different, but the rackets don't change. I know who to see, what to ask for, and how to ask for it. I've got a bachelor's degree, and in the land of the pre-GED, that makes me a fucking king. For almost my entire incarceration I've worked in offices, clerking for highly placed civilians. My security clearance is high, I'm not a sex offender, and I make people laugh. Climbing the ladder at Prison F will be almost too easy.

By tonight I'll be walking the yard, where I'll undoubtedly connect with old faces. I'll learn the best places to lock, the best jobs to have. They'll provide introductions to the right people, and I'll get juiced in with the quickness. That's how it goes for guys like me.

I'm tired of the road, tired of the lunch-meat stomachaches, tired of being shackled to strangers and dragged from one bull pen to another. I want to get my property, change into clean and comfy clothes, sleep on my own sheets, dry with my own towels, cook a good meal and eat until I'm full, receive mail, and make daily phone calls.

It is around noon when we pull off the highway and make our way onto smaller, more rural roads. Cresting a hill, the gray wall of Prison F rises to meet us. Everyone gets quiet, even those who've been here before. The wall stretches forever—more a feature of the landscape than one of architecture. Peering easily over it is a tan brick building, hundreds of yards long, four or five stories tall: the big house. It's like an old, dusky battleship floating on a sea of gray.

The bus hisses to a slow stop in front of the main gate, huge metal plates with chipped paint and rust spots. A tower guard steps out onto a crenellated turret, his assault rifle pointed at the sky. This is how prisoners are greeted at their new home. I can't speak for my peers, but I'm ready to kick the dirt off my boots and get inside. It's where I belong for now.

Back we go.

TWO

El Otro Lao[1]: Spanish for Users

*A sad, underground language, forever being lost and recovered.
I soon learned that Spanish as spoken in Mexico answered to
six unwritten rules: Never use the familiar* tu—thou—*if you
can use the formal you—*usted. *Never use the first-person
possessive pronoun, but rather the second-person, as in
"This is* your *home."*

—Carlos Fuentes, "How I Started to Write"

You're not ready to meet Lily, not in this state. First you
must travel through years' worth of madness. Standing with
your back to the brick wall, watching the guards in their high
towers, as they watch you and your peers amble around the
yard settling scores and copping drugs and doing time—you've
got quite a bit to learn, friend. But rest assured, you'll get
sorted out. The time will alternatingly compress and expand
into a soup of the day, a hodgepodge of years. Just flow with
it. With every passing day you'll grow less and less bewildered
by the commonplace events of your new life, and the Diag-
nostic and Statistical Manual-grade personalities that inhabit
these places. Your eyes will somehow grow accustomed to the
incidents, the surroundings, the people. You'll hear backstories.
You've come from a different walk of life, and are traveling a
different path. But the one thing you have in common is that
each of you was brought home from the hospital, a brand-new

---

1. Pronunciation, in street Spanish, of "lado," side.

person, and your loved ones stood over you in your crib. You were all fresh and innocent, cute, big-eyed little critters. And they stared at you lovingly and imagined bright, successful futures for you. What they didn't imagine for you was this life of crime and hurt and prison. Your company porter had once been a bank robber with dreams of paying off his brother's student loans. The bored man behind the mess hall counter once thought that the best way to provide for his kids was as a middleman in the coke supply chain. One of the chaplain's clerks was a roofer and alcoholic, who killed a man with bare hands. The old man who mumbles to himself and picks up cigarette butts in the yard, mumbled and panhandled in the *world*—before that he was a math teacher (they're all weird).

The freaks, fiends, and freedom-impaired; con men talking you onto wild rides; haunted houses bristling with razor wire—life *inside* often feels like a high wire act without a net. It's all a goddamned circus, you'll think to yourself sometimes, a concrete carnival. But if you didn't want to take the ride, you shouldn't have bought the ticket. So, say good-bye to normal, and if you can't be good, be careful.

Your bed in prison offers little comfort, the six-by-nine cell a meager home piled high with the handcrafted baggage of regret. You're bilingual now, but how's that cost-benefit lining up for you? Your neighbors bicker *en Español*, toilets flush at random, televisions and radios form an ugly aural tapestry. Indeed, it's an ugly place you now call home, but the behavior that led here wasn't always pretty either.

Supine, you rest an old, pleasantly musty copy of *The Stranger* on your chest. You were *this* close to reading the book in county jail, when it was taken on a shakedown (life *inside* allows for no more than twenty-five books at a time). You remove your reading glasses and rub the bags beneath your eyes. Camus's succinct prose sticks with you—you remember flinching in sympathy for the narrator (". . . loud, fateful rap on the door of my undoing"). The yellowed pages bear your marks, attempts, in the margins, at making sense of your own descent (". . . paths traced in the dusk of summer evenings may lead as well to prisons as to innocent, untroubled sleep"). One line reverberates like the cell banging closed: "From the dark horizon of my future a sort of slow, persistent breeze had been blowing toward me, all my life long, from the years that were to come."

Could it be that simple? *Una brisa mala*, like your neighbors say when *una tormenta* appears on the horizon? Was it a breeze from the future that had you take every good lesson and repurpose it for bad? Was it a breeze that blew you off course and landed you here? Maybe it was a force from the years to come that pulled you to *el otro lado*—the other side of words, sobriety, the law. Maybe the upright iambs of English never convinced you that they tell the whole story. Maybe it simply took you this long, on this gnarly path, to figure out how to be *humano*.

When you were six, your father brought you by train to his office in the city. On the brown expanse of the conference-room table, you played with an Obi-Wan Kenobi action figure: your model for God, when you were bored enough to imagine such things.

His secretary, Clara, treated you like one of her own, but also with the glad-handing due *el hijo del jefe*, the boss's son: colored pens, drawing paper, smiles, and candy. When your stomach said *lunchtime*, you found your way into your father's well-lit corner office. He brightened the room with a squinching-eye smile, and leaned forward to introduce you to his visitors.

The brightly appointed, rugged-looking immigrant couple applying for citizenship stood up, then bent down to greet their patron's son. They accosted you with browned forearms, big smiles, and the darkened silver outlines of third-world dentistry.

You coughed up a *Buenos días* and studied the carpet. As feared, they replied with fast, gregarious Spanish that left you spitting up facial expressions, looking to your dad, choking in the choppy wake of foreign jargon.

Your face melted with the heavily perfumed pinch of your cheeks and the declarative *¡Qué lindo!* This was the same reaction you had when your great-grandmother pinched your cheeks and *kvelled, Shana punim*, then gave your "sweet face" odoriferous *mwaw-mmmwaw* kisses. Your embarrassment in the undeserved spotlight, wanting to evaporate and just be rid of it all.

The stately hotel in Santo Domingo had suffered since the picture in the brochure, which failed to mention the smells of bus exhaust and din of traffic. You and your brother couldn't swim in the pool—the water was brown. Your father explained how plumbing works, and how it breaks. Your brother giggled when he next heard a toilet flush.

A bellboy who pulled double duty as a sugar-cane vendor offered you a sample of his wares, *gratis*. Holding the maroonish cane in one hand, he unsheathed a serious-looking machete, and *whiss-whiss-whiss*'ed the skin to the ground. You got a tremendous kick out of gnawing on the whitish baton of cane sugar. You asked your mom to make the next transaction for you, but she refused.

"Ask how much he wants for two—one for you and one for your brother."

"C'mon, Ma," you said with your seven-year-old stop-breaking-my-balls eyes.

"*¿Cuánto por dos?*"

She made you repeat it.

The bellboy heard your mom give you instructions, so he was prepared to sell you two when you clumsily asked. He quoted you a price in quick Spanish—you scrunched up your brow and cocked your head, like Scooby-Doo. He repeated the number, happily holding up ten fingers. You pulled out your *plata* and made the exchange.

Walking away, you felt quite proud at having transacted business in Spanish. The novelty wore thin by the third day, but the bellboy was so eager, you dug out your coins. Your shirt, frosted like your breakfast flakes, perpetually featured dribbled spots of sticky sugar. For this you earned the sobriquet *Chooger Cane*. The entire staff, from the concierge to the chambermaids, began to call you by the new moniker. They probably laughed at what a slob you were. Your kid brother became *Chooger Cane Baby* and your dad *Chooger Cane Father*. The American Family Chooger Cane.

Stateside, your parents repeated the story to family and friends and casual acquaintances, never leaving out the grating pronunciation *Choo-ger Cane*.

The sun went down on the airport in *La Capital, Republica Dominicana*. You were hot and tired and wanted to be in a hotel room already. You wanted to give your mom and dad some whatfor, but there was no use compounding things by asking annoying questions. You and your kid brother sat on the luggage, took turns playing your Donkey Kong handheld, and cadging bits of your parents' conversation.

The flight was canceled. A flight that was supposed to hop you over the mountains and land on a dusty strip at a rural airport *por el Norte*. You'd have to wait till morning.

Somehow, your dad summoned the airport manager, a podgy, sweaty human being with the air of high command. Reaching into the inner pocket of the tan sport coat he always flew in, your dad removed his thick, creamy business card and placed it in the swarthy palm. Your dad leaned in and, in rapid, muffled Spanish, delivered a pitch that hit the right notes of anger, frustration, important-American-person-of-consequence.

When your dad was done with his pitch, the manager straightened up, almost clicking his heels, then closed the distance between himself and the unhelpful ticket agent. Your dad winked and flashed his boyish smile, the moustache to his beard taking flight like an inky gull. Then the manager huddled with the ticket agent, the conversation nearly one-sided, growing heated until he slapped the agent and sent him walking.

The manager returned with a conciliatory smile. He spoke to your dad, who in turn ushered the family down a peg-board corridor animated by a sputtering fluorescent. The airport manager's windowless office featured a smorgasbord of furniture culled from at least five different sets.

"Boys, wooht yu like sohm-sing to drínk?"

"*Sí, uh, por favor,*" you answered for the two of you.

The manager returned with thick glass bottles of Coke for everyone. Your mom asked, "What do you say?"

"*Gracias,*" is what you and your brother said.

Over the manager's desk, he and your father quickly dispensed with business. Your mom reacted to the furrowing of your brow by giving an occasional muffled translation of the proceedings. The manager had arranged for a car to take you over the mountain and to the hotel.

Your father was being polite as the manager showed him pictures of his *esposa y hijos.* You picked out the phrase "*es posible,*" and watched your father write something on the back of his business card, then hand it to the manager. When your father was involved, almost everything was *posible.* The lives of entire families changed because of him. It was common for them to send a gift—*paella, pasteles, dulces, rón*—on the anniversary of their citizenship.

Curbside, the car wasn't a car at all, but an *autobús.* A rather modern looking *autobús,* or *guagua,* out of whose window you watched your father press a green bill into the manager's paw. Having the bus to yourselves seemed more ridiculous than luxurious. You sat in the front, each sprawling on bench seating built for two.

You awoke to the rhythmic tick tock of the *guagua*'s hazard lights. The interior lights were on, like a supermarket in the night. So dark outside you could differentiate the *shapes* of stars overhead. Sinister trees lined the road. Your mom explained that the bus had a flat tire that the driver couldn't fix. Your dad stood with the man on the side of the road waiting for a passing car that would surely never motor through this shadowy patch of nowhere.

When your brother awoke, you filled him in on the sitch, speaking quietly so as to not arouse the monsters lurking in the jungle.

When a car finally approached, the driver and your father stopped it and talked travel plans. The bus driver crammed your family's luggage into the trunk of the car. Was it a cab? Was it merely a guy returning home for the night? Both? Your father sat up front and gave instructions over the squeaky shock absorbers and loosened dashboard.

The three of you squeezed together in the backseat, the night air streaming through open windows helping to battle the sticky heat and the smell of car freshener to which your upper-middle-class nose was unaccustomed; also present were darker, more primal smells that years later you'll learn to attribute to cheap wine and rough trade. You and your brother were absolutely starving, everyone was absolutely starving. More instructions to the driver.

The eatery looked sketchy, but you knew better than to object given the hairiness of the past few hours. The driver pulled off the dirt-asphalt road, killed the engine and, again, everything was a vacuum of sound within the static of flying insects. The cantina was made of cinder blocks, the wall that surrounded it was cinder blocks, the painted decor was a smattering of yellows and turquoises. Along the walls were a few promotional signs for American beverages that, years before you majored in marketing, made you wonder how they wound up in the jungle, in a cantina with corrugated metal roofing and janitorial-closet lighting. A place that seldom, if ever, saw nonlocal traffic.

A hearty woman emerged from the hut's interior. She was all smiles, aglisten with forehead sweat, the progenitrix of all the housekeepers back home. Your mom's graceful, Castilian Spanish almost made the owner swoon. You were shown to one of the plastic tables while orders were barked to the kitchen help. Your parents spoke to the woman while you and your brother numbly stared at the scrawny mutt lying in the corner. Your thoughts were probably the same as your brother's: let's play with this dog until the food shows up; but this isn't your well-fed, happy, and clean golden retriever; this dog probably wants to be left alone, this dog probably bites.

A large plate of *tostones*, your new favorite food, appeared. With canine ferocity, you tore into the plate of fried plantains. You slowly became conscious that the talk in Spanish somehow involved the two of you. You looked up, wiping grease from your maws. Through your mom, the woman urged you to save your appetite. The adults laughed as you continued eating, only slower. You could always claim the message was lost in mastication.

The fried chicken was fresh, gamier than you were used to, but amazing with spritzes of fresh lime. The woman brought you special desserts, all very good and all very, very sweet. *Dulce de leche, dulce de coco,* a *flan* that you shared with your father. You said *muchas gracias* to the woman and earned an unpleasant tousling of your hair.

There was adult business to be tended to. The woman's husband was magically spoken into being and the couple asked your dad questions. He transformed from affable tourist into competent, savvy operator.

Of all the gin joints . . . What must this couple have thought of your father? Americans with connections were surely spoken of by the locals, but as the stuff of legends: A cousin of a friend of a friend who made it to *Nueba Yol* thanks to *una persona importante* who knew the right people. Standing before them was Hermes, a messenger sent from the gods north of the border, and he was there to receive a favorable impression. You could picture them later—rosaries in one hand, cream-colored contact information in the other—recounting to their friends and family how your father emerged from the dark road, glowing with power. They'd dare to imagine their future: a *cuchi frito* in Paterson or Washington Heights, change-of-life babies (automatic citizens), vacations back to DR wearing their brightest finery, their *hijos* growing successful in the land of opportunity . . .

Your dad handed his business card to the deferential husband. The woman doggie bagged *los dulces* and gave your arm a squeeze.

You were asleep in the cab only to be jarred awake by your dad shouting. Quite uncharacteristic of him. *"¡Alto! ¡Alto!"*

Your mom joined the chorus before you realized why they were screaming at the poor cabbie to stop: he was accelerating wildly, attempting to win a game of chicken with a train. Unlike back home, the railroad crossing wasn't blocked by black-and-white wooden arms. It was more of an honor system, a dim, red light pulsing lazily on a wooden post, which taunted the Dominican: *¡Olé! Vámonos*, got plenty a' time here, *amigo*.

Your dad finally yelled the cabbie's lead foot onto the brake, and the car skidded off the road to avoid hitting the clanging cargo train. The dust stirred to life while the train rumbled past.

Your dad cursed the driver *en Español* for his peasant valuation of your lives, words and tones that weren't heard around the dinner table on Spanish night. There would be no advice from Hermes, as there had been for the roadside couple. The driver realized he'd angered the wrong American, the type who could make life difficult with a well-placed phone call. *Probably coulda made it*, you thought.

The train faded away, towing the sound with it, and the driver sheepishly continued on. The remaining half hour of your car ride was silent.

The grand hotel loomed large and bright. When you were dropped off at the porte cochere, there was no proffering of a business card, and probably little in the way of a tip.

You were efficiently shown to your rooms. The exploring would have to wait for the light of the morning. It was very late and you were very tired. With fragrant soaps and fluffy towels you cleaned off the grease and stink of the past twelve hours. As your head hit the pillow, you realized that the difference between this bed and spending a night sleeping on luggage in a hot airport was the difference between fluent Spanish-speaking parents and abrasive monolingual gringos.

You weren't old enough to drink back in the states. But this was *Cancún*, for crying out loud, the land of the teenaged hooker, why shouldn't you down *una cerveza o tres?* As you had done countless times before, after your dad ordered drinks, you tacked on a *lo mismo*, make mine the same. You did this in Americanized, Taco Bell Spanish, not wanting to sound uncool for taking something seriously.

The cute waitress looked at your dad for the OK.

Your dad looked at you and chuckled, "Right."

"C'mon, Dad, we're on vacation."

The waitress brought you *un Coke* with a plastic sword full of maraschino cherries, which made you feel that much more juvenile.

When you saw the waitress leave work after midnight, you broke off from the kids you met earlier. The two of you walked along the light-blue moonlit beach. "*Hola*," you said over the surf.

"*Hola*," she giggled.

"*¿Habla Inglés?*"

"Yehs, a leetle."

"*Yo soy de Los Estados Unidos.*"

As the waitress's eyes went wide with visions of the Hollywood sign, Times Square, touristy whatnot, and green cards, you sat down with her on a beach chair. She was around your age and, like your housekeeper, probably watched *las novelas*, cheesy soaps, whenever time permitted. This *Carmencita* definitely entertained notions of tall, mustachioed *hombres* oozing machismo, sweeping her off her feet, rescuing her from a life of poverty, loving her for a countryside lifetime. But she'd have to settle for you.

By this age, you had already begun to shut yourself down— a self-preservation mechanism against a suicidal self-loathing that your coevals experienced as garden-variety insecurity. A consequence of this numbing: a diminished ability to feel for and with others. If empathy is the quintessential human characteristic, when you erode it, you erode your humanity, despite all the love you receive at home. For you—One Night Stanley—the opposite sex amounted to little more than tender, touchable, finger-poppable playthings. Your ability to love only stretched finger deep, and you lived it up to the knuckle.

"*Siéntese aquí, señorita,*" was the last complete sentence you spoke to her. She wanted romance, you gave her Señor Glick's Unit on Simple Commands filtered through *Penthouse* Letters. You were in her pants in less than five, and then spent the rest of your vacation trying to order beers and avoiding this waitress.

Freshman year of college, you registered for a unit of Spanish to fulfill a pesky liberal arts requirement, figuring it would be an easy B, *no problema. La clase* met *a las nueve por la mañana—un problema.* Way too early for your crapulent hangovers.

Your mom asked how you did on the midterm and you told her: "got a C," inflating by two letter grades.

"A C!?" your mom said over the phone's receiver. "But you *speak* Spanish." She was more confused than exasperated.

"*Yo sé,*" you told her, "*me voy a tratar con más fuerza, Ma.*" The "I'm gonna try harder" yarn that you'd worn threadbare over the years now worked because of the delivery.

El profesor was *un cabrón,* you reasoned—of course you didn't try harder. You weren't even able to scrape out a gentleman's D.

Your parents were not pleased.

Heralding your sophomore year were the warm colors of a New England fall. Prowling the quad, you learned some daffy campus organization was throwing a fund-raiser. The dorm flyer read:

MexiCali Buffet
Faculty Dining Hall
ALL YOU CAN EAT $7.50
Tonight

It was a weekday afternoon, you and your two *amigos* were *muy borracho,* powerful drunk, and thirsty for vicious mischief. Angry, on edge, coming down from the morning's Ritalin binge. The Valium not yet working its somnolent magic, your frayed nerve endings sparking like exposed wires. You grab the flyer off the bulletin board, hand it to the boys, and blindly paw the tabs off the flyers for rides home, rooms for rent, guitars for sale. It was agreed that you three will make this student organization very sorry for printing the words "All you can eat."

A trio of jackals emblazoned with Greek letters, you made your way to the faculty dining hall. You all paid your $7.50, then smiled wickedly piggy to each other.

Enrique, your Spanish professor from the year before, wearing a *Hello My Name Is,* gave you a genuinely warm *Hola,* which you returned with a *Whatever,* while bumping past him.

Veterans of the buffet scene, your crew took a table closest to the food. You were there to do damage, not get a name tag and be sociable. This was the serious business of your pleasure, and there was no time for small talk. You attacked the serving trays, piling your plates high with meat and cheese and lettuce and salsa and sour cream and guacamole and jalapeños.

When Johnboy grabbed a handful of bread sticks, you eyed him with disgust. "*Orale, vato,* starches are for suckers. Don't be such a piker, get your head in the game." He tossed them back into the serving tray.

With sleeves pushed up, you tucked greedily into your plates, leaning over the spotless white table cloth, and spraying brown juice from your dripping snouts. Everyone went back for seconds, then thirds. You drew concerned glances from faculty advisors and students.

"What kinda meat you think this is?" Spanky asked the table.

"Grade E," you replied between spicy mouthfuls. "Circus animals *con* filler."

"Filler?" said Johnboy.

"*Sí, seguro,*" you continued with increasing authority, "Chinese newspapers ground to a pulp."

Laughter sprayed food. General merriment as you all wound down. And, truth be told, you would have been OK stopping there, if it hadn't been for the cute blonde girl who began to dismantle the buffet table while the organization's boys watched nervously for your reactions. Personally affronted, your troika demanded to know the meaning of this.

You switched to mock sincerity, gently pleading with a faculty member that you had paid your hard-earned money to eat all that you could and you were not full (*"No estoy completemente lleno"*) and you were going to have to go to bed hungry and it just wasn't fair.

"It's OK, gentlemen," assuaged the dean's secretary. "We'll be bringing out a build-your-own sundae cart momentarily . . . oh, look, here it comes."

And so it did. You were allowed to go before the name-tagged others, and made obscene sundaes, grotesquely gooey affairs. After the initial surge of sundae goers, Spanky managed to snake the open box of Reddi-wip cans, which he tossed under the table with a giggle. Experts at taking whippits under pressure, you three reached for a can, broke-jammed the white nozzles, quickly inhaled the entire amount of pressurized nitrous oxide, then tossed the oozing whip cream cans back under *la mesa*.

The sweet air went straight to the brain, made everything warm and giggly light. You went back for whippit seconds and thirds. Then you were all standing, floating out of the dining lounge, wild-eyed and numb with oxygen-deprived brains and whipped-cream-spattered torsos. Drooling, arms flailing wildly, drifting out the doors, and down the stairs somehow. The laughter *wa-wa-wa*'ing in your ears, the sound of the brain eating itself. Into the men's room you twirled giggling.

Each in a stall, you did your worst to pee all over the place. It was Spanky who first shattered his toilet with three hard drop kicks. Capital; *¡Qué magnífico!* You stomped your Bass loafers against the rim of yours. The unit wrenched noisily out of the wall on the third kick, and on the fifth it hit the floor, shattering like so many white ceramic ice cubes while the water sloshed past your shoes and you *ooohed* and *aaahed*. Johnboy then disposed of his toilet. Then all went to work on the sinks, smashing ceramic to smithereens and laughing maniacally.

Out you walked, proud and victorious, and listened for anyone coming to break up the fun. Luckily, the kitchen was nearby, laying down a heavy cover fire of clanking pans. Putting your worst foot forward, you broke from the pack and spun back into *el baño*, running down the row of stalls, kicking the flush valves into permanent ON, spraying like geysers out of the wall. The boys agreed that was a nice coup de grâce as you walked out of the building.

Later in your drunken travels that night, you flew through the back stairways, and passed two Spanish-speaking women from the cleaning crew obviously talking about your earlier mayhem.

"*Animales,*" one huffed to the other.

"*Animales,*" the other *señora* slowly confirmed, bewildered as to the *El Niño*-like destructive force unleashed indoors.

You bit your fist to keep from laughing in their presence as you loped by. You wondered if there was a Spanish idiom analogous to the English: What kind of animal . . . ? Maybe, *¿Qué tipo de animal . . . ?*

To yourself, you quoted Dr. Johnson—the epigraph to Hunter S. Thompson's *Fear and Loathing in Las Vegas* past which you weren't sober enough to read—"He who makes a beast of himself gets rid of the pain of being a man."

In the next weekly issue of the campus newspaper, your hijinks received a special mention in addition to a spot in the campus police blotter. A couple of inches cowritten by the dean of students and the chief of campus police angrily described how much damage was caused (seventy five-plus thousand dollars was surely an exaggeration for insurance purposes), how it reflected poorly on the student body entire, and concluded with a stern warning that the perpetrators would not go unpunished.

The clipping made a nice addition to your scrapbook of destruction, a best-of your unnamed appearances in the campus police blotter. Aside from abstract financial ramifications, you reassured yourself that yours was a victimless crime (unlike throwing up on your RA's door). Just a little prank, boys being boys. You didn't initiate it, after all, and you were only following suit, no? Wouldn't want to let the boys down, right? One victim, of course, was your better nature, but you'd smashed the mirror before you had a chance to see the look on your face. The distinction between destruction and self-destruction becoming a thousand glittering shards reflecting nothing.

It was junior year when many of your friends went to study abroad. You knew your grades would preclude you, but figured you could finagle an official waiver, the way you did for courses that were already filled.

Your parents weren't easy sells. But you appealed to your mom, who spent a summer in Mexico City during college, and convinced her how much you wanted to live in Madrid and perfect your Spanish.

The school was a different story. "Young man," the head of the study abroad program admonished, "you've been on academic probation for three semesters. We don't *feel* you would represent the university well in another country. Why do you even *want* to study in Madrid?"

You should have been ready for such a question, maybe have something prepared to say *en Español*. Still coursing with last night's ecstasy, lit up with Northern Lights, you gave an impassioned plea, which centered mostly around your love for the Spanish people. Afterward, you remembered repeatedly referring to yourself as a "people person," an approach so stupid it practically drooled.

You relayed the school's decision to your folks. "*Qué será, será*," you said over the phone to your mom, while digging around the couch for a lighter.

Her voice rose instantly: "You're being awfully cavalier about this."

As she got angrier, you wondered if you had inferred an incorrect translation and been using it incorrectly all these years. *Qué será, será.* \ kā sîr'ə, sîr'ə \[Sp]: Life will kick you in the soft stuff. Repeatedly.

"No," your mom clipped, "no, that's not what it means at all. *Translate* it."

"Uh, *qué* means *what, será* means . . . uhhh—"

"You know what *sera* means. *Diga me.*"

"I don't know."

Now exasperated, she gave a quick lesson in the future tense. *Será*, future tense of *ser*, to be. *Will* be. *Qué será, será.* What will be, will be.

Damn future tense.

Yours was truly the unexamined life, the past and future tenses not your strong suit. As quick-witted as you were, you showed an incredibly slow uptake of big-picture stuff like past performance, meaning, and story arc. The world was your playground, people your playthings—any cognitive dissonance that arose, you easily drowned with liberal applications of substances, both controlled and non, from A to X.

By the end of the semester, your friends abroad began mailing you envelopes of opium or hashish or opiated hash from their wild weekends in Amsterdam. Smoking the goodies, you laughed at the crusty, turtle-necked administrator who wouldn't let you go to Madrid. You won, you tried to convince yourself, as the sweet smoke bubbled from the water and curled into your bong.

You were familiar with the reptile brain by face, if not name. You learned the quickest ways there, and with cost-efficient precision. While you didn't know how the old parts of the brain factored into pleasure addiction (slept through that Bio 101 lecture), you did know the precise mixture of water to heroin required for a smoke. You chased the dragon with your friends, floated weightless around your warm college apartment, sucked down warm, better-tasting cigarettes, oozed onto soft couches, came in warm kootches.

Back home after getting expelled from college ("Your behavior finally catching up with you," as your parents said), a mortarboard's toss away from graduation, your nascent heroin habit quickly grew to a mainlining affair. You burgeoned from single heat-wrapped dope-bags to ten-pack rubber-banded bundles. Searching for yourself in the wrong places, you wound up lost. And what did you lose? The direction, the plot, the person inside your better self. These weren't conscious decisions, you didn't think: *I like this path of debauchery, but to continue on it, I have to replace my empathy with an unflinching obeisance to my pleasure center.* The id doesn't speak like that (reason does), it just says: Me wantee, *yo quiero*. There was little to no forethought with you, little in the way of rational thinking—thanks to the drugs for lowering your inhibitions.

The Dominican dealers in the city liked your girlfriend and gave her decent deals. She was Sailor Moon pretty and junkie thin and threw around her sexuality. In the beginning, when you were only copping a couple of times a week, you could split a bag with the girl, and bring her to cop for the two of you. As a couple, you could've been mistaken for Al Pacino and Kitty Winn in *The Panic in Needle Park*.

When it became daily excursions, you learned to fly solo. You formed relationships with the runners, the hustlers, the dime bag chuckers. Cash changed hands, hands exchanged junk. You smiled a see you later, and nodded off on the *smoooth* drive home.

What you learned about copping: it's incredibly easy. Nothing to be scared of. Just pull up to the curb, let your guy sidle up to the window and "serve" you (like McDonald's, over one guhzillion bags sold). They're mostly Dominican, these purveyors, with a Puerto Rican every now and then. No need for your Spanish. You vibed Well-heeled Junkie, they strained to make their English presentable. They gave you cell phone- and pager-numbers, made sure you got into and out of the neighborhood safely, and made sure you knew you could call upon them almost any time ("Jus' not too late, Papi"). In their heads, they calculated your Lifetime Customer Value. That was their business and business was good.

After a few months, when the money became problematic, you broke out your Spanish like you were doling out pesos to sugar cane salesmen. You pronounced your dealers' fake names with reverence, trilling your Rs, paying heed to the accent marks.

Sweating, shaking, dope sickness. Desperate times called for desperate Spanish. You could always manage a pathos-wrenching

Ayúdame, while your eyes said: Help me. The pronunciation alone allowed you to purchase an $80 bundle (the standard 20 percent discount on ten $10 bags) for $75 plus some *plata*.

When that no longer worked, your dealer, Jesús, gave you eight bags for your $250 radar detector. You drove more carefully. *Tú me conoces,* you know me, is what you'd say when asking for a two-bag line of credit. On the strength of past dealings, and still bearing pin-striped respectability with its promise of better times, you could get a few bags *por crédito*, a little something to see you through the night. The friendlier dealers tsk'd, *Estabas jodido.* And they were right, you were fucked up, broke, and out of it.

Your girlfriend could cry alligator dope-sick tears and bat her eyes from the front seat. The dealer would toss her a bag. But tears are for those who still have hope. You couldn't squeeze any, and they wouldn't help even if you could. The flip side of being respected by a group is abiding by their mores. And in the land of machismo, men don't cry—*maricones* do. There was nothing left to do but curse God and get high, overdose and die.

You were a defective unit. *Un animal* propelled by dope-sick depravity, dangerous, saurian cunning. Of course, no animal thinks it's an animal.

Illegal operators or not, the Dominicans held on to Latino notions of trust and honor, placed you on a higher plane for communicating with them in their native tongue. This made it easier to game them here and there, getting over for a few bucks, and moving your copping to another neighborhood. This was your eight-hour myopia, a result of being chained to a slithering organism that required a thrice daily dosing of opiates, lest it start oozing fluids, cramping up, and behaving very, very badly.

There was nerve and coordination, *chutzpah* involved in handing a dealer a fin over a bunch of singles as payment for your $80 bundle. You would peel away from the curb, dodging the honking, oncoming traffic, with a bundle on your front seat and a very angry dealer in the rearview.

One autumn night, a dealer from back in the day flagged you down as you rolled through the neighborhood. You hesitated, played it safe. He assured that all was cool, *'stá bien, amigo.* Through the passenger's window he offered you a free taste of his new wares, asked about the girl, and made small talk.

Turning to flick a Marb out your window, you glimmed a figure sneaking up past your blind spot. Your side view showed a cartoonishly oversized revolver pointing toward your ear and a body tapering behind it. When you saw the gun pointed at your head, the breath left you like you had just booted an eight-bag shot. You wanted to shift into drive and scram, but remained frozen, stuck on stupid, as the hustlers say.

A voice boomed from down the block. *"Chino, calmate! Vas a calentar el bloque!"* Don't make the block "hot" by killing a white kid, it's bad for business.

Walking toward you was the owner of that voice. All swagger and home turfedness: a stomping grounds gait. An elder, perhaps in his early thirties, who never transacted street sales, probably a low-level supervisor, a Somebody.

Gently easing off the brake and quickly accelerating, you passed Somebody, who made his fingers into a gun and spit in your face as you drove by. You blew a red light and got the hell out of Dodge, shaking numb. In the lighted visor-mirror, you wiped the cold, beer-infused spittle from the darkened circles of your eyes.

You looked in the rearview the whole way home, flinching whenever you saw corner kids.

Like Colonel Kurtz, who went way off the path and was found on *el otro lao*, your methods were no longer sound. You were so far afield that you saw no way of returning home. But you weren't too far gone to remember what home felt like, to pine for it, to slam smack dab into the junkie's catch-22: you can't continue using heroin, you can't stop using heroin; you can't live with heroin, you can't live without it. Still, you'd never quit today what you could quit *mañana*. *Mañana y pues mañana y pues mañana . . .* There was a part of you that wanted to just avoid making the decision altogether, or to outsource it to someone. Someone like the kid who was about to scatter-paint the windshield with your drug-addled brains.

Todos sus amigos son falsos, todos sus enemigos son reales.

—Mexican Proverb

Sober junkies often say that if they didn't quit H, they would've wound up dead or in jail. You wound up in jail, the deaths weren't your own, and, after sixteen months, your stint as a junkie had ended.

You lived for H. You killed for H. A desperate act. An animal in a corner freaking out, needing its life-preserving feed, you did as an animal does—then found it's gone ahead and done it. You finally learned, albeit in a way none should, that it's rarely a sunny day in Youville when the reptilian brain gets up to bat.

You met the enemy and he is you. The moral of the story is that anyone is capable of anything at any time. But, that's not spoken. It's too scary to think that way about our loved ones, our friends, ourselves. Instead, the cautionary tale is given emphasis. A tale of the havoc you wrought will be told with a sigh by loved ones, for ages and ages hence. You *killed* for H. Life, as you knew it, had ended. Through the fog of your shock, you realized: You're never going home, there's no one to go home *to*; there's no return from such madness.

Like George Carlin said, "Just because the monkey's off your back, doesn't mean the circus has left town." You chased the dragon, now the dragon will chase you. It will appear in the form of "friends" and cellmates who offer you junk. It will force a reckoning in B-Block, where on the soft, white underside of your bicep, you had tattooed an incongruously cute, purple Puff the Magic Dragon. Let it haunt you for life.

Behind prison walls, you found what you forfeited years ago: liberty. A freedom understood by losing everything and beginning the slow process of finding yourself anew in your early twenties. You turned your time into a belated junior year, seeking knowledge and adventure, trying on new ideas. Going through the stages of grief, you learned about yourself, tested your mettle, pondered what kind of egg you'd been.

Meanwhile, 30 percent of the prison's population was Hispanic. A New World paella mainly stocked with Puerto Ricans, flavored with a smattering of Dominicans, with savory hints of Cubans and Colombians, and colorful chunks of Ecuadorans, Salvadorans, and Mexicans.

When you were housed in-between Spanish speakers for months at a time, it was the longest you were immersed in the language. You heard it on your neighbors' tellies *en las mañanas y las noches*, over the mess hall table, at work, *en la yarda*. You couldn't help but again become quasi-fluent.

Just like when you spent an extended vacation in the Dominican Republic or the several months you were able to last managing warehouses staffed by bustling undocumenteds, you began to have the occasional dream *en Español*. This always signaled an uptick in your fluency.

Maybe you tell yourself that when you get out in a few decades, you can use your Spanish and your sack of people skills (i.e. negotiation and conciliation) and do a snug piece of *negociós internacionales*.

You can be a pirate, a privateer, a publicly traded company owner.

Buying pot wasn't a bad way to ingratiate yourself with the legions of Hispanic drug purveyors operating in the yard like at a Middle Eastern bazaar. You paid your bills, your Spanish got better, and the sellers got a kick out of you.

If, in order to please them, you had started sucking up to them, agreeing with them, taking on their various mannerisms in order to win their friendship, they would have immediately figured that you were doing this out of fear and cowardice, and they would have made you their victim.

Instead, you remembered Señor Glick's eighth-grade Spanish class. The green, orange, and yellow-colored textbook. You cherry picked the information helpful to your new life, like the unit relating to *el supermercado*. Place your groceries *en una bolsa*.

You repurposed these lessons, translated your current slang into Spanish, asked for *una bolsa de verde*. Armed with *¿Cómo se dice?* and *¿Qué significa?*, you learned how to ask for *monas*, buds, and steer clear of *polvo*, shake.

Los tigres[2], the hustlers and savvy operators, sometimes called you *paisa*, thinking highly enough of you to consider you a countryman.

On a hot summer night in the yard, Coquí, your go-to for good greens, asked you to take a walk. Coquí walked you into the middle of the yard where stood a sinewy Puerto Rican in a yellow tracksuit. His painted-on hair and jaw-outline beard were edged perfectly like the hedgerows back home, his gold rope chain thicker than your pen. You would later learn he was one of the higher-ranking Latin Kings in the state. Next to him was a menace who needed no introduction, 'ector el Collectór, *el cobrador* who was sent to twist the arms of buyers with past-due accounts. Hector eyed you with his permanent scowl, both his hands in the deep recesses of sweatpants pockets. Juggling lint, possibly, or a razor. Or his *huevos*.

You looked to Coquí, but his face gave no clues. Your immediate concern was that someone in the yard had recognized you from back home, the maniacal junkie with the red Jeep. Someone you had ripped off for a couple bags had put a contract out. A poetic and chthonic ending to your tale.

---

2. Your Mexican friends prefer the term *tiburones*, sharks, rather than the Dominican's "tigers." This footnote is your splitting the difference.

To the bright yellow figure, Coquí introduced you as *mi gente*, vouching for you as "his people." Shaking the outstretched hand of Big Yellow, you offered a proper greeting: *mucho gusto*, a pleasure. But you lisped your S—*mucho guthto*—like a Castilian. The classy greeting didn't go unnoticed.

"Coquí say you real smart."

"Smart enough," you conceded.

"*Entonces*, they wanna deport my boy Hectuh back to the D.R. He's gotta immigration hearing coming up . . ."

In the months that followed, you translated Hector's rambling, guttural letters into a cohesive questioning of the pro-bono *abogado* handling the extradition hearing. You translated him through the process, not that it changed things—he still got deported. But Hector appreciated your help and let it be known that you were protected. More than once Big Yellow pulled you aside in the yard to say *Te lo agradezco*, I appreciate it. After making sure *el guardia* wasn't watching, he'd motion for one of his *paisas* to shake *su mano*, leaving in it *una peseta*.

You'd nonchalantly pocket the sugar packet full of *hierba*, twenty-five-dollars-worth of his appreciation, then nod and say, *Te lo agradethco.*

The years passed and you went out to the yard less and less. Your drug Spanish waned, but you kept it active enough to place the occasional order *por hierba: "Oye, amigo, quiero una peseta, tengo paquetes de Newport." Hierba mala nunca muere,* weeds never die.

More interestingly, you learned of the strict hierarchy amongst Hispanics. Cultural anthropology your new hobby. Spaniards are like royalty. Vying for second place are Colombians and Cubans. Then you've got all the other Latin Americans, followed by your Puerto Ricans. There's some jockeying for position and some instability in the ranks if, say, one country's *fútbol* team did spectacularly well in the most recent

Copa Mundial. Despite their fierce nationalism and bitter rivalry, they can all agree that the Mexicans are dogs, *perros.*

Miguel was in his early twenties when he moved into a double bunk cell on your company. The Hispanics called him *México*, but you preferred the dignity of his given name. His peers, Renzo and the detestable Chui, worked him like a pack mule—cooking, washing clothes, sewing—in return for table scraps. But you watched him learning quickly, lifting whole phrases from the English speakers. You saw the injustice of his being smarter than his peers, but always the odd man out. His being called "*abrelata*" (can opener), no better than calling a woman with an ample bosom "cans."

Tutoring Miguel with his English began organically. You were baked, *estaba arrebatado y drogado*, and feeling even more friendly and helpful than your norm. You had him write a paragraph *en Inglés* detailing how he crossed into *Los Estados Unidos.* Then you made a few minor corrections and had him write it over. You gave him a few lessons in usage and grammar.

Later that night, you realized that you had just taught someone, performed a completely selfless act. You basked yourself to sleep in the warm feelings of altruism. It felt good to be good.

You continued helping Miguel and vowed to help him pass his GED. Like most novice teachers, you often put more into the study than the student. You gave him a copy of Junot Díaz's *Drown* to show what was possible, then gave what passed for tough love. On a piece of paper, you wrote: YOU MUST CHANGE YOUR LIFE. A Rilke quote that you had used as a retooling mantra. Underneath, you had him translate it. *Se tiene que cambiar su vida.* You nodded, he smiled. You taped the paper to his wall.

At times you hear the gentle plucking, two cells away, of Daní Cavallero (whose name you absolutely love)—*un viejo,* an old man with an acoustic guitar that's faded from use along the neck.

The pleasant notes reverberate and waft your way like diaphanous patches of cotton candy. This south-of-the-border rendering of Kansas's "Dust in the Wind" soothes like a golden dream sequence of dry-ice clouds and angels' harps. It is practicing more than playing, reminding you of a Mexican café, a cantina during the day, from back before life got crazy.

The cantina is nearly empty. Dark wood chairs, tables, floor, and ceiling beams. Dust lazily spirals in the several shafts of post-noon light. Everyone relaxes in the worn, wicker chairs, your father's camera bag hanging from the back of his. Your mother puts her purse on the table. You and your brother decimate the bowl of tortilla chips. Your waiter pours from a sweating pitcher swaddled in white cloth. The water is cool and sorely needed and tastes heavier than the water back home. The band—one of whose members is partly visible around the gentle corner of the bar—practices for nightfall. It's slow, languid, and serene. One *tocadero* practices finger work for a song's bridge. One plays with lyrics, seeing how the changes sound to his ear.

This is what hearing *El Viejo* Daní does for you. You regularly compliment him on his playing and tell him how nice it makes you feel. He always eye-smiles, bespectacled, rheumy, and pats your arm, repaying your compliment.

You listen to the gentle music. Daní's muffled singing is so low that one can hardly tell what's what. The rhythm and melody are very Mexican—*muy auténtico*. Each bar ends with a dulcet drop of melancholy, like the upward inflection of a sentence-ending question. Breathtaking, life affirming.

You lie quiet behind steel bars, beast no longer, caged nonetheless. You close your eyes and sip the air. Listen. Think. *Feel.* Your brain is slowly rewiring itself. Learning how to be a human being again.

THREE

Decibel Hell

*The mind is its own place, and in itself
Can make a Heav'n of Hell, a Hell of Heav'n.*

—John Milton, *Paradise Lost*

No one will ever confuse me for the revolutionary George Jackson. He was a Panther. I'm a pussycat. He dug Ché, Lenin, and Giap. With seven years into my prison term, I'm relatively content to be living in Prison A, and am more into chai, Lennon, and the GAP. But on the subject of noise, we're brothers. A couple years before he was gunned down in San Quentin's yard, Jackson wrote this about noise:

> It destroys the logical processes of the mind, a man's thoughts become completely disorganized. The noise, madness streaming from every throat, frustrated sounds from the bars, metallic sounds from the walls, the steel trays, the iron beds bolted to the wall, the hollow sounds from a cast-iron sink or toilet . . . This is Saturday: There is so much noise on the tier that even my earplugs are useless. Grown men are acting like high-school girls. The guards have some kind of sports on the radio.[1]

---

1. George Jackson, *Soledad Brother*

The state-sanctioned violence in prison has become a lot less blatant over these past forty years. The noise, however, hasn't changed a bit. Five feet from where I sit reading there is a barrage of Spanish yelling. It is not a fight, but rather an ugly colloquy concerning sports teams, movies, and the associated characters. Bad noise from bad men. All that separates me from this aural assault are the steel bars of my cell and the bed sheet I have hanging as a curtain. That is to say, nothing separates me. The noise owns me. I realize that I've been reading the same line repeatedly for the past half hour. Sitting at my desk, trying to lose myself in a book, I look to escape from Prison A the most productive way I know. Twenty minutes ago, before the noise, I was in a 1920s Princeton dorm room courtesy of F. Scott Fitzgerald's *This Side of Paradise*. Now I'm back in prison as three animals mill around a table regrettably close to my cell, and I want to scream.

My mind leaves the page and quickly grows dark: *Let the yelling lead to violence. Let one stab another. That'll quiet shit down.* Violence in prison is always accompanied by silence. Tense silence, but silence. Because I understand a fair bit of Spanish, I know that this spirited debate is asininity followed by misinformation with upside-down exclamation points smacked onto each word. No, there will be no violence here. Just more shouting until they disperse to watch TV or eat. Such is the tyranny of the boorish and their pedestrian desires.

Almost as a rule in prison, a point is made not on the merits of one's argument, but on the vociferousness of one's delivery. It's not just the Latinos, it's everyone. In the course of life, you will find that the people with the least intelligent things to say are those who say them most loudly. These clowns invading my space are but ghetto versions of right-wing radio hosts. Being hyperaware of your surroundings helps keep you alive and it definitely helps your writing. But it's a nightmare in a place like this, where you can never close a door on the noise. I've often fantasized about a loss of hearing that I could somehow control.

The line I've been trying to read: "Tom was deep in his work, and inside the room only the occasional scratch of a match or the rustle of leather as they shifted in their chairs broke the stillness."

Noise, everyone hates it. That's why it's called noise and not ice cream sundae. The word comes from the Latin, *nausea*, seasickness. Listen to how luxury car commercials tout "quiet interiors" more stridently than Dolby sound systems. Unless you're enjoying the collective effervescence of a large public gathering, you likely want the noise kept at a minimum. It's why dampers of all sorts were invented. Owing to their construction and inhabitants, prisons are noisy places. Metal, stone, concrete, brick, and safety glass—all bounce sound. And since there's no carpet and nothing soft to damper the sound except human bodies, the noises of prison crash around and land hard in your eardrums. Gates banging shut are grating until one gets accustomed to the sound—then it becomes mere annoyance, like a car's horn. Antiquated steam pipes knock and bang in what is called a water hammer, a perfectly descriptive term.

But the bulk of the noise is from the prison's residents. By most standards, these are close quarters. An average company is roughly 250 feet long, the cells are six feet wide and separated by quarter-inch steel. You share this company with forty-four men. If you're unlucky, your prison is very old and is made of multiple "open tiers." This open tier design is familiar to anyone who's seen *The Shawshank Redemption*: companies stacked on top of each other, with a grated metal catwalk between the floors. Your noise level then increases by a factor of three (or more) floors. (You'll experience this when you follow me to Prison F.) And if you're really unfortunate, the open tiers face their mirror image thirty to fifty feet away.

I count myself lucky not to live in such a place. In Prison A, there are stone floors that separate me from the floor below. Still, there is constant noise. Papers shuffling, toilets flushing, teeth brushing, the human digestive system working, TVs and radios blaring. There's cursing, coughing, threatening, and cajoling. Mad men holding conversations with themselves. And this passel of Puerto Ricans. They have been the bane of my existence for the past several years and I've taken an ugly, unsophisticated, and quite racist view of them.

My chief antagonist is called Chui (pronounced "Chewey"), a nickname often bestowed on men named Jesús. Chui is a complete narcissist and one of the loudest people I've ever encountered, someone with no concept of an indoor voice. He lies in bed and yells to a neighbor fifty feet away rather than get up. Even writing about him makes me angry, because I can hear you, reader, thinking: *He can't be that bad.* He can and is. And now I must explain myself or appear vicious. Seriously, I can't refrain from saying a few words about this man, as he is the apotheosis of aural torment, the ne plus ultra of noise. Ladies and gentlemen, hurry, hurry, step right up, I give you Chui.

I've tried diplomacy, asked if he could wear headphones. He said, get this, "Oh, my TV bother you?" Like it's my problem, not his inconsideration. When he was screaming outside my cell, addressing himself to his peers less than three feet away, his booming voice penetrating through my headphones, I stuck my head out: "C'mon, man. You're screaming." He said that no, he wasn't screaming, then returned to screaming at his friends.

Pause for a moment of quiet reflection with me. The headphones I mentioned are of the noise-canceling type. I managed to get a pair for the sole purpose of canceling such neighbors, so you can imagine my devastating chagrin, can you not? They were *developed* to counter the monstrous whine of twin turbines, yet Chui's booming irrelevance renders these headphones practically useless. I've tried to get others to totally ignore him, but it seems I'm the only one cold enough to pretend this scumbag doesn't even exist, to stare a fucking hole through him.

Chui continues on, uninterrupted. He speaks a loud, uneducated, frenetic Spanish. English speakers would call him a motor mouth; in Spanish it's *ametrallador*, a machine gunner. His words are punctuated by long *uhhhhs* and *ahhhs*, and I want to hit him and say: *Hey, stupid, slow down, think about what you want to say, then say it—SOFTLY*. And the topics of his conversation are the night's TV schedule, pop-stars' bodies, and the most outlandish conspiracy theories you'll ever hear. He butchers his own language with talk about nothing. He lives several cells away, but has found a willing ear in my Dominican neighbor, Renzo, who happens to be a great guy, but is a magnet for noise. Chui is a tall, husky fuck. With slightly crossed eyes, he appears to be a mix between Mongo the fat, dumb cat on the cartoon *Heathcliff* and Saddam Hussein. I recall taking a shower in the stall next to him over the summer. He turned the water off on his side, then I noticed a stream of yellow sluicing down the drain. That's textbook narcissism: not only peeing in a communal shower, but doing so *after* the water's been turned off. A douche bag coup de grâce. Like Saddam standing on a balcony and firing off his shotgun into the air, he is a walking assault on the senses.

Chui is the obnoxious lady reeking of perfume who wedges herself into the elevator, never bothering to hang up her phone. He applies scented oils to his lamp, and the smells waft twenty feet in either direction. He perfumes himself with this oil, so that if you happen to be in his wake, you can actually taste this sweet shit in your mouth. It's for Chui that someone coined the term "Puerto Rican shower." Somewhere, there is a family of people very happy that he is locked up. They can enjoy their breakfast in peace.

Someone like this is the activity director at a resort. He's great behind the mic, going apeshit, screaming himself hoarse, exhorting the sunburned Americans onto a conga line, clapping his hands over his head and blowing a fucking whistle.

He has an infectious laugh. But you don't invite the loud activity director to your table for drinks during the calmer evening hours. The hotel management knows to keep him locked away when it's quiet time.

This past summer the Latinos got into an almost daily routine of making *morir sonyando*. It's the Puerto Rican Orange Julius, and translates: "to die dreaming." Chui would herald the arrival of the drink (or, as was often the case, manipulate one of his peers into making it) by screaming *MORIIIIIR SONYAAAAANDO* like that idiot soccer announcer. I found myself fantasizing that the drink actually did cause death. Die dreaming? I don't care. Die gurgling on poison, die vomiting up frothy orange drink, but just die quietly, away from me. Nice, right?

A word on your author. I am quiet. Not shy, or even reserved, but considerate. My free time is occupied by reading and writing. In this way, I am an alien in a landscape where most of the reading is along the columns of TV listings. Decades ago, Piri Thomas described the scenery of his incarceration in *Seven Long Times*. "Bayamon, Zorro, L'il Henry, and Juan de Jesus were engaged in animated conversation." *Animated conversation*—that's one way of putting it. Piri, I initially thought, you give them too much credit. But a few sentences later, one learns that Juan is holding a *New York Times* on which the conversation centers. I once left a *Times* on my neighbor's table, thinking one of his crew would find something of interest. When I returned, I saw Chui with the paper. It was rolled up and he was using it to scratch his back. So, before you judge me, imagine yourself in a serene yoga studio, doing restorative back poses, *Ommmmmm*. Now *crash!* One of the walls crumbles down and exposes the frenetic, noisy kitchen of a Mexican restaurant. This is my life. It is hard enough to lead an intellectual life in a place so devoid of rational thinkers. Add to that the near constant distraction of inconsiderate thugs, and one must attain a Zen mastery of his concentration.

I loathe Chui for the aural assaults, but I resent him for the ugly things I feel. I recently wrote to a cousin and asked if his Puerto Rican friends were not preternaturally loud, boorish people. He wrote back laughing off my racism, saying that they're not that bad and I should chill out. Easy for you, I thought, you don't have to live next door to them. But then I remembered Puerto Ricans from college with whom I was friendly. They were caring, intellectual folk. There are Latinos on the company who are paragons of consideration. Daní, the sweet old man, whose gentle guitar work takes my breath away. My boy, Yas, for whom I have love like a brother, is half Puerto Rican. Yet all these positive examples are eclipsed, at least for the moment, by Chui.

Aside from violence, which I will not do, there is no dealing with a bad neighbor. Someone like Chui is operating on such a different plane that there's no making him see reason. You can ask him politely to respect your airspace. If you're lucky, he quiets down for a few, like he's doing you a favor. And in his mind he is. But the next time you ask him to keep it down, the testosterone rages. He says, "Why don't you move?" "Why? Because I was here first, I like it here. AND WHO THE FUCK ARE YOU?! Why don't *you* move?" Nothing good comes of this exchange. From here on out, you will feel like he is making noise to spite you. And he is.

In Dante's inferno, each sin's punishment is a *contrapasso*, a symbolic instance of poetic justice: the soothsayers were made to walk backward, because they claimed to see the future during their lives. If I were inclined to believe in a literal karma, I'd say Chui has been thrown at me by the universe for the noisy tortures I inflicted on dorm-room neighbors. Or, for the people who lived above me off campus, who were subjected to the DJ's thumping soundtrack in my living room during the weekend-long bacchanals. And more recently, when I was relatively new to prison, the nights spent "on the gate," standing at my bars and joking with a friend who was also in a giggly pot stupor. Chalk it up to a matured sense of empathy or to temporary lucidity, but I learned my lesson on the spot one night. An old timer, housed a few cells over, called: "Hey, kid, it's eleven o'clock, wanna get the fuck outta my house?" His logic was unassailable and I make further amends now by urging you to find and read his work ("Ryan's Ruse" in Bell Gale Chevigny's collection, *Doing Time: Twenty-Five Years of Prison Writing*).

But Chui is, finally, but the loudest truth amid the truly noisy world I now call home. Some years later, during my first visit with Lily, she asked if I could describe the essence of prison. Chui came to mind, but rather than invoke him, I took a moment to construct a suitable analogy, then told her the following: Imagine the high school boys' locker room after a football game the team has won. Loud meatheads towel snapping, raucously cutting farts, and belching an endless array of dick jokes. Hear the lockers banging open and closed. Smell the stench of sweat and ignorance. Imagine the noise-makers minus twenty IQ points. Now picture yourself living in between those rows of lockers—forever. My work done, I smiled at Lily, who looked like she was going to be sick.

Even what's quiet in your world is loud in mine. Chess is a popular game in prison. But you will notice one chief difference in the chess played here: the inordinate amount of trash talking. Here's a sample: "Yeah, my horse's gonna fuck yo' queen, yo. Wassup, you don' wanna move theh, yeah, gonna fuck yo' shit up." And the recipient of these taunts will return in kind. What would have happened if some rogu-ish programmers at IBM coded Deep Blue to shout curses at Kasparov? I remember the game my grandfather taught me when I was young, the strategy and quiet reflection. And then I open my eyes and see a guy move a bishop as if he were slapping a domino.

Bill Moyers interviewed a social scientist who had devoted much of his life to prison reform. The man described the ingenuity of a group of inmates who played chess in their cells, with boards and pieces fashioned out of office supplies and wet toilet paper. Then he described how wonderful it was that they could call out of their cells, down the tiers, and carry on games from afar. Ingenious, he said. Inconsiderate, I thought; my heart is with the poor schmucks who lock between the chess players, the guys who wanted to take a delicious nap or bask in the solace of a good book.

There is so much useless talk in here, salutations issued from numb minds. George Orwell, in "Politics and the English Language," argued that clichéd language begets clichéd thinking. Such stale imagery "makes it easier for us to have foolish thoughts." In my bid for Elitist of the Year, I admit to living a life of the mind amidst the mindless. My inner monologue is the sweet melody of Schubert compared with my neighbors' discordant idiocy. It's similar to *Waiting for Godot*: in the absence of meaningful speech, the denizens of prison (employees as well) opt for nonsense[2]. It is speech to avoid thinking. They ask, "What're you up to?" often more than once, hoping that you'll fill the air with something other than their brain-dead rot. They are terrified of the silence of their inner worlds, so they banish it from their lives with TV and radios and meaningless drivel. Socrates worried that reading would undermine dialogue. If he lived on my company, with its intellectual squalor, he'd have a different attitude. *The printed word*, he'd tell one and all, *that's where it's at*. It's not just the loud guys, but the bores, the ones who talk ad infinitum about their trial transcripts to anyone who'll listen, and

2. *Waiting for Godot* was performed in San Quentin on November 11, 1957. The inmates enjoyed it tremendously; as a group, we know better than most the truth of Pozzo's dictum: "That's how it is on this bitch of an earth." We also know what it is to be waiting and waiting.

the run-of-the-mill gasbags, like my one-time cellmate, Jimbo, who belch out one gripe after the next. And we can't forget about the belligerent know-it-alls vociferating for hours about why a sports team lost their last game. In prisons throughout the land there are conversations that may as well be scripted, for all the times they've been rehashed. They are going on now, as you read: lengthy discourses on how the guards "don't even like themselves," how "they used to feed us real chicken," "it's cold as a muhfucker in here," "it's hot as a muhfucker in here." When the argument turns to how much Jay-Z is worth, I know it's going to be a noisy hour. They'll progress to the richest men in the world. A hoarse voice will reference a list from *Fortune*. That dude in Mexico, someone else will say, I forget his name. *Carlos Slim*, I scream in my head, *now shut the fuck up!* After being down seven years and hearing these discussions almost verbatim from different men in different locations, I've become disoriented. It's one thing when you think you've said something before. But when the déjà vu is external, and frequent, a lost-in-the-funhouse effect takes hold.

And then there's the peculiar phenomenon of shouted laughter. *In the world* it appears as caricatures of high school bullies who knock books from the hands of the bookish and give a HAW HAW!! But even that doesn't approximate the shouted laughter of prison. Some years ago, a friend referred to it as a "Box laugh." He explained how, in the Box, guys yell to each other all day, telling endless, pointless stories as the seasons change. Normal laughter can get loud, but it won't travel. Hence the shouted laugh, so your partner will know you're listening. These denizens of the Box eventually get sent back to population, bringing with them their war stories, new psych-med prescriptions, and the Box laugh. HA! HA!! THAT SHIT'S FUNNY, SON! Yes, well. Even funnier is a recent export from the Box: The elongated repetitive yell. YO! YO! SON, TELL 'IM I GOT THAT, III GAHHHT THAAAAT. (It's reminiscent of the scene in *The Warriors* with

Cyrus's "Caaan youuu diiig iiiiit?"—amusing on the screen, aggravating from your neighbor.)

Whistling, banging on metal tables ("making beats"), tossing a tennis ball against a common wall. If I were alone, on an island, I would do these things too. But I don't do them around others, because there are *others around*. More than annoying, it's inconsiderate and childish, it is to say, I am doing what I want to do ("Doin' *me*, son," in local parlance). But so it goes in the land of misfit toys and wayward boys, home to more sociopaths per capita than any other place in the world.

A question: Would you rather live in a cell next to a harmless eighteen-year-old doing time for shoplifting, who listens to loud gangsta rap all night, or a bona fide serial killer, who is quite pleasant and hardly makes a peep? While you're making the wrong choice, I'll tell you, from experience, that the right answer, without a second thought, is the quiet serial killer. Any day of the week.

You're reading now, likely in a calm environment. Let us then imagine that you are transported to a busy street corner in the inner city, with its attendant noise and danger and multifaceted assault on the senses. Now try to concentrate on the next sentence. Welcome to my world.

They should design a place for the noisiest people. A harsh place where their noise will only bounce back at them. Then I realize that they have designed such a place—and I live there.

Prison has taught me just how low a tolerance one has for discomfort. When it takes so much to eke out a comfortable existence in here, he who shatters my idyll triggers an ugly racism. It is the frustrated, covert racism of a liberal, someone whose formative interaction with people of color was predominantly with domestic help who feared being fired.

Several times since seeing *The Departed* last year, I have maliciously delivered a line to groups of friends. It is from the first half hour of the movie, when DiCaprio's "cop magnet" cousin returns to the car after a drug sale, and says: "Puerto

Ricans—they think they're so smart. If they knew so much, they wouldn't be Puerto Ricannnnn." When black folk were the chief noisemakers in my life, I offhanded a line from *Trading Places*. Upon seeing Eddie Murphy singing to himself in a bath, one Duke brother says to the other: "They're a *very* musical people." And when white people were the cause of my aural harassment, I voiced such pleasantries as: "They're Italian (or Polish, Irish, Greek); you can't expect any better from them." Or, "They're poor white trash, noisy is just how they roll." The Asians, now there's a group my ears can cotton to. So serene, so reserved. Loud talk is disrespectful to them.

I am mad at these louts because Spanish used to be a special language employed sonorously by my parents when we were out of the country. Now all I hear are boorish colloquialisms, day in and day out, worn thinner than my patience. *"¡Oye me!" "¿Qué pasa, 'mano?" "Tranquiiiiiiiiiilo."* This talk makes me many things, tranquil isn't one.

When I encounter truly vicious racism (usually from a guard, who assumes I'm of the same mind because of our shared skin color), I realize how low and hurtful such ideas and speech truly are. I constantly remind myself that inconsideration is not a Latino, black, or white thing. It's just that prison is a place that self-selects for bad behavior, for people of all colors and creeds who have a notoriously poor track record for showing consideration to others. Furthermore, in prison, as in any place where humans are brought together like cattle, you get aggravated and sometimes even hate others more readily than in the *world*. End of discussion.

Changing Pascal's formulation, I will note that most of my botheration comes from my peers' inability to sit still, alone in a room.[3] Living a productive life in prison is hard work. It entails being battered by the waves of peers who shout along

---

3. Blaise Pascal—"All of man's troubles come from not knowing how to sit still, alone in a room."

with Spanish *novelas* or rap videos or Jerry Springer—while I huddle with a book, cringing. I'm also constantly explaining myself to guards who view books as a place to hide drugs and weapons, and who think that the only writing inmates do is either mail fraud or gang related. And to actually produce creative work is no walk in the park. As Vincent van Gogh noted: ". . . if, however, we want to work we must submit both to the stubborn harshness of the time and to our isolation, which is sometimes as hard to bear as exile . . . One must seize the reality of one's fate and that's that."

If I'm drawing, I can put on headphones and listen to music. Not so when I'm writing or editing. The creative juices flow on their own schedule, yet I must work around the noise of my neighbors. Lately, I've been making a Freudian slip: typing quickly, "here" comes out "hear." It is not uncommon to hear of the guy who stays up all night writing so he can find some quiet. Jack Henry Abbott keyed on the solace of the late evening in *In the Belly of the Beast.* "The noise which literally vibrates your brain is gone. The distractions disappear. The freaks' faces are not in front of your cell. You are with yourself again. Until dawn, at least."[4] But breaking night is for the netherworld of county jail, and for prisoners who don't have a job, who don't have any responsibilities.

I am happier when I'm producing, be it art, writing, or folded paper. It's how I help imbue my life with meaning. Unfortunately, the vast majority of my peers have given up on positive meaning making. They will tell you that life starts

---

4. Jack Henry Abbott, *In the Belly of the Beast:* "You'd be surprised to learn what a little old-fashioned oppression can do to anyone. All day there are arguments and threats hollered all over the place. It is not too different, really, than the 'monkey houses' or the zoo . . . It is who can shout the loudest over the longest period who dominates the situation. It is the only situation I have knowledge of in which a scurrying coward can impose himself *directly* upon other men. The *vileness* of such men is in no other case so exposed to view. There are not that many such men, but they dominate relations between men in cages."

when they hit the streets (in this regard, they are not much different from people *in the world* who believe life starts when they turn twenty-one, or when they graduate, or get a job, get married, get divorced, retire). Noisy and stressful as it is, this is my life. And while I understand that people with diametrically opposed styles of living will get under each other's skin, it makes the situation no easier to tolerate.

It is difficult, mentally engrossing work to write and edit a piece. It's why writers find a quiet place in which to ply their trade. There was a notice in the *New York Review of Books* from the New York Public Library seeking fellows. The copy promised facilities for writers to complete their work. Upon reading, I envisioned an upper floor in the vast public library. A floor on which the general public is not allowed and the low-pile carpet has extra padding. It is warm and quiet and sunlight pours in. When you encounter a fellow traveler, you speak in whispers.

And then there are the writers' colonies advertised in the *New Yorker*. One pays thousands of dollars to get away from noise, to be around other creative types. It's laughingly opposite the world I inhabit. Like Huysmans's elitist, jaded sophisticate protagonist "Des Esseintes" in *Against Nature*, I'm often "overwhelmed by an immense weariness, by a longing for peace and quiet, by a desire to have no further contact with the heathen, who in his eyes comprised all utilitarians and fools."

That writers don't like noise shouldn't be news to anyone. Reading and writing involves imagining yourself into another world, and it requires some shut mouth. This holds even for a personal essay that chronicles one's own world (going back in time, reflecting). As you read this, your brain is concurrently making sense of the letters, forming them into words, painting the scenery, querying my meaning, and comparing this all against a vast repository of past experience. Loud noise—the intermittent banging of someone thumping along with music, the shouted laughter—brings you out of the headspace and into the meatspace. Try it with me. If you're at home, turn your television to Telemundo or Univision, adjust the volume five slashes louder than you would normally. Now return to the page. This will work especially well if there is a commercial on right now. Maybe there's a talk show with shouted Spanish catch phrases. *¡Ayyyy, Dios, mio!*

You've suffered enough. Turn off the TV if you haven't already done so.

Throughout the history of prose and poetry, you will find innumerable descriptions of quiet, solitude, and noise. Frost wrote "Stopping by Woods on a Snowy Evening," not "Listening to My Neighbors Scream Themselves Fucking Hoarse." "The only other sound's the sweep/Of easy wind and downy flake." Beautiful. When it gets really loud in here, and I get so I want to break something, I've taken to using "easy wind and downy flake" as a mantra.

Luckily, I have some freedom of movement, and can sometimes relocate when it gets too loud. One day I was in the dayroom, two hundred feet away from Chui, yet I heard him. He was cooking, extolling his rice and beans as the best. Noise for the sake of noise. When Melville lived among the inhabitants of Tahiti, he made numerous mentions in his *Typee* of their "unintelligible gibberish."

With an angry shudder, I stared out a window and remembered something I read about Roger Ebert, who, after a series of operations for thyroid cancer, could no longer speak. To communicate with friends and loved ones, he wrote notes on squares of paper. Words were the most valuable thing in his world. Idle chatter would be like lighting cigars with C-notes. For Ebert, every word held meaning.

I've taken to using literature as something shored up against the lapping tide of idiocy in which I float. They're books, my friend are books, I read them. But these escapes are fragmented: rarely do I get more than ten minutes of being completely immersed in a text. It gets choppy.

While writing *The Corrections*, Jonathan Franzen some-times wore earplugs and earmuffs. The noise in his digs, I can safely assume, was nowhere near mine. I might try the earmuff thing, though. I've got a pair.

Jonathan Safran Foer published *Extremely Loud and Incredibly Close*. I'm tempted to read it, just to see if he's writing about my neighbors.

Kevin Brockmeier wrote a wonderfully quirky short story of mysterious silences titled "The Year of Silence." In it, "the jails were unusually tranquil." He gained a fan with that line. I thought: *Here's someone who knows what it's like inside.* The piece was aural porn. Brockmeier describes a silence that was "plain and rich and deep" and I came in my pants. Spoiling my fun, he wrote that a "hidden longing for sound" sprung up, so a "noise club began operating, tucked away in the depths of an abandoned recording studio." A room full of Chuis no doubt, talking as if they were at a sporting event, whistling, drumming on flat surfaces, shouting their laughter. I imagine one final noise. Dressed as Wile E. Coyote, I lay dynamite at the building's exterior, and spool out detonation cable. With a wink at the camera, I blow the "noise club" to smithereens.

One of the main reasons I dislike the noise is that it drives me into my cell, where I don headphones, retreating from my friends—disrupting a family gathering, as it were, temporarily severing the life-sustaining connections. When it isn't too loud, I can enjoy elaborate meals at a table with my close friends, Whit, Yas, and Doc (permit me to give them a proper introduction later on). We share ideas, and escape from this place via the warmth and compassion of others' words. Those are times when my nerves aren't on edge, when my neighbors are behaving like they live amongst people with a working sense of hearing, and in those times, I begin to think more rationally. They're not preternaturally loud, they're responding to stimuli from one loud friend. They've taken to communicating through noise. One slams his bowl of food onto the empty table: *I am here, alone, come join me.* Plus, most of the inhabitants in prison come from the inner city. They spent their time on the block, a loud environment where people speak loudly to have themselves heard over the din of traffic and the hum of commerce. I grew up in the suburbs, and the loudest thing we contended with was the occasional car alarm. My home was quiet. Not insanely so, as were the houses of some of my friends. Houses ruled by a self-important captain of industry who demanded utter silence whenever the door to his study was closed, or a mom who would nurse a midday hangover and shriek if we made a peep before her Valium began its velvety magic. No, my parents weren't tyrannical, they understood that kids make noise. But if my brother or I became too loud, we would be told "ee-nough."

Because the dayroom became noisy, I retreated to my cell. This lousy animal Chui is whistling as I write this. Loud, intentionally annoying whistling. Do you now see why we couldn't pass him over in silence? He is more than fifty feet away, in his cell watching garbage TV, lying in bed, and whistling, because no one is paying attention to him. With my pen I create a golem that stomps down to Chui's cell, grumbling the song of evil. Propelling itself bodily into the cell, the creature kicks Chui's fucking teeth in, and growls "Ee-nough!"

Like everything else, my perception of noise is determined by the context of the situation, my attitude toward the noise-maker. Were I to hear my newborn nephew's cry, I'd think: *Awww, little guy wants to be fed.* But when Chui mimics a baby (a very fat, ugly, swarthy baby), with his shrieking cries and contorted face—all this to poke fun at one of his friends—I want to throw him out with the bath water.

A time and a place for everything, thus the admonition to use one's indoor voice. So it's not about Puerto Ricans, or even noise, when we finally get down to it. It's consideration and the tremendous lack of it. Everyone, as Fitzgerald suggested, suspects himself of at least one virtue. Mine is consideration. If it were possible, I'd trot out for you now all the neighbors I've had in prison over the years. They'd tell you that they hardly knew I was there. Yes, I was more Chui than church mouse throughout college, but I matured. Sure, some of that came from seeing guys get their faces sliced open first thing in the morning because they played their music loud the night before. But with upgrades to one's modus vivendi, a win's a win. Finally, I'm no longer the Beastie Boy willing to *fight . . . for his right . . . to parrr-tay.* Minimal footprint, that's the new me. I get up and walk to my friend's cell rather than yelling out a question. I make every effort not to invade the space—aural, physical, and olfactory—of those around me.

But when the judge sentenced me to twenty-five-years-to-life, it wasn't twenty-five-years-to-life on a beach. It was twenty-five-years-to-life living next door to a Chui, listening to loud inanity and gross ignorance day after day after ear-ringing day. Little can one imagine the excruciating drudgery of hardly ever being alone for even a minute during all the years of one's imprisonment. It was Schopenhauer who opined: "Amongst the evils of a penal colony is the company of those imprisoned in it." To which I rejoin a "You ain't lying," and add: no one oppresses like the oppressed. A guard walks and the louts turn down their music, only to blast it louder when the coast is clear; *they'll show him.*

I'm aware that if I were in constant physical danger, I wouldn't worry about noise. And, for this, I am thankful. On *The Simpsons,* Sideshow Bob once lamented to a courtroom that the prison book club consisted of prisoners clubbing him with books. He then lifted his jumper to reveal the bruises. Perhaps all my musing here is a luxury of the privileged, i.e., the relatively safe. An upside to this noisy downer is that my Spanish is better than it's ever been. Still, I'd rather be less-than-fluent like my brother, who'll dust off Rosetta whenever he needs it. There's always sleep, when the sound between my ears goes blank, like the borders of this page.

Sometimes I dare to dream of a life other than prison. Most of these meditative scenes have me alone, in a white room filled with sun and staticky silence. Or a forest clearing where I sit half lotus and get serenaded by random bird calls. After Lily came into my life, she naturally came to inhabit my quiet meditation space, though, as we sit on the fine sand, our toes in the gently lapping surf, there is none of our normal banter.

Rudimentary versions of these musings have appeared in my notebooks over the years. Those attempts at coping were a lot less polished, a lot more vulgar. The ethnic groups changed. But it was a recent reading of Seneca's "On Noise" that prompted me to have a more serious go of things. I found it somewhat reassuring to read his words from some-time around the year 30: "Here I am with a babel of noise going on all about me." His thesis was that quiet isn't as nec-essary to the studious type as it was thought to be in his time.

One, the noise in Seneca's life emanated from a public bathhouse over which he lived. It was a bathhouse/sauna/gym. White noise compared with the vociferous lunacy of prison. Further, Seneca was a stoic and wrote the essay to prove a point: sometimes we must grin and bear it. He closes his short treatise, however, with an offhanded admission that the din is the reason he "shall shortly be moving elsewhere." He merely wanted to test himself and see if he could hack it. I call bullshit on you, Seneca. When there's an end in sight, there is almost nothing you can't deal with. Knowing you can move anytime you wish, you can bring on the horrific neigh-bors, just to assess your mettle.

Not so for prisoners. As soon as a cell opens up, resi-dents begin silent prayers for a quiet neighbor. But it's no use. Nature abhors a vacuum and so does prison. Should Chui find himself moved, his replacement will eventually be as obnoxious as he.

Seneca's living conditions bring a memory to the fore: On vacation with my family twenty years ago, we were booked into rooms above a bar that was used for nightly band practice. Being the Dominican Republic during holidays, we were treated to a nonstop loop of "*Felíz Navidad.*" When it got late, my father called the desk. The band knocked off early that night. In the morning we were shown to our new rooms, and given baskets of fruits and goodies for our troubles. Ahh, the good old days.

But what's the use of dwelling on unsolvable problems? The alarm bell is ringing: it's time to stand and be counted. How many thousands of days like this are still ahead of me? How many Chuis?

FOUR

CREWED UP

Sometimes you gotta punch a gift horse in the mouth.

—RAY

Chui wasn't the only person who kept himself turned up to eleven. Alas, it's impossible to move throughout this chapter of my life without putting Ray's name on it, or I would, quite gladly. You see, everyone has a Ray in his life. Your Ray probably isn't named Ray and may not even be male, but mine is. It is safe to say that there are more incarcerated Rays than there are Rays romping around the free world, which is probably a good thing for decent society. He's loud and aggressive and unaccustomed to hearing his requests denied: on the heavy side, but not fat; sweaty, hairy, shaved bald (finishing the job genetics started, saying Fuck You to his lost hair follicles—*Thinning hair? Huh. That's not bald. I'll fuckin' show you bald!*). And Ray is the name that appears on his birth certificate, not a civilized Raymond. I find this fitting, like he was tagged in the womb as a force of nature. Rays are usually preceded with a pejorative adjective: Crazy or wild or angry. Rays are nice places to visit, but you wouldn't want to live there. They're the bottle of mescal you buy knowing damn well you shouldn't. The girl you bring home from a dive bar, who lies about everything important, then steals your wallet while you shower.

Inevitably, I become close with a Ray. I become his consigliere, the business-savvy operator with a taste for the edge who acts to dull Ray's sharp practice and mellow his harsh pronouncements. Someone who can deliver unpalatable news with a soft hand, then strategize a way past the obstacles. Ray's all iron fist, I'm the velvet glove. There's a symbiosis. Every tough guy needs one person in his life who's not afraid to tell him to *Shut the fuck up* every now and then *and* allow him to save face. And in here it's nice to be the right hand to someone who's feared. Like Robert Duvall in *The Godfather*, I'm no wartime consigliere. My best advice concerns business ventures, wives, and girlfriends. When someone has to be made to pay, with resources other than fiscal, I'm *good for nothin'*, or so I'm told between mouthfuls of spaghetti marinara. But what a Ray really likes to have me around for is medical advice. (I'm not a doctor, nor do I play one on TV.) What I am is a recreational pharmacologist with a working knowledge of every drug worth knowing. I can also be counted on to perform some emergency trauma work in a pinch. (In our world, "a pinch" is anything you don't want the authorities knowing about.)

When Ray first came to this prison over a year ago, he landed on my company. I identified him as a Ray even before I knew his name—Rays have a certain way of walking, moving, creating a swath of chaos in their slipstreams. (Dr. Robert Hare, the Sigmund Freud of psychopathy, on his first day at work at a maximum-security prison in Vancouver in 1960, met with an inmate around whom the "air seemed to buzz." In his account of the incident, Hare called the inmate "Ray." Go fucking figure.)

On his second day, he caught an elbow to the eye, the result of some Ray-type beef, and then proceeded to smash the instigator's face repeatedly into the concrete floor. The guards didn't see the incident, but they had to remove Mr. Bloody Pulp. While they did, Ray hid out toward the back of the company. Like the mouse prepared to remove the splinter from the lion's paw, I walked up to Ray, and told him to follow me to my cell. Adrenaline-buzzed, he was in no condition to argue with a stranger and meekly did as he was told. Rays are good at sensing fellow travelers.

Me, I was playing to the gallery of myself, channeling Dr. Seuss's fix-it-up chappie, Sylvester McMonkey McBean: "I've come here to help you. / I have what you need. / And my prices are low. And I work with great speed. / And my work is one hundred percent guaranteed."

With my maroon sheets hung against the cell bars, I flipped on the harsh fluorescents. I prefer a pair of forty-watt desk lamps, making the white walls look golden warm—but for technical work they just don't cut it. I mixed up acrylic paints to match Ray's skin while he sat on my bed staring at me with fat reptilian eyes, then applied the paint around the already-purpling eye socket. The hacks would be on the lookout for anyone with cuts or bruises. Ray sat perfectly straight and still, his hands on his knees for support. I leaned in close enough to hear air whistling through his nostrils as I painted. My color matching was spot-on, the angry bruise hidden under DIY flesh tone: titanium white, cadmium orange, burnt sienna, alizarin crimson, and just a dab of cadmium yellow light. (Toxic cadmium has no business on anybody's skin; think I shared this fact with Ray?) I put the remainder in a container, about a week's worth of stay-outta-trouble, and showed him how to apply it. We spoke very few words as this scene played out, this Clinique-counter-come-to-jail surreality. Leaving my cell, he shook my hand and we exchanged names.

I don't know why I helped Ray. Maybe it was because I just sensed his Rayness and knew that it's usually a good idea to preemptively help a Ray. Or maybe it was because the fuck that he duffed out was Chui's boy, a piece of shit who was making my nights miserable—running a game of dominoes mere feet from my cell, yukking it up, thunderously slapping each domino, and causing an involuntary twitch as I lay reading. Prison teaches you just how low a tolerance you have for discomfort. And available recourse isn't always pretty.

That night, Ray repaid me in spades. As a greeting, he asked, "You get high?" I played coolish, said nothing, got up, stood inches from his face, and looked at his eye.

"Nice paint job, Ray," I said as I sat back down on the bed. "Yeah, I get high, anything but junk. Whaddaya got?"

Putting six dompers in my hand, Ray sealed our friendship. He set the tone for all that was to come. He thanked me sincerely, assured me that he "don't forget." Rays are always good tippers, they always show their appreciation in gratuitous and conspicuous fashion. And me? I'm a hungry, hungry hippo who gobbles up drugs like the world's ending at dawn.

My relationships with Rays usually end poorly. I tire of the visit to Crazy Rayville, look to move back home, and they resent being the one who gets slowly left. They feel used and look to settle the score. That's just how it goes.

The last Ray I invited into my life was a hulking Italian called Lou, a smartish killer-for-hire. For a couple of years we shared a table in the yard, talking about life for hours each night as the seasons passed overhead. There was always a cast of hangers-on to laugh at our jokes and ask our opinions, but Lou and I *were* the crew. One night he angrily accused me of cheating him out of a few dompers. We were a day away from learning that one soon-to-be-having-holes-poked-in-him junkie had "dipped" Lou's pocket, so, in the meantime, Lou threatened to "bloody my mouth." It was the first time he'd threatened me. Reproaching myself for my poor choice of associates, I vowed it'd be the last. I stopped coming out to the table as much (no loss, since my boy Ant had just gotten jammed up for drug possession, and transferred out via the Box), and started staying in my cell and reading more. Some flunkies looking to ingratiate themselves with Lou talked of jumping me, but he gave me a pass. There were a few awkward, precarious weeks. Then out of the blue, the gods in the Office of Movement & Control transferred Lou to another prison. I made my way to a better block, supposedly having learned a lesson about the true cost of keeping up with My Joneses.

Dompers are a pharmaceutical of dubious provenance: an upper, a downer, an all-arounder. You won't find dompers in a *Physicians' Desk Reference*, but they exist nonetheless. They kill pain, ease anxiety, and, in general, make life worth living. Other than at the beginning of a sentence, dompers don't start with a capital d. They're white and circular and come in two dosages: small and large. The small is roughly the circumference of a pencil eraser, the large about the size of your pinky nail. The pill has no number, identifying mark, or brand name on its face. A generic of a generic, the pill itself is often worn uneven by the time it reaches your sweaty palm. More often than not, dompers are in disrepair because they've been hidden in and spat out of a patient's mouth, then made their way through multiple hands and damp, linty pockets.

You won't be prescribed dompers by your doctor. Unless, of course, you happen to live in the poorest of poor ghettos or find yourself in prison. We love them in here. The market for dompers is quite active, the price fixed at one pack of smokes for six small domps. Officially, a pack will get you three large domps, but you'll rarely make that deal. Big dompers are given to guys in big pain, guys who can't afford to sell their meds.

When I heard a nurse refer to the pill as a domper, I gave up looking for more information. Dompers are dompers. Made by the makers of dompers, marketed solely on an invoice that few will ever suffer the boredom of rubber-stamping. When I used to overhear militant blacks rant about the CIA funneling drugs into poor communities, I would laugh scornfully (to myself). Those were the days when I was seen by good doctors, prescribed brand-name meds that came off my co-pay, when the doctor's office phoned in scripts that would be waiting for me on the pharmacist's counter—when I was a card-carrying member of the anointed class and the drugs rocked me good like Big Pharma should. Now, I'm not so quick to deride these conspiracy theories.

Dompers make my weeks go by. They are the serious business of my pleasure. I make it a point never to turn them down, but I tend toward weekend warriordom.

"I can get you a needle," Ray matter-of-facts.

I brush the offer away with my hand, turn my head, and look out the panes of a safety-glass window. I'm in his cell on a Tuesday night. Sitting on the bed, I look out into the yard four floors below. Under stadium lighting, a hundred or so of the block's finest bumble numbly around the yard. Looking for drugs or beefs or boy pussy or just some conversation. Most of the figures wear muted earth tones blasted dull from years upon years of exposure to the elements.

An immediate brush-off is my gut reaction, but the voice inside mulls it over. The beast inside awakens with a soporific grunt. I stare out the window, so Ray won't see me thinking. The needle offer hangs in the air, attempting to pierce my defenses. An old voice speaks up from the darkest recess of memory. A voice I gave birth to the first time I stuck a needle in my arm. It speaks in an opiated, scratchy whisper: *It might be fun.* The beast is not my friend.

Ray the consummate finagler has recently finagled, from some guard who owed him a favor, a half gallon of light beige paint. One of his flunkies painted his cell. You can still smell the fresh coat behind the floating blanket of our cigarette smoke. Next to the TV on his locker are pictures of Ray's wife and kids. On the wall are enough pinned-up tits and ass to keep a ninth-grade basketball team entertained for a few hours. A red-clad throng of Bloods walks by in the window-framed view of the yard. Junkie to junkie, Ray's more aware of my ambivalence than I am. "A clean settta works," he continues. "Brand fuck-ing new."

"No, seriously," I say, "thank you. But I appreciate your thinking of me."

Ray wonders aloud what it would be like to shoot some dompers. I tell him I've done it. "*Really?* How was it?"

I tell the story of how several years back, in the dark, light-shafted mess hall, a guy handed me a set of works under the table at dinner. Back at my cell, I copped some bleach off the porter and cleaned the rig. I tried to sharpen the needle on the coarse emery board of my toenail clippers, ever so gently, without damaging the spike. Shored up the plunger— a jail-made wooden job—with tightly wrapped *Scootch* tape. Crushed six dompers, mixed with water, carefully drew the milky liquid into the needle. Poked into my old go-to—a partially collapsed vein on the topside of my left hand, the least painful reminder of my junkie days. A telltale plume of crimson fluttered in the barrel of opaque liquid, and gave me the green light. I depressed the plunger with my thumb and . . . nothing. It jammed. Jammed! After all I'd been through, after all the built-up excitement. Jammed for a poor schmuck who had an incredibly hard time finding a working vein. Not wanting to lose the vein, I shifted my body, used my thumb and forefinger to grip the syringe proper, put the butt of the plunger against my desk drawer, and applied increasing pressure. The syringe shook, my fingers trembled, sweat pocked my forehead—only partly from the late summer sun. I felt the plunger begin to acquiesce, to move in my favor, then—blunt force trauma.

My fingers slipped, the needle punctured the vein, ricocheted off wrist bone and jutted cruelly back out of my hand like some ridiculous new spot for a body piercing. After catching my breath, removing the spike, cleaning off and checking a still-trickling stream of blood, I carefully emptied the syringe's contents into a plastic spork. Disgusted, I looked at the by-then-bloody liquid, slurped it down, then began to cry—at first because I wasn't able to mainline the dompers, then because I'd even attempted it in the first place.

Self-consciously pushing my watch up onto a scarred wrist, I leave most of the details, especially the unsuccess and crying parts, out of my retelling to Ray and Tommy G.—for Tommy G. had eased into the doorway somewhere during my description of the used needle; I winked hello at him while saying "*Scootch* tape." Instead, I tell them, "Eh. It was awright, not worth the effort."

Undeterred, Ray is smiling, licking his chops and wringing his hands cartoonishly. "Wonder what it'd be like to shoot some dompers." He's heavy into the dompers, needs ten a day. Ray is prescribed four dompers a day for legitimate back pain. The six-pill overage is what medical professionals call off-label use, the tendency to gradually walk-up dosage levels. He's sweating and sneezing now because he's "only" eaten seven today.

"Look at me," I tell him, "and believe me when I tell you: This story doesn't end well."

Tommy laughs in agreement, loudly says, "We're *here* because of needle stories not ending well!"

Or, did he say, "He's *here for . . . ?*" *The* "he" *meaning me? Tommy knows that Ray got his kicks through a crack stem. How much of my bio has he been privy to?*

Tommy G. is a burly Irish kid and self-described sociopath. The kind of guy D.H. Lawrence might have described as "isolate, stoic, a killer." Stocky, with an I-don't-care haircut, uniformly short black hair like an Asian fifth-grader. Matching purple eye luggage and the wanton facial hair—rarely clean shaven, not quite a beard, not quite the douche-bag chic popular with actors in between "projects"—of a guy who's got a long road ahead of him before eventually expiring behind the wall. He reminds me of the cleft-chinned sergeant in *Tour of Duty*, the late eighties Vietnam War TV show that opened with the Stones' "Paint it Black." He's a few years older than me, a soldier in Gulf War One while I was a spastic high schooler. He said he was in a marine intel unit attached to a Force Recon platoon. In the month since I was introduced to Tommy G. (by Ray, the inveterate matchmaker), he has shown a tendency toward the exaggerated. He's slept with "over five hundred" women—this he told the prosecution's shrink. He then proceeded to justify his numbers to me the way he did for the shrink: This many girls per weekend, times this many weekends.

It's the same with some junkies I meet—they remember that one weekend when they shot two thou' into their veins. As preamble to their tales of junkiedom, they beam that they were thousand-dollar-a-day junkies. I don't make the same aggrandizements, I give my stats as they actually were. But I had the benefit of a B-school education and its lectures on smoothing versus teasing-out data points, and dollar cost averaging.

Everyone's bona fides are suspect *inside*, it's what market researchers tactfully call the self-reporting bias. I believe what I believe, discard what I see unfit. Sure, there are times when I'm misled, but that's the price of being a trusting person. I'd rather be misled by a few little half-truths than go around in a funk thinking everyone and everything is suspect. You meet a guy in here, he seems nice, he might tell a few tales, you might be wise to it, you rationalize: OK, he's lying, but he's a nice guy. And the acceptable lies aren't designed to defraud, they're designed to bolster one's image, which comes back to insecurity, a topic I know well. We're all misfit toys and way-ward boys. Some more misfit and wayward than others.

Tommy, Ray, and I have different reasons for entering the dompers market, different styles of enjoying the high. Ray eats them constantly in an attempt at dampening the pain and stifling his rage. He's turned the domp high into a default setting and gets sick when he runs out. Needless to say, Ray is not a pleasant character when he's coming down. Tommy and I go up less frequently and make it an event. For us, the high is a pleasant stroll down memory lane, a selective revisiting of a past that doesn't end with a murder.

Like any neural path, the more you tread on it, the more distinct it becomes. As you strengthen the connection between drug and pleasure center, other, healthier roads to happiness begin to grow obscured with weeds and creeping vines. This happens on a transactional level as you opt for narcotic happiness over, say, playing Frisbee in the park. At the cellular level, these narcotic rides to Pleasantville actually rewire your brain.

When I eat these pills, it is like cruising at night on the service road running parallel with a highway I'm not prepared to enter. Past the sunken shoulder, the highway is dark, desolate, cracked. Convenience-store detritus skitters across the road surface, occasionally levitating in a vortex of bad wind. The toll required is nothing less than a bag of junk, which can be scored in the yard on any night of the week. The highway is the permanent pleasure pathway I've seared into my brain with heroin, the I-Something I cruised on through a year and a half's worth of altered states. (The service road, dompers, is not the same.) Someday, years from now, the heroin highway might be bulldozed into oblivion, replaced by verdant meadows with warm sunlight and chirping birds. Maybe that's wishful thinking. It will likely always remain cut across the meat in my head, a perpetual reminder of the death and destruction I visited on the world. No matter how long this road goes unused, if I pay that toll, I have a feeling gears would creak to life, lights would come on, and it would be as if I never hit the off-ramp those years ago. Such is the nature of junkiedom. In this regard, I believe Tommy and me to be quite similar. Then there's Ray's brain, which, I imagine, is less a matter of highways and service roads, and more like one large bumper-car-fuckaround. Each car powered by a substance: crack, dompers, liquor, etc. Ray jumps around from car to car as soon as one loses its juice. This is a ride he'll probably never get off. Ray's an all-or-nothing guy and I don't see him taking the I-was-healed-through-the-awwwwesome-power-of-Christ route.

Despite our inebriation-related idiosyncrasies, the lowest common denominator is that we're all trying to feel *better than*. Better than the back pain which accompanies sleeping on a two-inch-thick "mattress" in an environment where all is cold concrete or steel; the de facto radiant cooling exacts a creaking, popping toll on our joints that only worsens over time. Better than the memories that our bad pasts, and the realities of our ugly presents, allow. Sobriety is indeed a cruel mirror for those who have destroyed like we've destroyed, who have inflicted pain—both physical and emotional—on victims and loved ones alike. Better than being without dompers. Better than the gray pain of a colorless palette. Better than merely being alive.

The pill is our nepenthe, the potion that temporarily obliviates suffering. I can repurpose Nietzsche here: "Drunken joy it is for the sufferer to look away from his suffering and to lose himself . . . (in) that brief madness of bliss which is experienced only by those who suffer most deeply." (Now, there's a pairing: Ray and Friedrich. Ray comes in wobbly from a night of hard drinking. Wanting a nightcap, he swipes a glass-bottled sedative from Nietzsche's nightstand: "Thanks, Freddie." "But, Ray, I need zis for my insomnia." "Right. Got any more?")

It comes down to intentionally losing the plot every now and then. Temporarily forgetting that I don't know if I'll ever see the *world* again. Getting a puppy, "reestablishing" myself, finding a woman who'll love me, starting a family—at this, pre-Lily juncture, we can hang a question mark behind each.

What I know, and don't have to be told, is that Tommy G. is really smart and, in here, smart is hard to come by. That he's a tad loud—I asked him if he was hearing impaired—and his humor skews toward the cheesy, well, I just chalked that up to him being from Ohio. (When an Ohioan laughs,

I expect to hear a laugh track in the background, or see an APPLAUSE sign drop from the ceiling.)

In my first real conversation with Tommy, he happily admitted that he's a sociopath, that he has to consciously work on empathy. In the waning afternoon sunlight, with summer a recent memory, we sat side by side on my bed, Tommy slouched forward like a bored chimp.

What are the odds on Tommy being correct? Fifteen to 25 percent of our prison population is affected by the pathology of moral emptiness that mental health professionals interchangeably term *sociopathy* or *psychopathy*. Among other tendencies, they exhibit a parasitic lifestyle, pathological lying, conning, proneness to boredom, shallow emotions, lack of empathy, poor impulse control, promiscuity, irresponsibility, record of juvenile delinquency, and criminal versatility. As a defense against such menacing scoundrels, the brain may be hardwired with an ancient "intraspecies predator-response" system. This reptilian fight-or-flight mechanism stands your hair on end, makes you uneasy when in the presence of a true psychopath, someone who views you as no more than a life obstacle. Being away for all these years, I've had the chance to run into people who trigger this reaction. Ray and Tommy, however, don't set off my predator alarm. And, because I can empathize and read people fairly well, I can tell you that I don't set off this alarm in others. (Or, maybe I'm being dishonest with you now—something a psychopath would do.)

"You're not a sociopath," I told him, in a tone a father would use after his son admits that the boys at school call him stupid.

He cited medical professionals: "All the doctors, my side and theirs, after performing *baaaaatteries* of tests, came to the conclusion that I am." He told me about the Rorschach, Stanford-Binet, word association, MMPI, thematic apperception, and a few more. This was the time Tommy told me how he told a prosecution shrink that he'd banged over five hundred. We were both looped on dompers—my eight to his six—talking blue streaks, jawing at not-quite cross purposes, smoking like it was going out of style.

I let him blather on, self-praising in a demented way, found my conversational hole, and inserted, quickly, without pausing for a response, "Isn't it *cool* to have all that attention? All those eyes staring. Probing. Asking *you* questions about *you* and getting paid one-sixty an hour to do it? Taking notes on your life, asking questions that show they've been actively listening, having you go back over some detail so they can clarify its place in their notes. It's a fuckin' wet dream for the self-involved."

I said this as a personal observation, a way of showing rather than telling that I know what he's been through. I think Tommy took it more as my commentary on his sitch, not an admission of mine—so much for that conscious work on empathizing, Tommy Boy. He was amused by the insight, rubbed his chin and said, "Hmm. I've never thought of it that way, but you're right. Yeah . . . you're right."

In questioning his sociopath label, I said that a label-happy therapist friend of my grandma's told her that I was a sociopath. I didn't feel like one, and told Tommy, in my Lionel Hutz, Esquire voice, "Your Honor, the term 'sociopath' is thrown around so often these days, that it's lost all meaning."

He insisted that he's the genuine item. I tried to dissuade him, thinking I have a vested interest in proving that sociopathy, like depression or ADD, is overdiagnosed. Trying to prove to myself, in the process, that I'm no sociopath. He stuck to the collective diagnosis and so ended my pitch.

Why are guys so enamored with that sociopath label? He's not the first to pathologize his behavior, and merrily proclaim it to me. It's like sociopathy is a badge of honor in here, or some catch-all defense of all of one's bad actions (much like the poor conversationalist with the attention span of a gnat, who blurts out that he has ADD). Or maybe it's justification for the gnarly path their lives have taken—*It's not my fault, it's this faulty wiring, this goddamned sociopathy I gotta deal with.*

For some reason—it's not a religious one, because he isn't—Tommy doesn't even entertain the thought of suicide. Maybe sociopaths aren't suicidal. (If that's one of the criteria, yours truly is no sociopath.)

It was during this conversation, our first bonding session, when his extreme slouch-forwardness enabled me to see him as a child. Before my eyes he shrank, lost the facial hair, kept the posture and the boyish haircut. One hand held a retro can of Coke, the other maniacally worked the bulky black Atari controller, killing eight-bit space invaders, yelling over his shoulder: "In a minute, Ma . . . *Jeez!*"

We've moved beyond nighttime needle stories that don't end well as I sit on Ray's bed. He and Tommy are arguing over a batch of pork chops they acquired on the black market: Who bought what and who owes who. Between sociopaths, there's no such thing as professional courtesy. This is their standard mode of conversation, and incredibly grating to someone who didn't grow up in a household where yelling was standard communication. The boys yell for yelling's sake. Standard jailhouse shit. The louder you are, the more serious your words. The more dangerous or important.

Ray tells me the chops are of a really good cut, winks as he invites me to their upcoming pork chop meal. To make sure I recognize his largesse, Ray adds, "Nice, right?"

"Very," I tell him. "I'll speak to a guy about hooking up some apple *shauce*." By "shauce" the boys are fighting again. About what day the meal should go down and whether rice or pasta is more suitable. I know some type of rice pilaf is the better choice, but don't want to get involved in this no-winner.

On Ray's TV, *Zodiac* is ending, the credits rolling to Donovan's "Hurdy Gurdy Man"; I hum along with this catchy tune, and know that I'll be doing so for some time, that I'll probably incorporate it into a yoga mantra. The song also drifts over from the TV of Ray's neighbor Claude, an affable, heavyset black man who murdered enough prostitutes for the local news to dub him a serial killer.

My new tattoo itches. I dig my nails into the inflamed skin surrounding this dancing pig that looked better in my head than it does on my forearm. This has the desired effect and Ray stops yelling long enough to look at the piece more closely. During the who-did-it-and-how-long-did-it-take line of questioning, Tommy walks away, presumably to his cell, the sociopath's dwelling where all is hectic and precariously stacked and dusty.

"Ray, I really wanna go up this weekend. The three of us."

The first claim couldn't be more true, the second, well, I'm trying to close a deal. It's an old junkie script that I find myself reading. The emphasis is hung on the sense of sharing the high, like, *I enjoy hanging out with you, but the domps would make it even better.* I'm willing to work the proposition of getting high with Ray and Tommy into the equation of dompers. We love each other like stepbrothers: in small doses. For these lovely characters, I've forsaken my real friends, Whit, Yas, and Doc—rather than joining them for nice, leisurely meals, I keep my stomach almost empty, so as to not interfere with my drugging as I hang out in the darker precincts of the cellblock.

Reader, are you rooting for me to go up this weekend or do you think I'm taking advantage of Ray? I can tell you that in matters such as these, past is prologue and I *will* have those hits by Saturday, be all jake by the tweakend. The hanging out together—I'll give you fifty/fifty odds on that happening. I'll hound Ray into feeding me, while not appearing to do so. That's another symbiotic element to our relationship: Ray needs to feel like the Great Provider, and I allow him to be. Or is this just a junkie rationalizing his drug hunger?

Ray starts throwing numbers around in his head, pantomiming a juggle of figures with his mitts. I tell him I'll pay for this round of domps if he can put them together. He gets a daily dose, but for my request will have to source some additional hits. The money is a problem, he's spent his packs on those pork chops and I'm in the hole on account of something else (a little pot last week that I didn't let the boys know about, since I shared it with my friend Marty, a dead ringer for the photographer Terry Richardson). Ray determines that we need three packs to make the festivities happen. This is who we are: worshippers of Dionysus, sharp practitioners of recklessness, decadence, self-destruction, and waste.

Ray asks, "Why don't you go see the Old Man?" He means, Why don't I see the Old Man, watch him jerk off, collect the three packs as payment. I've done this more times than I care to admit, all in the name of copping dompers.

The Old Man's been down forever: a disgraced investment banker or some such who went away in the late 1970s for raping and killing his friend's six-year-old son. Ray chiseled a few packs out of the guy a while back on some deal. Ray's the one who told me the Old Man likes having young guys watch him jerk off. "The pay's good and you don't have to get your hands dirty," were his exact words. I'm the one pushing for this weekend's deal to go through, so I'm the one who'll have to see the Old Man: the disgusting, dirty old man who calls me Billy as he's coming. The fuck who makes me light a cigarette for him after he's done and before he gives me my three packs. However, aside from the gross-out factor, and feeling like a hooker, the gig ain't bad. Like Ray says, "Three packs is three packs," and all I'll have to do is sit there. It'll be over in less than ten minutes.

"I dunno," I tell Ray. "There's this guy who wants a portrait drawn of his son. That could earn me five packs by week's end. And I wouldn't have to watch that sick fuck jerk off."

Ray laughs. "Well, I need to give the packs to my guy by tomorrah, Thursday the latest. Can you have 'em by then?"

"I'll make it happen. By Thursday the latest?"

"Thursday the latest."

Tommy walks back in: "Ray, you fuckin' asshole, you owed me two packs from the last time we bought pork chops."

They argue some more about things wholly unrelated to my quest for dompers.

I try to bring them back on topic. "Hey . . . HEY!" They quiet and look at my uncharacteristically raised voice. "Wouldn't it be cool to all drop at the same time—go out to the yard, and all be on the same page?"

They're game, but don't share my enthusiasm. I can see they're about to resume their arguing.

"Think about it. We'll drop six apiece in our cells, when we meet in the yard we'll be *niiiice*. We'll suck down a tonna cigs, and I'll bring out some candy. Blowpops and Twizzlers and Smartees. C'mon, we'll eat on empty stomachs, the pills'll hit in thirty." I'm on a fucking roll here, settling into a natural Always Be Closing mode, full-dress madness as I propose this lame attempt at a Trimalchian feast. "Let's be men about this."

"Odi, I've seen how you eat your domps," Tommy says. "And I'm *definitely* not the man you are when it comes to that shit."

Odi: the name I go by when I'm partaking in things I shouldn't be, the sender of purchasing messages like, *Tell him Odi wants to see him.* Odi the drug monster thinks about overdosing. Right now, Tommy's referring to the other night when he watched me eat two dompers in Ray's cell. I crushed them, let them melt under my tongue, and after a time washed them down with a shlook of Ray's water—Odi's patented sublingual dissolve method, borrowed from the summer I learned to administer glucose to diabetics. "*Brootha*," I say, "when it comes to *droogs*, few are the man that I am."

Tommy takes that as a boast, so I correct him: "Kid, I'm a *fuck-ing pig*, I've got issues and I'm not proud of it. We're just stating facts here."

He accepts this, and then resumes arguing with Ray.

Me: "Are you two birds gonna cluck all night or we gonna make some plans?"

Tommy roars, "Fuuuuuck you, Hymie!"

Ray laughs.

Pointing to each anti-Semitic douche bag in their turn, I calmly say, "Massengil, Summer's Eve, it sounds like we've got a tentative plan to go up this weekend. Now, I gotta get back to my floor before I turn into a pumpkin."

We pound fists good-bye. I am smiling inside. There's a slight trickle of anticipatory dopamine that washes over my service road to Pleasantville, leaving it clean and inviting, ready for a weekend drive. Although my attitude toward getting altered has improved a good deal since going away, this happy anticipation is a response conditioned since my pre-bar mitzvah bong hit days. It will take a long time to decondition myself. If ever.

Walking down the company away from Ray's cell and toward the stairs that lead back to mine, I hear my friends laughing and know, because I *know* these jackals, that Ray has just told Tommy about the Old Man.

Under the cold, muted hum of old fluorescents, guys do their time. From the periphery—it is bad form, and sometimes dangerous, to look into someone's cell uninvited—I note darkened cells with bodies tranquilized by the lambent blue light thrown by black-and-white televisions. Then there are those who hang out on the long company, moving about, leaning against cell bars, or sitting at tables. The furniture has been handed down repeatedly, we are the last stop on the product life cycle before the trash heap. The Formica tables have colors—vom orange, pus yellow, split pea green—that were all the rage in the seventies, and now lay dead in forgotten greasy spoons and bingo halls the country over.

A band of cutthroats sits around the poker table. One wears knockoff Ray-Bans and ear buds that snake to his Walkman—a move undoubtedly copied from the plethora of televised poker players with their Wayfarers and iPods. Their faces are focused, glum, deadly serious. Passing the poker table, I see one of my "guys" flash a real shit-eater as he ups his ante. I'm into this mug for two packs behind a couple of joints he sold me last week. I know he sees me, but going by the chip stack in front of him, his luck is dripping strong. He doesn't want to invite my kind of luck to the table, and, besides, my two-pack debt pales in comparison to the twenty packs in chips he's fondling. We both know he'll collect.

I'm almost off the company when I hear Ray's distinctive yell. "Oh!! 'ey!!"

I turn. They're giggling, doubling over. Tommy yells after me, "Don't get any on ya!"

Et tu, Tommy? It'll be that much easier to go Machiavellian this weekend and eat into your share of the domps. I turn back around, continue my walk, and by way of offering my second good-bye of the evening, shoot two birds over my shoulders.

The Old Man locks on the floor beneath mine. A heavy, dark red blanket hangs on the inner side of his bars, completely obscuring the view, blocking the morning sunlight. I'm conscious of the irony in asking if he's decent before parting the curtain and stepping in. The Old Man sits smoking in his chair, his blue-veined legs dangling from a thick robe. The not-unpleasant smell of yellowing newsprint permeates the dark, still cell, like the attic you clean out after an old relative dies. *Sesame Street* plays on his TV—mood music. Moving a pile of *Wall Street Journals*, he makes a space for me to sit on the bed.

He begins to inch his chair closer to where I sit, but I shoot a look that stops him. He's old and frail, I'm young and capable of doing damage; he doesn't know that I've never punched anyone in the face. As Count von Count heralds the number of the day, the Old Man opens his robe and starts fondling his purple, uncircumcised prick with a satisfied wheeze.

Detach, go numb, move outside yourself, try to figure out who's on the cover of The Economist *sitting on the floor.* The Count: *one, hahaha, two, hahaha . . .*

The three packs of Newports on top of the tellie will pay for my weekend's numb. But something feels different this time. Going numb is what got me here.

The Old Man works into a rhythmic wheezing and shuffling.

The Count: . . . *seven, hahaha* . . .

As a boy, the same age as the Old Man's victim, I had family and teachers who showed me affection, talked of my potential. How absurd a comparison between then and now. Yet here I sit, a degenerate, getting paid three packs of cigarettes to watch an even bigger degenerate jerk off because I need money to get drugs that, amongst other things, help ease the pain of the wrongs I've done, and continue to do.

What am I doing here? Sitting here is easy, but living with it is hard, emotionally taxing. A thought: In much the same way that I'm with Ray and Tommy, I'm also crewed up with the different facets of my character—reason, desire, self-destructiveness. Like the lives of my friends, these elements are often intertwined: my desires are often self-destructive and employ reason to rationalize my bad behavior.

If I often find myself crewed with a Ray, lashing my wagon to a plummeting star, it's the self-destructive in me, what Poe referred to as "the imp of the perverse." Like the beast, there are some voices that will always lie dormant in me, waiting to be summoned forth. I may not be able to walk out on them, but I can at least leave them undisturbed, *leave their loneliness unbroken.*

The realization gets me to my feet. Still whacking away on his greasy dick, the Old Man's eyes go wide: "Whereyagoing?"

Go, I tell myself, *don't look back.* Instead, I sit back down. "Thought I heard a guard walking."

He listens for a second. Satisfied that all is clear, he gets back to work.

Let's not be rash, the emotional damage is done. In for a penny, in for a pound. Might as well get paid. I slouch forward, impersonating a little boy, hoping it'll move things along.

"Uh, uh, uh, Billy, oh, Billy—thwack . . . thwack . . . thwack—unnnnh." Folding in on himself with a spasm, the Old man comes into a dirty sock. He closes his robe with a wheezing cough, puts a trembling cigarette to his lips. Without waiting for him to ask, I wave a flame from my Bic. He closes his eyes and draws hungrily, the cherry flaring bright orange. On the tellie, Elmo squeals something to his fish Dorothy. The Old Man breaks into a fit of coughing. I use it as an opportunity to stand and grab the three packs. He stops coughing and gasps, to my back, "Come back sometime, kid."

Parting the curtain, I wince in the midmorning sun. Let the Old Man find someone else to play Billy—the cost-benefit no longer adds up. Stopping a ways down the company, I move to an open window and breathe deeply from the clean, outside air. The sun warms my face and it feels good.

Tommy and me and Ray, we'll have our party, and that'll be a better time than this.

Act as if. Always, at all times, act as if.

FIVE

MALE GAZE

I never returned to the Old Man's cell. It's the only thing I *am* glad to know of myself regarding that sordid business. Years afterward, I would come to view that morning as another mile marker on my journey to a better place, a place that would eventually lead to Lily. Much still lay ahead of me, things I had never conceived of, things I had never foreseen. But while the stale miasma of the Old Man's cell still lingers, let's chew the fat on that old standby, the admonition, *Don't drop the soap.*

Dig it: after one of my numerous cell moves, I landed on a company whose porter, Amir, promptly began "cracking" on me. Once I awoke from a nap to catch him staring at me, pretending to sweep in front of my cell. During my first few months there, that weird shit was Amir's norm. While I was reading in my cell, a captive audience, this middle-aged, closeted man would stop on some obvious pretext and engage me in tedious conversation.

Seeing him propped against the push broom one day reminded me of the time in honor block, when an old timer bumbled into my cell, his shower shoes sliding against the terrazzo floor, and accidentally knocked over the miniature broom propped against the wall. It fell with a crack and startled Ralphie—a cherubic, cartoonish man in his midsixties—while merely annoying me: sitting on my bed, spending a weekend afternoon contemplating a strange photo essay in *Grand Street*. So as to avoid bending over, he attempted to pick up the broom with his foot. It was like watching someone at an arcade dipping the metal claws on a stuffed animal and coming away clutching nothing. "Dude," I said, "you're pissing me off, just leave it."

He looked up, and gave me an exaggerated pout.

"Leave. It."

With a step toward me, Ralphie affected a *West Side Story* street tough: scrunched-up face, lowered head, outstretched arm from which he'd just flicked an imaginary stiletto. "Blood on my blade," he growled, "or shit on my dick."

"*What?*" I said, laughing with incomprehension. I knew this to be a prison saying—threatening, graphic, and disgusting— a phrase that could only be coined (and survive) in prison, a prelude to rape. Caught off guard in an unsupervised area, a shiv in your face or blade at your throat, you needn't any help with the uptake. *Your* blood, *his* blade, or *his* dick up *your* ass. But what brought on this horrific non sequitur, I hadn't a clue.

He sat near me on the bed, while I just stared.

"Eh, I'm disturbing you," he said.

"You're not disturbing me—you're just plain disturbing." I cracked a smirk.

After a few beats, Ralphie laughed himself into a smoker's coughing fit.

I always feel bad when I'm short with Ralphie. He's been down since the sixties and will likely die behind the wall, it pains me to say, if the parole board has its way (which it most certainly does). A teenage junkie pulling burglaries to support his habit, something went horribly wrong and he killed two people with political connections. Contrite, compassionate, and a gifted painter—it's miraculous he's not hopelessly institutionalized.

"Tell me," I said, "what brought forth such pretty talk?"

The broom falling, it turned out, had unspooled a string of memory. A fresh-faced newjack, Ralphie found himself in a maximum-security prison that would be familiar if you watched old movies: dreary cellblocks, hard men doing hard time. An austere place, no televisions to opiate the incarcerated masses. Violence occurred much less frequently, but when it did, the outcome was often punctured organs, or death. Rape was a lot more common. On the bus rides upstate, the old timers would scare the youngsters shitless with tales that needed no embellishment: psychopathic, marauding homosexuals, taking it however they could get it, claiming young men as their chattel. One such creature, called Mother, was so predatory that his brutalities are still given mention decades later. These young souls were instructed never to let their guard down, to always be ready to defend against such advances, to use as a weapon whatever was at hand.

So it went with Ralphie. He was sweeping out his cell—"Wasn't in the jernt a week"—his back to the open doorway, when he saw a piece of candy land on the bed. (A move from an earlier time, akin to roses and chocolates, though a lot more direct. The gesture still carries meaning today, but is employed jokingly by friends with a twisted sense of humor.) No sooner did it register that he was being "cracked on," than Ralphie felt a hand violently grasp a fistful of shirt at the small of his back. This hand was pushing Ralphie into his own cell. Ralphie managed to lunge, then spin around and crack the broom over his attacker's forehead. Frightened, Ralphie wailed on the guy for a bit until he was safely unconscious. Some men who lived on the tier dragged the guy away and left him in the shower, bleeding. Ralphie earned himself some protection—the predators can always find easier marks—until he eventually aged out of the tender "boy pussy" demographic.

The thread of memory loosened, Ralphie began remembering details, people from back then. In the meandering style favored by the old timers, he interwove narrative lines across several decades: *I didn't see B again for twenty years, until we both landed at Prison G; he went to the Box from there; I heard he's out now, living with his daughter, tending a small vegetable garden. He's the guy who gave me this sweater back when we were in . . .* Not uninteresting, but my own memory was triggered, and so left Ralphie to his reminiscences while I retreated down the rabbit hole that is the hippocampus.

In my head it was a warm, spring day. I sat in our car's backseat with my brother, our mom drove. We were returning home from some event at the elementary school. I was in fourth or fifth grade, my brother three years younger. As we pulled into the garage—a garage with garden tools lining the walls—my mom remarked that pretty soon I'd have to beat the girls off with a stick. She must have been watching girls watching me. It was very embarrassing to hear my mother talk about such matters. I had a "girlfriend" at the time, a Persian girl named Shari; we kissed and held hands like it was going out of style.

Because one sometimes hears the phrase, "too pretty for prison," I note that I was an attractive young man, the kind that girls would sometimes refer to as "beautiful." You won't hear me bemoaning my objectification. While my friends honed pickup lines, I merely floated about, a fish caught by others. (The lessons I learned from this translated poorly to other areas of my life, the results often disappointing, calamitous, or ruinous.) I felt neither beautiful, nor a catch, instead fostering an ugly self-image. Attention from the opposite sex warmed me (as it does to this day), reassured me, if temporarily, of my worth.

It wasn't all yearbook signing and phone numbers on my arm. There was a downside. I was sometimes picked on by boys who didn't like my competition. On occasion, they'd float the rumor that I was gay. And I was cracked on by older men. Of course, I didn't call it that, I often didn't know what was going on until it became all-too-obvious. While registering the heightened attention, I marked it differently from what I experienced with girls. *This* was awkward and uncomfortable.

During my first months as an inmate of the county jail, looking younger than my twenty-three years, believing the pop-culture dictum that pretty boys quickly became the property of others, I did my best to grow a goatee. The result was comical—something you'd see in the parking lot of a convenience store, sported by a gentleman wearing a HOOTER PATROL T-shirt. It was, I decided, masculine.

In the public's reductive consciousness of prison, there stands no mightier evergreen than rape. This is thanks to the disseminators of pop culture. No easier means for a screenwriter to convey the horrific powerlessness of prison than to paint a scene in which a man lies unconscious in the shower room, the hot water washing his blood down the drain. The prison rape scene is employed as an objective correlative, a showing rather than telling that immediately evokes emotion— in this case, fear, powerlessness, horror. (It is also an accessible metaphor, familiar to anyone who's come up against an omnipotent system: *This is what it's like to be bent over by the Man and reamed up the ass.*)

If the trope of prison rape self-reinforces as a recurring plot point, if it just isn't a prison story without a little rape, it's worth considering why. Put simply, we're dealing with morbidity unchained, our most base instincts allowed to roam free, our nastiest fantasies realized—death and sex, but for criminals whom it's OK to hate. "We deny our sadism," wrote the psychologist Neville Symington[1], "by projecting it back" onto the criminals in our story. It doesn't say nice things about our society that the topic has become standard fodder for comedy. Adam Gopnik, writing in the *New Yorker*,[2] noted: "The normalization of prison rape—like eighteenth century japery about watching men struggle as they die on the gallows—will surely strike our descendants as chillingly sadistic, incomprehensible on the part of people who thought themselves civilized. Though we avoid looking directly at prisons, they seep obliquely into our fashions and manners."

The Shawshank Redemption looked directly at prison and, with nuanced realism, did it well. In the bright and dusty prison yard, Red alerts Andy to the attention of Boggs and "the sisters." But, I'm not gay, responds Andy. Red explains: Neither are they. Shortly thereafter, Andy gets cracked on, and eventually, wailed on. Oftentimes, Boggs and company would move on to easier prey. Because Andy was an asset to the guards, they disposed of Boggs. That's not unheard of.

A couple years into my sentence, I was awoken one night to a neighbor—K, a boyish black kid in his late teens—loudly intoning: "Oh, hail no. Hail fuckin' no!" He'd gotten the attention of neighbors, who'd adopted him as a kid brother. Apparently, a middle-aged black man, whose cell was directly next to K's, was helping the kid with his legal work. Not uncommonly, one of them held a small shaving mirror outside the bars, so they could see each other's faces while speaking (it allows for quieter conversation, important at night, and especially with legal work, which you want to keep quiet). At some point, the man tilted the mirror to show the kid that he was jerking off. I would've recoiled in embarrassment, kept mum, and had no further contact with the guy. But I was a little older than K—he might have perceived the overture less as disrespect and more as an overt threat.

---

1. Neville Symington, "The Response Aroused by the Psychopath."
2. Adam Gopnik, "The Caging of America," the *New Yorker*, January 30, 2012.

The next morning, as the porter pushed his broom past our section, my neighbors stopped him, and engaged in a bit of whispering. The porter went to the front of the company and—I'd later learn—got the OK from the guard to handle this amongst ourselves (if later asked by his superiors, the guard could shrug and say he stepped away from his post for a moment). The porter—a huge, muscular man with a keloidal scar that looked like a fatted leach stretching from mouth to ear—was at the man's gate when all the cells opened for breakfast. He pulled the man out, grabbing him securely around the waist from behind, lifting him off the ground. The mess hall was serving waffles that morning, so I had to walk past, pretending not to see my neighbors line up to land haymakers in the guy's crotch. He was tossed back in his cell, and transferred to protective custody by the afternoon. Like with Boggs, that was the last we heard of him—as goes Shawshank, so goes life inside.

More often than not, however, pop culture serves up caricatures. Scene: outside of a prison cell. Scrawny white man, filmed from behind, holds prison-issued bedding. A guard, club in hand, stands next to him, says something menacing like: *Bubba here's been lonely.* Up the drama. The guard motions to a coworker out of the shot, yells: "Crack thirteen cell!" The new prisoner is given a slight push into the dusky cell; we hear the gate bang closed as a large, hairy beast (often black) stands to full height and dictates which bunk the new guy will be getting. Because the newjack is shot from behind, the viewer is partially shielded from the dangerous bunkie, but then he moves, and, with jump cuts, the camera switches from him bending over to the bunkie looking lustily. Now that the ominous foreshadowing (often a misdirection) has been dealt with, the guard makes a jackass remark, *You two play nice,* and walks away.

My peers and I groan when we watch such paint-by-number scenes. We groan because we know that our family and friends are watching: their perception is not our reality.

For those who have lost much, there's a particular sting that accompanies the thought of losing further power and dignity in the eyes of our loved ones.

Hours into a pleasant conversation during a visit, Lily once joked that her friend warned against kissing me, as I'd undoubtedly contracted untold sexually transmitted infections during my incarceration. I laughed it off—we'd been kissing like high school kids—but every so often, I feel the vague need to reassure her that I'm not hosting parties in my mouth.

In the prison yard, however, like in any family, we can make those jokes amongst ourselves. Mikey Pancakes once made the mistake of telling the table that his bunkie in the Box, a forty-something outlaw biker, used to smuggle dope and weed back from visits, and offered to share more generously if Mikey let the biker blow him. Jackals that we were, junkie that Mikey was, I spoke for the group: "So, I guess the only question is, Did his beard chafe your thighs?" And we all laughed ourselves teary, even Mikey.

Yet, clichés are cliché for a reason: always a basis in fact, a pit of truth within the pop culture peach with which we get our faces sticky. Rape happens in prison because there are rapists here—and I don't mean "rape-ohs" doing time for raping a woman or helpless child, who are, for the most part, made meek with fear of their captors and peers. I refer to the violent sociopaths, creatures whose reptile brains call the shots. They have *gone away* for purse snatching or multiple homicides and everything in between, and deal with the powerlessness of the place by inflicting fear on others, exerting dominance in darkened stairwells and the steamy far corners of shower rooms. We have slang for such men and their proclivities. They are "booty bandits," or simply "bandits," who "take it" ("it" being the ass of the unwilling). Bandits exist as real-life bogeymen, characters used by old cons to scare and prepare the newjacks. Eventually, he targets the wrong person and meets a violent end. Staff will agree, off-the-record, that he had it coming, and that's the end of that ugliness.

Sitting in a crowded mess hall just two years into my bid, I caught one such animal staring at me across the table and it caused instant alarm. He was a known bandit. At a previous meal I'd heard him say to a chump (an openly gay man), apropos his rear, "Damn, girl, look at that fat pussy!" Despite my goatee, I felt like a scrawny, pale lamb. I became conscious of how I was eating (could it be viewed in any way as feminine?), stared ahead, my expression a practiced version of numb anger. Given the chance, the guy would crack on me and eventually do worse. He'd gotten in the practice of waiting in the law library stairwell in the evenings, rumor had it he knocked out a white kid earlier, and I made it my business never to be in an isolated situation with him. And so I managed to avoid any unpleasantness. Truth be told, he wasn't gunning for me. There are usually enough willing participants around that; anecdotally, in Prison A's population of two thousand men, I'd peg the incidents of rape at no more than ten per annum (though certainly, if you're one of the ten getting corn-holed, probability means shit to you).

And to think how scandalized I was during an eighth-grade house party when a girl approached and handed me an envelope, which she'd been asked to deliver. It wasn't addressed to anyone and the return bore the logo of a gay and lesbian group.

"Who'd you say sent this?"

"The guy from Pure Records."

Pure Records was a small, independent music store new to town. They specialized in overpriced poseur wear and beaded jewelry, and maintained a good selection of non-mass-market music. The counter was manned by an affable thirty-something, a big dude with a dark red beard whom I regarded as an arbiter of good taste. He'd appraise what I brought up to the register with silent nods, and sometimes a subtle wince. If I received more of the latter, I'd vow to select more tastefully when I returned. He gave me a 20 percent discount, which I accepted as one would a birthright.

"The guy from Pure?"

"Yeah," she said.

"And he said *me*? For you to give it to me?"

"Uh-huh," said the girl, who then walked up the damp lawn and went inside.

Standing off from my peers, I nonchalantly ripped open the envelope. Inside was a form letter from the organization, inviting me to attend one of its meetings. I returned the letter to its envelope and then slowly ripped the thing to pieces. Crouching at the mouth of a sewer, I tossed the shreds down the drain. Was this a prank? No, I concluded, the girl was a friend. Mistaken identity? No, he used my name. But how did he know I'd be at the party? How did this girl know I'd be at the party? What would've happened if I wasn't there— would she have showed the letter around, naming me as the intended recipient? Why would he send me such a thing? Did he think I was gay? Did he—a hip, older person—know something I didn't? This was all unsettling, the type of thing my peers could really run with . . . totally screwing up my gig.

Cautiously, I went into the house. No one spoke of the letter. The messenger, whom I considered asking for discretion, was well on her way to becoming drunk. I banked on her forgetting everything.

I never again stepped foot in Pure Records, and the owner did me the favor of going out of business not too long thereafter. Instead, I shopped for CDs at the local Tower Records, a much larger, less personal space where the cashiers couldn't have cared less what I bought. A beautiful girl worked there, stocking the racks, answering questions, getting hit on. Her body—curvy, perky, tight—played against the fabric of her uniform. Smelling of light, sweet perfume and gum, she had straight, blonde hair. Glossy lips. This was a girl who fucked. At least sixteen, this heterosexual icon wanted nothing to do with me.

Rape is one of the few prison issues for which the public has an appetite. In 2003, Congress passed the Prison Rape

Elimination Act (PREA). This translated, at the local level, into mandatory training sessions for staff who now say, whenever the subject arises, "The Department has a zero-tolerance policy for sexual abuse." Also, each inmate was given a pamphlet explaining how to avoid such abuse ("don't accept gifts") and what to do if it happens ("report it"). Collectively, there hasn't been as much smirking since the abstinence and clean-living pamphlets proffered by our high school health teachers. My friend, Angelo, who worked in the print shop, mocked up the PREA handout, having it read: "Everything will be fine so long as you stay seated and keep your mouth shut." It's better than nothing, but PREA is almost meaningless in practice. "Too often," reads the PREA Commission's report, "in what should be secure environments, men, women, and children are raped or abused by other incarcerated individuals and corrections staff." Departmental PR flacks dismiss inmate claims of staff sexual abuse as patently false, they suggest that inmates are crying rape after routine pat-and-frisk searches. Granted, some of the claims have been made fraudulently, or less than objectively. But all of them? I've been pat frisked by sadistic officers (with a latent homosexual vibe) and felt violated. After literally hundreds of pat frisks, I know the difference between routine frisking and inappropriate touching (my balls being maliciously squeezed, for instance). Fearing retaliation, I've never reported these incidents.

Anyway, in men's maximum-security prisons, sexual contact with staff is more often consensual (even though, as wards of the state, inmates aren't capable of giving consent in the eyes of the law). I'll never forget a fall afternoon early in my bid: sick with what seemed like the flu, I was allowed to leave work early and return to my cell. Making my way up the flights of steps in the block, I came upon Cheri, the most sought-after trans woman in the prison, kneeling in front of the officer's cage, blowing a guard through the bars. This was an off-hour for facility movement and they obviously thought they'd be undisturbed. Not wanting to be recognized (and possibly targeted by the guard), I sprinted up the steps three at a time, and briskly walked to my cell.

But, the rougher stuff tends to happen in women's prisons and, more so, juvenile facilities, which produce a steady, yet underreported, trickle of staff-on-inmate molestation and rape—exactly what PREA is designed to combat. It will be harder, however, to eliminate instances of inmate-on-inmate abuse, especially gang rape, since PREA concerns itself with reporting requirements and statements of zero tolerance, rather than calling for the installation of ubiquitous surveillance cameras.

The price of prevention is dwarfed in comparison to the human cost exacted upon the lives of those unfortunate souls who have been brutalized. T.J. Parsell[3], now in his fifties, was seventeen when he was gang-raped on his first night in a Michigan jail in 1978. Parsell attempted to rob a photo shop with a toy gun. "I deserved to be punished," he said. "I didn't deserve what I got when I went there . . . Being gang-raped in prison has scarred me in ways that can't be seen or imagined." After twenty years of therapy, he's still haunted.

The men who do such horrid things are, almost as a rule, experienced gamers of the system and thus preternaturally adept at staying below the radar. They choose from the meek and bide their time.

Many prisons make double bunking a requirement for stretches of up to one year. More often than not, this is where the rape is going to happen. According to policy, the Department will not double bunk someone who has been designated an "overt/aggressive homosexual." Needless to say, oversights abound.

I was double bunked for sixty days when I first went upstate. A string of bunkies were taken in and out. Luckily,

---

3. Robert Gavin, "Cruel, but not unusual," *Albany Times Union*, March 28, 2010.

none wanted to rape me (though, a gargantuan of a Puerto Rican, who bunked with me for two weeks, was having issues with his psych meds, and I worried that he'd smash my face with a foot locker as I slept).

Growing up, my bed was large and extremely comfortable, unlike the guest bedroom's, which was only slightly wider than my bed in prison. Because of this, when friends—boys or girls—spent the night, they did so in my bed. By mutual, unspoken agreement, we slept back-to-back, conscious (at least I was) of not crossing the center line.

Thus, when JT drove me home—both of us lousy with drink—and I said he shouldn't get back on the road, it was my bed in which we eventually passed out.

JT was in his mid- to late-twenties, a tall, light-skinned black guy with short dreadlocks. He grew up nearby, and at some point ingratiated himself into the periphery of the social scene of my high school. JT was a likable sort, and made a great impression on our parents. He drove us around before we had licenses, helped us buy beer, and borrowed money that he'd never repay. Someone would "adopt" him for a while and then he'd move on.

I awoke to him scratching my back. Drunk or not, I'm a sucker for a back scratch. Still, it's not the kind of thing guys normally do for each other. To quell the dissonance, I pretended to be asleep. Son of a bitch if he didn't slowly work south, eventually slipping under the waistband of my boxers—a move that I'd pulled on countless girls. As icky as it felt, it didn't occur to me to say NO, then GO, and TELL, as the public service announcement exhorted. I was embarrassed at being put into the situation. In a move borrowed from the girls, I grumbled some displeasure and scooted away. After a minute or so, his hand returned to my back—been there, done that—and furtively traveled to my waist. Boozily, I got up and left the room.

"C'mon," he called as I closed the door.

The bed in the guest room was uncomfortable, but small enough that I didn't worry about JT sneaking into it.

I'd like to say that the experience caused me to behave differently with the girls, to not be so grabby and blindly goal-oriented. But that would imply a degree of self-awareness I wouldn't possess for another ten years. I even continued hanging out with JT, though I never again let him crash at my place, thus maintaining my policy of denial and avoidance.

Since going away I've been steadily cracked on. Shortly after getting out of a double bunk cell, I was assigned my first job: schlepping wheelbarrows of steaming asphalt for a paving project in the prison yard. After finishing, we'd troop to the gym for a communal shower (boxers on is the unspoken rule), then sun ourselves on the soccer field. On one such afternoon, Jazz sat near me. A genial black kid prone to bouts of debilitating stuttering, he was into cinema. So we spoke about that until he leaned closer and lowered his voice. "Duh duh duh duh duh—"

I did as I try to do with all stutterers: resist the urge to complete the thought for them (What is it, boy—trouble at the old mill?), and make my face a passive mask showing neither exasperation nor sympathy.

"Do you muh muh muh muh—"

And it clicked. Jazz was cracking on me, asking if I messed around (with boys). Like anytime I'm cracked on, my default reaction is embarrassment. Couple that with the painful awkwardness of the protracted pitching of woo, and I just wanted done with the entire episode. *Do I mess around? you're going to ask*, is what I thought. But I didn't say this on the off chance that he was going to ask if I messed with drugs. Wouldn't I look foolish then? He's trying to sell me a joint, I misinterpret his motives, he calls me a freak, a fucking homo, or just punches me in the face. So, I waited for what felt like minutes until he did indeed ask if I messed around.

"Nah, man. I'm straight. But flattered." (Did I really say that? Such a narcissistic moron.)

"Wuh, wuh,wuh—"

"Don't worry, it stays between us."

In between aspersions cast on each other's heterosexuality and the endless rounds of dick jokes that pass for meaningful conversation between sexually frustrated men, my friends urged me to work out with them, to toughen up.

Truly, it wasn't my scene, but when in Rome, hit the weights. Weekday nights, weekend mornings—heat, rain, snow, ice, whatever—I joined my crew in the weight pit, a section of yard with thick rubber matting, weathered wooden benches, dumbbells, and free weights. It was like Muscle Beach, if Venice got snow. My peers spoke of protein powders and the latest pronouncements from their bible, *Muscle & Fitness*. The scene interested me as it would an anthropologist: traits, tropes, and trappings. I learned of an illicit and quite lucrative market for creatine, which was snuck in and sold by guards or concealed in coffee creamer jars and shipped in through the package room (though they eventually got wise to that one). A tourist in this most stereotypical prison tableau, I observed it all. The flexing of shaved musculature; endless talk about who has the biggest biceps, tightest pecs, most "shredded" abs; the guys who stood embarrassingly close as they spotted a partner on the squat rack. And Rizzo, a funny, meatheaded Italian kid who shaved his chest and was openly "into the chumps."

A bright weekend morning, I'd left my water bottle beside the bench press. Midworkout, I took a long drink from my bottle and came away with a fruity taste, which was odd since I hadn't any candy. Rizzo, doing preacher curls while he smacked on a Starburst, smiled and gave me a wink. I thought: *You dirty cocksucker*, and left my bottle in the snow.

Admiring his smooth, flexed forearms, Rizzo would slam his workout-gloved hands together, making loud, hollow claps. He shouted hoarse encouragement, and barked out rep numbers to a hulk of a workout partner, who all assumed he was blowing. Rizzo was a tough kid, but wasn't taken as seriously as he would have been had his sexual proclivities been kept under wraps.

There's an uproarious line in *Road House* that has become comingled with my memory of Rizzo. Patrick Swayze, as a less-than-believable tough guy, about to indulge in a spot of bar brawling, tells his opponent: "I used to fuck guys like you in prison." The line is the lecherous uncle of "Too pretty for prison." Amusing myself, I imagine Rizzo out in the world, sharing a tender moment with his partner, lovingly burbling that he used to fuck guys like him in prison.

Jean Genet published his *The Thief's Journal* in 1964, and it remains one of the better-known prison writings, amongst a field that includes George Jackson's *Soledad Brother*, Jack Abbott's *In the Belly of the Beast*, Bell Gale Chevigny's anthology *Doing Time: Twenty-Five Years of Prison Writing*, and H. Bruce Franklin's anthology *Prison Writing in Twentieth Century America*.

What differentiates Genet from the pack is his portrayal of prison sex as consensual and loving. He very much romanticized the hard scrabble life of the petty thieves he fell in with, several of whom became his sexual partners. Genet described relatively short stays in French prisons as little more than a smorgasbord of tube steaks slathered in condiments (Vaseline, I learned, was once packaged in a metal tube). Stripped of the pretense and trappings of the world, however, he experienced truly tender moments of love and companionship. It made his life behind the wall livable.

Some years ago, a couple appeared in the writing workshop I called home. One had legally changed his name, taking the last name of his partner, Mr. and Mr. Benton. The first two workshops they attended were somewhat tense: an openly gay—and interracial—couple draws all types of unwanted attention in prison, and they expected no different from the dozen or so workshop members. On the whole, my peers and I were cool with them so long as they respected the room, and didn't jerk each other off under their desks (something not unheard of during certain weekly religious gatherings).

Jameson, our instructor, the Patron Saint of Prison Writers, drove hours each way, only to be subjected to the harsh realities of Prison A—all in the name of helping us, The Lost Boys. He taught us craft, but, more importantly, showed us to be tolerant and selfless. As such, we treated the Bentons as we did all new participants, making them feel welcome, modeling good behavior, and seeing what they had to offer. In measured tones, they told of the taunts and harassment from the guards. I quickly came to admire their courage. Their peers—in workshop, at work, in the yard—didn't give these tough young men any guff. The white one boxed golden gloves as a teenager. Reading an in-class assignment, he described himself through the words of someone in the yard: *He's a homo, but good wit' his hands.*

The couple were doing different sentences and had little opportunity to be physically intimate. But there was a strong bond in their companionship.

Guards quickly got wise to their presence in workshop, and they both, mysteriously, began having difficulty getting out of their cells on those evenings. In short order, they were transferred to different prisons—it's likely that a separation order, usually reserved for enemies, codefendants, or partners in crime, was placed on their permanent records. I'd like to think that, Departmental separation be damned, they kept their long-distance relationship alive using third-party mail.

The Bentons were a rarity, and the system responded as it normally does with rarities: as would be done to Lily and me, it cut them away and tried to paste them back onto the straight and narrow. Open sexual relationships are more common in women's prisons. Natalie, who we'll meet in a bit, had done time in Washington, and corresponded with me for a spell, told of open, and largely stigma-free sex with her peers (she did a snug piece of business selling artisanal dildoes).

Natalie also mentioned special friends who seemed to be ersatz sisters, mothers, aunts, cousins. That's quite common for men inside, as well. Over the years, I've learned to soften and be grateful for platonic love. Ant, my funny, fucked-up cousin, who got the boot from Prison A after some weed was found in his cell. Whit, a wise, simpatico uncle I'll never forget. The stepbrothers best taken in small doses, Ray and Tommy G. The men who have stood in for my kid brother: Chris, my writing workshop mate who had a brain tumor, and my boy Yas. We share jokes, hopes and dreams, express our fears, open up about our crimes, and cry together. Safely. Inside these familial bonds, we are shielded, albeit temporarily from the harsh realities of prison.

One evening I was painting on a canvas taped to my cell wall. Engrossed in my work—in what the social scientist Mihaly Csikszentmihalyi (six-cent-mihaly) describes as a "Flow" state—I slowly became aware that there was someone in my space. Pretending not to be startled, I said, "W'sup man," to Shabazz, a portly black Muslim who locked a few cells away.

"Just watching," he said.

Shabazz had cracked on me the day before, then got weird when I told him I was straight. Perhaps he feared I'd "blow it up," endanger him by telling one of the enforcers in the Muslim community, despite my assurance that I wouldn't. His proposal came on the heels of an earlier conversation that he subtly steered toward a few trans women in the prison. I told him that before moving to the block, I'd been friendly with Cheri on the strength of shared points of reference (megaclubs back home, rave DJs, and name brands of ecstasy). Shabazz laughed about Cheri's antics in the yard, the nightly displays of intoxicated "faaaaabulousssss." I'd later come to realize that this conversation was a feeler. Had I responded in the conventional vein of "Fucking homos," he likely would not have cracked on me. I've since become wary of guys steering to a gay topic—prison experience has borne this out to be subterfuge.

It's not uncommon for people to watch me draw or paint, but Shabazz was unsettling me. His thumbs were hooked into the waistband of his sweats and he wore an odd expression that I couldn't place. Was it a weapon in his waistline? Was he going to expose himself? (The possibility that *he* was nervous didn't enter my mind.) Hand at my side, I slowly rotated my paintbrush so the (dull) point stuck out of my hand, ready.

He looked at me.

I him.

He moved a little closer.

"You're fucking with my light," I lied. "I need you to take a few steps back."

After a moment, he complied, taking one step back. And I'm glad he did—the paint brush was a poor Plan B.

Again, in the interest of lighting, I asked him to step back. Comically, we played out this routine until he was outside my cell.

John was well read, college educated, a farmer from upstate who grew good pot as a hobby. There was a twenty-year age difference between us—classic rock was the soundtrack to his youth—but shared interests in music and literature fueled our conversation as we walked in the yard. Thing was, he began talking more and more about porn, specifically a practice he had developed in his forties while visiting a friend from college. During these wife's-away weekends, the boys would watch porn in the same room and jerk off—he stressed that they never touched each other. For whatever reason, I found myself thinking of the (non-ursine) characters in John Irving's fiction: cross dressers, closeted wrestlers, and precocious gay outcasts; men whose sex lives are but one long, experimental drama. It's only embarrassing if you make it so, I told myself. My perceived unflappability, unfortunately, was (is) viewed as a green light. I knew what was coming.

But not exactly. He made his advance, I made my well-worn and unequivocal reply about being straight and not interested, and figured we'd move on.

"I'm straight too," John said. "We can just help each other out."

In 1948, Alfred Kinsey proposed a highly controversial theory of sexual orientation. Everyone, according to Kinsey's scale, fell somewhere on a six-point continuum. Zero being completely heterosexual, three bisexual, six completely homosexual; one, two, four, and five are the various shades in between. (Forced to self-identify, I'm a one or a two—over the years there have been instances of my groin warming at the sight of two or three strikingly feminine trans women.) Despite how we self-identify, Kinsey said the majority of us are not zero or six, but rather someplace along the continuum. Further, these numbers are not always consistent over time (see, perhaps, that one really weird drunken night with your college roommate). This dynamic nature of desire would seem to explain the overly simplistic pop cultural dictum that prison (and the navy) "turns you gay." A more nuanced explanation might be that prison and the military produce a formula—bored men, a lack of women, long stretches of time—that often leads to homosexual opportunism. It's a numbers game: get enough humans under these conditions, and the behavior will manifest itself, just as it does during drunken late-nights in college or on a wife's-away weekend. In the absence of opportunity, those who prefer the opposite sex, but harbor homosexual leanings, may choose to indulge them. As Hannibal Lecter said to Clarice, though in a different context, you covet what you see around you. Like John, these men are adapting to a change in circumstance, outing a latent tendency: "helping each other out." Boys being boys brought to you by the creators and users of the glory hole: blind, dumb pleasure (*Could've been a girl doing the sucking . . . yeah, probably was a girl*).

I was in the mess hall, eating lunch when an attractive trans woman swished past. Seated catercorner at the metal table, a friend volunteered that if he were "doing a longer bid," he'd "get with that." I told him it was an honest thing to say (and kept to myself the belief that this man doing a two-year stretch has likely gotten with that). Shifting talk to the thematic, I proposed a prisoner's theory of relativity: what constitutes a "long enough" bid to engage in this behavior changes from person to person and situation to situation. Just as there are people who kill themselves rather than even going away to prison, one sometimes hears the rationalizations from those who "mess around": *I'm doing life, never gonna see the streets again.* But I've also known "long enough" to mean fifty years, twenty, five. As behavioral economics teaches, we're irrational creatures, poor at predicting how we'll behave under different sets of circumstances, adept at post-game rationalization. Tweak the set (of people involved), setting and situation, and your capability to do anything (or anyone) will out. That should be the takeaway from Kinsey's work. Deep down, I think we all know this. Yet, as Joan Didion pointed out, "We tell ourselves stories in order to live." The fairy tale in this instance being that we're all quite normal, all of the time. Kinsey came under harsh criticism for his research methods, namely, the overrepresentation of prisoners and prostitutes in his sample population. Decades later, his data was "scrubbed"—out went many of the cons and pros—yet the results remain largely unchanged. Zero to six it is.

John tried again, leaving his offer on the table: "We can help each other out." I fell back on a scripted reply: "Fair enough."

He was good about not revisiting the subject. And, as usual, I pretended it never happened.

After my weed connection got busted and sent to the Box, I got introduced to D. A black man in his forties, D was short, muscular, and quiet in a menacing way. The second time I bought off him, he sent me to retrieve the small bag off his footlocker. As I did, he stepped into the cell behind me. I pocketed the weed and turned to leave. Practically body-to-body, he made no attempt to let me pass. Instead, he reached behind me and gently pinched my ass.

The reaction of my peers—of the street—would be to uncork a swift uppercut, beat D bloody, take the weed, then consider the matter closed. Hell, I had friends who doled out such beatings at the slightest hint of an advance. Me, I managed an awkward waltz, and our positions were reversed. "I'll have the packs (of cigarettes) for you tomorrow."

"Nah," he said. "We can work sum'in else out. I'll take care a' you."

Hanging out in bombed-out neighborhoods during my junkie days, I was never propositioned to make a few bucks the hard way. And it's a good thing, too, because I'd have done whatever to avoid being dope sick. Any junkie who tells you otherwise is lying.

"Eh, I'd rather pay." With this, I left, and went to my cell to smoke away the surreality. My mind ablaze, residual adrenaline in the blood, I tried to make sense of what just went down. D did business with a select group, I'd learned. Certainly they paid him, or at least most did, in money, not sexual favors. So why would he crack on me so boldly, in such an all-or-nothing way? I'm no tough guy, but I'm also not viewed as a lame—well regarded, in fact, by some heavy hitters. Yet D felt confident enough that I'd be game that he put himself into a potentially violent situation. To further complicate things, I was surreptitiously vetted by D before the introduction was made. I sometimes smoked with a bizarre old Cuban—he began to double his orders and procured for me from D, eventually making the introduction. Did D agree to do business with me with rough trade in mind? What kind of signal was I emitting? I'm aware that in this alpha-male, testosterone-fueled environment my otherness is apparent: not participating in sports or consistently working out, not adorning the walls of my cell with naked women, and not engaging in chest-thumping self-expression. But I'm not the only one who behaves thusly. Perhaps it was that behavior paired with my looks that caused D to do what he did. *Fuck knows*, I thought, ending the solipsism and trying to enjoy the high.

Instead, I found myself thumbing through newly remembered trysting scenes from my youth. How grabby I was. Poor girls. They gave me a kiss, I copped feels galore.

The following day, in what felt like the most awkward drug transaction I'd ever made, I paid D his packs, forcing a smile like nothing had happened. "Here you go," I said and turned before he had a chance to speak. And so began a little vacation from smoking.

It's only fitting that I got cracked on while writing this. More than three years have passed since the exchange with Ralphie that began this line of thought, even longer since the incident with D. I've recently landed in a new cell in honor block. My neighbor, Levonne, a pleasant fellow more than a little into pop music, seemed to make a show of his dexterity when passing items to me through the bars of our locked cells. His disembodied hand would snake around, leave the item on the metal lattice of my bars, then give a tap like "Thing," that hand on the *Addams Family*. Surely he was demonstrating his ability to give a "reach around." I knew it was just a matter of time, and was not surprised when he passed a note, inquiring if I were gay.

"No," I wrote back, "just artsy."

More recently, I was cracked on by a swarthy, unctuous Italian in his fifties who had an early Jerry Lewis gestalt and spoke with the smoker's baritone of a late-night radio DJ (which he happened to be before going away). I got a kick out of this one because I was able to write in my journal that Gay Jerry Lewis cracked on me. But it quickly became annoying when he'd stop at my cell and literally beg me to disrobe. I finally got him alone in the stairwell. "This business of stopping at my cell—that ends."

"Oh, c'mon," he said, laughing it off.

I played a card I normally don't. I addressed him as a convicted murderer speaking to a guy doing a nothing bid, played the role of young, dangerous, and nothing to lose: "Look at me," I said with all the dead seriousness I could muster. "Are we gonna have a fuckin' problem?"

Imploring laughter: "Whaddaya mean?"

"You know what the fuck I mean. What I need to hear from you right now is that you're done cracking on me. If yes, then we're cool, and none of this unpleasantness ever happened. If no, then we have a problem."

"You're really gonna hit me?"

I just stared, passively malevolent.

"I won't do it again."

"Good."

And he didn't.

Passive malevolence—that wasn't always my modus operandi. Certainly not in eleventh grade, when a friend let me in on a well-kept secret: each semester, Dr. F— offered an independent study in music history with a guaranteed A, which would give my GPA a sorely needed boost on the looming college applications. The friend's older brother, a wildly popular party kid, had taken the independent study. That I knew essentially nothing of music created earlier than the eighties didn't matter—all I had to do was convince the man that I'd be a good student. Dr. F— was a well-regarded, gregarious man, a gifted musician who gave private lessons in the homes of my classmates.

He showed me past the choral risers and into his cramped office, a place cluttered with sheet music and musicological bric-a-brac. We sat in chairs by the window, and he spoke kindly of acquaintances we had in common. At some point I asked if I could take his independent study. "Of course," he laughed, and returned to discussing my peers.

During the semester, we met in his office once or twice a week after school, fifteen minutes, half hour tops. From the beginning it was awkward. Not only do I feel compelled to please people and be well liked, but I overanalyze body language and facial expressions. The chairs were arranged uncomfortably close, I could smell his bad breath. His hair was straightened and slicked into place, glistening skin the color of dark chocolate; beneath glasses, his eyes bulged; a moustache on a boyishly round face. The aesthetic, encompassing his cheery demeanor, was Muppet-like. Dr. F— had me talk about how I spent my weekends. Often, he'd laugh aloud, grab my knee, and proclaim: "You Doc's boy!" Doc's boy thought it would be impolite to move his chair away.

A friend took piano lessons from him, so I asked if he thought Dr. F— was gay.

"He's married," my friend chuckled, "and has kids. He's just weird."

I did not relish the time I had to spend in that office. It did, after all, feel like work. Even though we never spoke more than superficially of music, I worried that he'd eventually make a blatant move. I spoke of girls I'd hooked up with, in what I thought would be a talisman against his advances.

On a few occasions I brought classical music CDs and asked him to help me appreciate them. He'd listen with his eyes closed, nodding sagely at a lull or shaking out his arms as the orchestra boiled over.

One afternoon a few weeks before the end of the school year, Dr. F— said that my independent study had drawn to a close. He was genuinely sorry, but with the graduation ceremony looming, he'd have to earn his keep. "What do you think your grade should be?"

Presuming this to be something near a rhetorical question, I chuckled and professed ignorance.

This made him laugh and pat my shoulder. Apparently he did want my input. He asked again.

"Something in the nineties?" I offered.

"Of course!" More laughter.

"Ummm . . . ninety . . . fff . . . a ninety-eight."

My seriousness amused Dr. F—. Patting my arm, he agreed to ninety-eight and, by way of justification, told me I was "real cool . . . *real* cool."

We shook hands and wished each other a good summer. I left quickly, afraid that I'd finally have to earn my grade.

"I'll leave you alone," Ralphie said as he stood up.

"Sorry, old sport." My friends had grown accustomed to my staring off into nowhere, but I still felt like a poor host. I thrust out my pen. "Blood on my blade, right?"

He smiled. "Right."

When he was gone, I picked up the small broom and returned it to the corner. Over the years, I've gone through stages: from absolutely clueless I was being cracked on, to merely naive; in my late twenties becoming so overly suspicious that even the slightest uptick in attention from a peer would alert me to an advance; finally, settling into a comfortable zone where I'm (usually) able to see an advance in advance. I've been lucky never to have been bent over a slop sink and violated, as one loathsome character in county predicted would be my fate. In my late thirties, with time under my belt, I'd like to believe that the chance of getting raped is in my past. But I'm not complacent.

I remember looking at the broom in the corner and snorting out a chuckle. My mom was only half right. Given the givens, it won't be girls I'll have to beat away with a stick.

SIX

THE WOMEN OF (BLANK) COUNTY JAIL

Do you remember the last time you had sex? How about a pre-Y2K tryst? If they're one and the same, you probably would.

At age thirty-two, I realized my last roll in the proverbial hay had been almost a decade earlier. On top of my green-and-white striped comforter, Jenny and I went at it like doggies. Facing a wall-length mirror, our eyes momentarily locked in disbelief: *We're actually fucking.* Junkies both, our sex life after two years together was that of a couple married for twenty years. We were good-looking kids and, like so much else, things weren't supposed to be this way. Early on, the bliss of heroin replaced orgasms. Climaxing became a maddeningly protracted affair. During the daily chemical withdrawal, coupling was the last thing our sweaty, achy bodies craved. When sex happened, it was not loving, but rather alternated between spastic and drowsy. One or both of us would be on the verge of losing consciousness. If there exists a fetish for zombie porn (and there likely does), I imagine it would look something like what was going on in my bedroom that long-ago afternoon.

Within the month, I'd be arrested for murder.

Shortly after arriving in Blank County Jail, I was placed on suicide watch. In the small hours of my first night in a cell, I was awakened by a guard and escorted to the infirmary. He stood in the doorway as I sat on the cold gray cushions of an examination table, slowly taking in my surroundings. The walls were faux-wood paneling, the room was chilly and quiet, and the fluorescents bothered me. The nurse—a young, attractive woman—wasn't warm and flirty with me as had been nurses and dental assistants from my life before. Thus, the system drew its boundaries, and pronounced me no longer worthy of the special attention I'd taken as my birthright. She addressed me in clipped monotone, as one would an intelligent animal. *Lift your shirt.* The stethoscope's smooth, cold head on my chest gave me goose bumps. *Deep breaths.* Her hand swept across my back, and I warmed from the human contact. The nurse cinched a blood pressure cuff around my biceps and stuck a thermometer in my mouth.

The guard tried small talk with her while the machines took their measure of me. The nurse had short blonde hair, windswept with gel. Her lips were pink and glossy. Moby's "Natural Blues" played from a radio in the anteroom, a soft, haunting melancholy. The last time I heard it, I was driving home from the city, a bundle of H and syringes under my seat. The song gave me chills and I wanted to cry.

Instead, I waited till the thermometer was out of my mouth and asked for something to kill the pain. And, for the first time, the nurse gave me a smile, and said: *Yeah, right.*

Suicide watch was more commonly called one-on-one, and meant literally that, a pair of eyes on me around the clock. Along with two faceless men, I inhabited Admin Seg 1 (Administrative Segregation 1). Admin Seg 2 was diagonally across the hall, into which I could see the beginning of a cell just like mine. Ours was a small, windowless tank containing three six-by-nine cells, a three-foot walkway serving as our front porch. Welded to the cell wall was a wooden bench too narrow for my "mattress," so I moved that, and myself, to the cold, dusty floor. The soundtrack to domestic life— random mumbling, toilet flushing, and shuffling feet—let me know that the two cells to my right were occupied. Less than twenty-four hours in, I didn't know enough to wonder why these men were segregated and not in general population.

But it was apparent that I was the only one being closely watched. A small desk had been brought in, along with an old, cushioned desk chair, and placed in front of my cell. Every eight hours a new guard parked his or her ass in that chair and read the paper.

This wasn't a bad arrangement for me. Being one-on-one gave me time to adjust to incarcerated life, away from the criminally mature men in general population, to learn things on my own. I got to know the guards and they got to know me. Some better than others. There were a few hard asses who wanted nothing to do with me, and spent their shift reading and avoiding any human exchange. But most were decent and many weren't much older than I. We seemed to strike an unspoken, mutually beneficial arrangement: I'd keep them awake and entertained, and they'd treat me like a human being. Already, I was relying on Willy Loman's mantra: *Be liked and you will never want.*

On my second night, a big woman had watch. I'd become adept at surreptitiously reading their tiny name tags. "Hi, Miss Haynes."

She was standoffish. But, with eight hours together, her chair three feet from the bars, we spoke and became comfortable with the other's presence. At some point, I lost myself in silent contemplation. I was withdrawing from methadone—nauseated, sweaty, achy, feverish—and very uncomfortable. At seemingly random moments, the guilt of what I'd done would pierce the veil of shock, flash across my mind, flood the inner recesses of my being. I would cringe and whimper. Fear, loathing, and self-pity? Sure, there was some of that.

In my puddle of misty despond, I reached up from the floor and asked Haynes to hold my hand. I couldn't believe that I asked, or that she actually obliged me. She extended several fingers, which I held through the bars. Sobbing, I thanked her, and curled into a ball.

It's a trick of memory that I remember more female guards than male, likely a result of having little cause to remember their male counterparts in the years since. Was I just lucky to have women assigned to guard me? Perhaps they requested it, felt that watching me was less stressful than working the tiers in general population. Faces started repeating. Each shift change became like a lottery: would I draw a dud for the next eight hours or a winner? An uncaring uniform who would barely acknowledge my presence, or someone whose sole focus wasn't the bars between us?

Keno laughed like a smoker. She had oily skin, a button nose, and big dark eyes like anime. She was a boyish lesbian a couple years older than I. To save my life, I can't explain how we came to discussing her dildo collection, but there we were, laughingly enumerating the finer points of her variable-speed, clitoral-stimulating, multicolor-beaded, sleek new rabbit vibrator.

Lesbian or not, I imagined her using said vibrator, working herself to an enthusiastic climax. And so it happened that my libido returned. A twenty-three-year-old newly sober junkie, I literally came from stiff bed sheets—a peculiar side effect of being junk sick. Being closely watched, however, drastically curtailed my ability to find sexual release.

The most privacy I had was during my shower every other evening in the intake room. The guard sat five feet from the curtain and had me call out occasionally. That old shower, with its dun stone-chip tiles, and hard, hot water, became my masturbatorium. For a while there, I went at it with the anticipatory excitement of a young boy. I think that, to my dying breath, the scent of down market shampoo will trigger a rush of warmth to my loins. Granted, this was wanking at its most utilitarian. So as not to be disturbed in flagrante Pert Plus-o, I'd call out a hello before I started, buying myself at least five minutes.

As was often the way with female guards, Kelly had a male coworker spell her while I showered. Kelly was a cute, short, pretty blonde who was friendly with me from the beginning. I could make her laugh and there was quite a bit of flirting back and forth.

The A-game is my default setting: play hard or go home and Always Be Closing. I was used to validating my self-worth through the eyes of the fairer sex, but my needing to be liked took on a further dimension. The local news had painted a pretty gruesome portrait that I felt compelled to overcome.

With Kelly, however, I got the sense that she saw past the televised perp walk. In fact, she began sending me some not-so-vague sexual signals. I noticed a heavier application of perfume. As crazy as it sounds, Kelly began wearing tighter-fitting uniform pants. (I am aware—more so now—that these changes could just as likely have been directed at a coworker, and closely watched me was merely a lucky secondary audience.) I knew enough to keep my hands and dirty thoughts to myself. Call it self-respect, situational awareness, and a desire to continue receiving such pleasantries.

When she kicked back in her chair, and rested her boot on my bars, I could see smooth white leg. "Nice socks," I said.

"You like?" she said, pulling it up to reveal cartoon animals.

That I was beginning to get aroused by this interaction made me feel like a pervert.

She took to resting both feet on my bars, tilting her chair against the wall. A rather obstetric pose. The inseam of her gray pants culminated in a tightness in the crotch that split clearly defined labia. I had a box seat to the vulva show and was going mad trying not to stare.

One evening, this display became too much to bear. Kelly, distracted behind a *Cosmo*, didn't notice me slowly making ready my provisions . . . easing under the blanket with my feet pointed away from her . . . removing my underwear . . . tenting my knees . . . pretending to stare at the ceiling . . . and silently working myself to a climax while stealing glances at her business. In the post-climactic rush, I felt dirty and gross, and knew there would never be an encore performance.

It was Carrie, however, who really threw me for a loop. I was in jail less than a month when she first worked one-on-one. Acknowledging the coworker she relieved with a mundane pleasantry, Carrie sat down and riffled through her lunch cooler.

Her skin bore the patina of a salon tan. She had big eyes and good features like a figure skater or a small-town beauty queen. Carrie licked a spot of mayo off her lip and, with a "here," handed me a branch of grapes.

I was transfixed and hungry and horny. "Thanks a lot," I said, popping grapes onto my tongue.

"No problem, dude."

She called me "dude" and proceeded to be bubbly and flirty. It triggered a dissonance. This was how I'd grown accustomed to being treated by girls (and Carrie couldn't have been more than five years older), but there were so many barriers. The bars, our respective uniforms, the abstract label of me, the murderer.

Every shift change was a crapshoot. I was always hopeful for her eight-hour presence. Carrie pulled one-on-one no more or less than the other women, or so I recall now. But, she inhabits a brightly lit corner of memory because our conversation, at her direction, took a turn for the bizarre.

The second time Carrie worked, I learned that she was married to a state trooper, and—her words—hated fucking him.

We talked briefly of sexual partners. Before long, Carrie admitted to being "fascinated" by serial killers. I didn't know whether to be more disturbed by her admission or the fact that I had an inkling she was lumping me into that deranged category.

Murder occupied her thoughts. Being that the subject is given soft-core gore-porn treatment in pop culture—Lifetime movies, *20/20*, all the *CSI*s and *L&O*s—I took her interest to be merely on the lower edge of normalcy. Until, that is, Carrie began bouncing ideas off me on how to kill someone, say, her husband. I was confused and uncomfortable, and tried to shift the conversation to a piece I had been drawing before her shift. But Carrie was undeterred. She talked of blood-spatter patterns, weapons, and DNA evidence. She'd wear a garbage bag, she said.

Carrie wanted to be a state trooper, and spoke of ways to confuse the battery of psych tests given new recruits. She was smart, seemingly promiscuous, and had connections (not the least of which, the husband she fantasized about killing)—I wouldn't be surprised if Carrie not only became a statie, but has risen through the ranks.

Bubbly Carrie, with the pretty face and conspiratorial talk, was almost certainly a plant, one of several people (some confirmed, some not) the district attorney had indirectly placed near me to gin up some evidence.

There was no shortage of women writing me letters, strangers who read newspapers. The feminine script on the envelope got my pulse racing, and charged my imagination. Such a vivid, hopeful, unrealistic imagination . . .

My soul mate would learn of my presence through an article. She would see past my worst. A relationship would blossom through the mail, and we'd eventually be married. There would be a kid, maybe. When, if, I got out, we'd retire to a modest home someplace far away . . .

And then I opened the envelope: garishly perfumed, poorly punctuated lunacy from fundamentalist Christian freak-azoids. They prayed for my soul and hoped to hear back soon.

Joan, the bringer of goodies, was a civilian employee of the jail, who did light clerical, oversaw the laundry, and pushed around a canvas-sided laundry cart delivering the commissary items we ordered. Superficially, Joan was a troll of a woman, but her personality was sweeter than the Butter-fingers she dropped off weekly. Once, when I ordered boxers (plain white), she bestowed on me what looked like shorts from the seventies, dark blue with white piping. The tag read Bob Barker, and they were likely shipped to the commissary by accident. While she didn't say it, I suspected that Joan gave them to me because I was still being made to wear a diaphanous yellow suicide smock (that and foam slippers with smiley faces: disposable hospital gear that would be replaced when it began to fall apart) with a pair of ill-fitting briefs. Those shorts were one of the most practical gifts I received in county, and I retained them for the duration of my yearlong stay.

Not long after receiving Joan's gift, there were a series of "incidents" on the upper floors, a place that occupied a very dark patch of my imagination. The administration needed cells with which to segregate the combatants. In other words, I needed to be moved. Since all six Admin Seg cells would be occupied, and they still considered me a suicide risk, I was moved to an isolation room, which happened to be on the women's side of the jail. The room had been built recently—likely to comply with a newly created standard—to house cases needing medical isolation (TB patients, for example). Air-handling units kept the room very cold, but aside from that (not insignificant) fact, the place was a veritable palace compared to what I'd been living in for the past month or so. It was roughly fifteen-by-fifteen, two beds (free standing metal platform on legs on which to place a thin mattress—just moderately more comfortable than sleeping on the floor), a color TV, pay phone, and bathroom with shower. The guard set up a small desk and chair in the air lock, and propped open both doors.

By this point, the powers that be had me wearing a blue ballistic nylon smock. It was thick, unwieldy, and had Velcro straps at the shoulders. If Fred Flintstone were asked to design a post-modernist housedress in a superintelligent shade of blue, this would be it.

I finagled an undershirt and had those blue shorts, courtesy of Joan, and I wore the smock rolled around my waist, reaching almost to the floor and covering bare legs. You wouldn't be insane to term it a dress, but I thought I looked rather like a samurai.

It shouldn't have come as a surprise that on the women's side there would be female inmates delivering my meals. When one came in with a tray, I didn't even have time to compose a proper flirt. Face-to-face with this short, bouncy Puerto Riquena, all I could manage was: "Uh, wassup."

She was flirty, treating me like a curious visitor to her territory. As Roxy left, I stared at the panty line on her pert, round ass in an orange prison jumper.

The next meal, she slipped me a note from her friend, Melinda. It was dripping with sexual frustrations. Melinda described herself with erotic innuendo, and said that she'd seen me when they went out to the yard, and wanted to get me alone. Possessed with a humming charge, I read her letter over and over, imagining wilder and wilder fantasies. "Hey," I told the guard, "I'm going to jump in the shower."

Across the hall from the Iso Room was a dorm that housed a couple dozen women with less-serious charges than Roxy and Melinda, who were housed in cells. Every so often, we'd wave. Once, a woman lifted her jumper and flashed me—areolas the size of saucers hung like udders inches from her plump belly's button. With a polite wave, I thanked her and turned away. "Caged Heat" and "Jail Babes" they weren't. These were women whose hard lives registered a toll in dog years: "pros," addicts, barroom hustlers, or the occasional woman who tired of her "old man" beating on her, and did something the court understood, and maybe even sympathized with, but still considered a violent felony. What I saw paraded past my door every day were big, often beastly women, all scars and missing teeth.

But not Melinda, who, to my delight, filled in for Roxy a couple times a week. She was attractive, tall with shortish hair, in her late twenties; a South American mestiza aesthetic. "Hey, sweetie," she'd say, handing me my food.

"Hellooo, beautiful," I'd cartoonishly reply as our hands touched.

The guard always stood close by. Not only was I on suicide watch, but I was a hungry young man living amidst ravenously horny women—they understood that I needed to be watched even more closely.

Jails are frenetic and unpredictable places, however, and one morning, returning from the yard, I managed to be in the hall alone, while Melinda was mopping.

"Come here," she whispered, and grabbed my arm. A door closed and I stood with Melinda under a dangling incandescent in a musty supply closet. Immediately, our hands were in each other's underwear, and we kissed with gusto. Only when the guards banged on the door that I held closed with my sneaker, and began threatening us with "trouble," did we come out.

That, at least, is the story I told my awestruck peers for the next several years. In truth, the guards were banging on the door as soon as it shut. We stood close, holding hands, giggling silently—fucking with the guards instead of each other. Melinda and I were back in the hallway in under a minute.

Not too long after that, my two-week vacation living amongst the Amazons came to an end, and I was moved back to my previous cell in Admin Seg 1.

Red moved me. She was stocky, and had hilariously dyed red hair, a bowl cut. Red was definitely uncool and certainly not charmed by yours truly. When I unpacked a black garbage bag given me to move my few possessions, she noticed the colored pencils that had been given to me by Carrie. "Where'd you get those?"

"I dunno. Just found them." Technically, I was given several things by guards that I wasn't supposed to have—food, reading material, drawing supplies, details of their personal lives—but I wouldn't repay the largesse by diming them out.

Red took away my colored pencils. I was on suicide watch, and couldn't be trusted with them.

I repaid the inflexibility by not giving her a courtesy flush whenever I used the toilet.

When I was taken off suicide watch after more than two months, I was moved upstairs to Z-tier.

A guard sat at a desk up front. He let me into the sally port—a secure entryway that consists of a series of gates—which contained a shower and slop sink, and then swung closed the heavy, steel-bar gate. Standing in the caged enclosure holding my black garbage bag of possessions, I saw men on the tier, walking around, sitting at tables. They looked at me, then went back to their business.

"You'll be going into the first cell," the guard said. He opened the panel box, and the gate between the sally port and the tier whirred noisily on its tracks. Two steps out of the sally port placed me in front of 1 cell, my new home.

I tossed my bag on the bed, then went about meeting my neighbors. They weren't a bad bunch. I learned that Z-tier was considered a close-watch tier, housing psych cases, rapists, men in protective custody, and those whom administration didn't want in general population for whatever reason. All in all, it further eased my transition to incarcerated life—I didn't have to worry about an eighteen-year-old corner kid sucker-punching me because I didn't surrender my candy bars. There were sixteen cells on the tier, mine included; four metal picnic tables, with benches, were bolted to the floor; TV on the cat-walk, viewable through the bars; a pay phone; the aforementioned shower and slop sink. On the other side of the bars that enclosed the tier, was the guard's walkway (the "catwalk"), and then cinder block walls with the periodic high window, small and frosted.

At 1 cell, I was the closest watched of the closely watched. It worked out great.

Rachel worked nights, eleven to seven. She was cute in a bookish way, two years my junior, and finishing her bachelor's. She'd worked one-on-one a few times, and we had an easy rapport. Owing to her Irish surname and our shared love of *The Simpsons*, I dubbed her McGarnagle, a character voiced by Phil Hartman, whose life on the show lasted less than ten seconds. The obscure reference was an incantation that produced laughter whenever one of us uttered it.

Shortly after eleven, I'd hear the sally port whir open, the outer gate unlatch and swing, and Rachel would slide her chair in front of my cell. I sat on the edge of my bed and we talked through the bars in the dark, thick as thieves. She wasn't the only guard who did this with me, and I sometimes wondered if they told each other that I was a good means of staying awake, the way a trucker might share some speed with a fellow traveler outside a diner. But Rachel was the only one to scratch my back.

"McGarnagle!" I said the first time she pulled up her chair.

"Hey, Jimmy," she deadpanned—our call-response, part of the same obscure *Simpsons* reference.

After some hours of talking, she turned her back, and asked me to rub her shoulders, while she read a sociology textbook aided by a small clip-on lamp. To loosen the collar, Rachel undid a button of her blue uniform shirt, then pulled her strawberry blonde hair up in a bun. I kneaded and rubbed her shoulders and neck, constantly fighting the urge to crest her collarbones and play high school boy, gradually moving toward tit. When my arms grew tired, I told her as much, then proposed a win-win. So it came to pass that we reversed our seating arrangement, and she scratched my back through the bars while I skimmed the sociology text, marking with highlighter the important parts for her. To think: Andy Dufresne, Red, and the boys thought they were lucky because they got to tar the roof of Shawshank prison, and drink one lousy bottle of beer in the summer sun for their efforts.

We spent countless nights in this fashion, and it remains one of the most pleasant (and surreal) memories from my stay in county.

Two of the metal tables on the tier sported the painted remnants of game boards, faded and deliberately chipped. A guard, "Ms. Grace," showed up one afternoon with pints of red and black Rust-Oleum and asked if anyone wanted to paint checkerboards on the tables.

Can you guess who volunteered?

Ms. Grace was the unofficial activities director of the jail. This forty-something with a hoarse voice, slight moustache, and unpronounceable Italian surname, provided movies and board games.

I kept on very good terms with her, and Ms. Grace allowed me to add a movie choice or two to the dreck that was played each weekend.

Like many of my peers, I got into the habit of sleeping late into the morning. If you're not meeting with an attorney or going to court, there's little to do in county jail besides play cards and jerk off, and there's only so much one can shuffle that deck.

I began to notice a couple neighbors leaving the tier shortly after breakfast, and returning before lunchtime lock-in. They came back from "school" carrying books, art supplies, and enthusiastic positive talk.

For an application, I drew my sink four times on a piece of drawing paper, each a different style: cartoon-faced, cubist, contour-lined, and photo realist. Along with a brief cover letter expressing interest, I sent the drawing with a neighbor and instructions to give it to whoever made decisions regarding attendance.

A couple mornings later, I was called down to school after breakfast, and greeted by Fawn, an artsy, spunky, forty-something. She was pretty, with great big boobs.

By the end of the morning, I'd become the unofficial teacher's assistant for a GED class of twenty.

Five mornings a week I spent in that classroom helping my peers on computers, collecting and correcting composition books, and supplementing Fawn's art lessons.

Fawn encouraged my art, and pushed me to produce more consistently and in a studied manner. She gave me good drawing pencils, a twenty-five-stick set of oil pastels, and proper drawing papers. I did figure studies and made two pieces of finished work a week—everything that I didn't do in my drawing course freshman year in college.

Fawn also plied me with a speedy little painkiller each morning (a pharmaceutical I would come to know as dompers several years later). I'd drawn my line in the sand with heroin, but, in those days, everything else was fair game. Fawn wasn't the only staff person to give me (unsolicited) substances: two guards gave me painkillers, and the occasional joint. I can only assume now that they themselves were users, practicing the Golden Rule. At the time, I didn't question the motives—hungry hippos don't look gift horses in the mouth.

Fawn made sure I ate the pill in front of her (like a true junkie, I began skipping breakfast, to increase the pill's efficacy). Sometimes she'd join me, and swallow half a Soma. We talked art and artists, drew for each other, and got fucked up before noon. Fawn instilled in me a love for the work of Mark Rothko; to this day I get absorbed in his large, warm blocks of color. She also encouraged me to borrow books from her shelves, damn good lit that I'd neglected growing up: Huxley, Hemingway, Conrad, Faulkner, and Fromm.

Michelle was another teacher. In her midthirties, with silky blonde hair, she dressed like a grad student from an eighties movie, long skirts and sweaters. Michelle was a sexy flirt of a pothead who I could make laugh. We often sat next to each other at the bank of computers, and told tales of debaucheries past—my college years and time spent in the rave scene, her past weekend.

When she showed me a fading red splotch by her right thumb, and laughed that she'd given her boyfriend poison ivy along with a hand job, I couldn't stop picturing that hand at work. My imagination played like "The Tell-Tale Heart" by way of *Penthouse Letters*.

There was a dissonance for these women. I was educated, personable, attractive—and awaiting trial for murder. Though, they managed to see past that (or, at least, acted as if), and made for me a welcome, stimulating environment.

I was a narcissistic people pleaser who looked for acceptance and comfort in others. With these women, it wasn't about sex. Well, for the most part it wasn't about sex. They provided approval and lavished me with the comfort that I've always found in the succor of the opposite sex. I felt the constant need to be at my best, most talented, charming, and gifted—not merely to humanize the monster, but to prove worthy of their treatment and ensure its continuation. Thus, the curtain rises on the tragicomedy of my narcissism: the drive to know all, help all, love and be loved by all will often be confounded by the past weight of my senseless crime, a hole I'm forever digging out of.

The third teacher was Claire, a matronly figure in her late forties. While she was the least cool of the trio, Claire was still quite decent, paying me in good chocolates to do her grunt work. Grading papers earned me a handful of Godiva; making spreadsheets and organizing her personal life paid off in Toblerone. I was helpful, attentive, and polite—the only difference between me then and in photos at four years old, was that I wore more chocolate on my face in the photos.

Having a cell to myself allowed my born-again libido to stretch its legs. Put plainly, I was masturbating like a teenager. My storage bin held a minor trove of porn I'd inherited from friends when they were transferred to state prison. Oh, the collective hours spent panting over those brightly colored, fleshy pages.

But the creative hemisphere of my brain was also marshaled into service, recalling scenes with girlfriends past, or manufacturing assignations with the women of Blank County Jail. These were all improbable scenarios with the same driving logic and plot arc of most porno flicks: find myself alone with a woman who happens to be really, really horny.

Carrie (or Kelly or McGarnagle, and sometimes two or three) works the midnight shift, opens my cell, and takes off just enough of her uniform for me to access the areas of vital import. Alone in a stairwell with Melinda, we do what I'd been hinting to my peers that we'd done, only better. I arrive early to the classroom, only Fawn (or Michelle) is there, and we screw furtively behind the filing cabinet.

Fawn didn't dispel those fantasies when, after telling me about it for weeks, she brought in *Harold and Maude* for the class to watch. My peers deemed it silly, and looked askance at the quirky, platonic love between characters with an age difference measured in dozens of years. I looked at Fawn and thought: *Are you thinking what I'm thinking?*

Alas, my life wasn't all peaches and cream and masturbatory fantasies. Roxy's boyfriend, Juice, locked on the floor above mine. Apparently he got it in his head that I was too chummy with Roxy, and sent word that he was *gonna fuck me up.*

The chance of our coming into contact was unlikely. I did, however, worry about someone looking to score points with Juice, someone with whom I did come into contact, like one of several teenage gang members in the GED class. The preferential treatment I received from female staff made many of my peers envious. And not just my peers. A sleazy guard who often worked the women's side of the jail took vicious delight in passing messages from Melinda. "Hey, your crack whore girlfriend sends her love." "Your crack whore misses you."

His ad hominem editorializing vexed me, and I wanted to defend this girl. Not responding to the guard was the best I could do. It had never occurred to me to wonder what Melinda was in jail for—she likely *was* a crack-smoking prostitute.

And there was the incident with Mrs. Smith, who, unlike the sleazeball, was a good person. Both she and her husband were guards. A handsome black couple in their early thirties, they were born-again Christians, a lifestyle choice I tried not to hold against them.

Missus had worked one-on-one more frequently than Mister. We were on good terms. Leafing through the gilded pages of a Bible at her post on Z-tier, she'd call me over and earnestly quote verses. To her, it was very simple, the answers were right there in black and white, everything was in accordance to plan, and it was my turn to be saved, to be forgiven my sins. In my estimation, however, the dead can't offer absolution. On the strength of our past dealings, I was polite as I made my exit. Usually.

On a particularly dark day, I responded to her born-again *mishegoss* by launching into an unkind deconstruction of organized religion. This quickly morphed into a blue streak of choice blasphemies mocking her belief system. My pent-up jeremiad only ended when she began to cry.

That evening, Mr. Smith had me brought into the hallway, where I was left standing against the wall. When he walked over, I believed I was in for some time-honored abuse at the hands of a guard. His face inches from mine, Smith said, "Whadju say to my wife?"

Hoping to make it no worse, I explained, in a manner less cogent than I use here, that I was having a bad morning and the proselytizing became too much to bear; I was rude and am sorry.

He weighed my words for a moment, then told me, in no uncertain terms, that I was not to speak to Mrs. Smith. All things considered, I got off easy. Were he to have punched me in the stomach, I wouldn't have blamed him.

Returned to jail after my van ride to court for sentencing to twenty-five-to-life, my status was changed to "state ready." In a week or so, I'd be transferred to a state prison reception center. I had grown accustomed to the faces and routine of the small county jail, and was in no rush to leave. The next van ride would lead to a much larger, more indifferent place, which filled me with vague fears of the unknown. Also, I'd miss the women who'd softened my transition from street to incarceration. Something told me I would never again experience such kindness from female staff.

Fawn asked to keep several pieces from my portfolio, and generously mailed the rest to my brother. My art had really progressed through her mentorship. As a going-away present, she gave me a big hug and a handful of pills.

Claire brought me a chocolate orange and, true to form, asked that I address and personalize her holiday cards. Fawn and Michelle thought it was gauche of her, but I didn't complain. And since she made the mistake of letting me seal the envelopes without her inspection, I was able to personalize the cards as I saw fit. If the name on the mailing list spoke to me, I'd add a daft non sequitur ("Spay and neuter your pets," "Last night a DJ saved my life," etc.), wholly uncharacteristic of Claire, and which likely prompted a perplexed reply. To a gay couple, I penned: "Have a happy and healthy prostate. Love, Claire."

Several days before Christmas I was taken by van to Prison E, the reception facility. A light snow fell as we drove on roads that seemed familiar. Thankfully, it was a short trip—the holiday music was more cloying than usual.

The difference in staff attitudes between county and state was made clear in the first bull pen. I was less a person than a pair of wrists that needed to be uncuffed. This place processed in more inmates in one day than were housed in the jail I'd come from. The high turnover meant that guards kept their distance; they hadn't the cognitive energy to treat us as people with a past and future, we remained synecdoches, heads to be counted, cells to be checked.

Six months later, when I was sent upstate to the maximum-security Prison A, the distance from staff only increased. In their eyes, I was farther from a past life of respectability, my ID number showed someone who'd been incarcerated for roughly two years, a fucking newjack. To be sure, there were friendly guards, but nothing like in county. The few female guards weren't my age, but ten to twenty years older. Some were very attractive, but I took my cues from the old timers: *These hillbillies will kill you for looking too hard at a female.*

Over the years my enforced celibacy became easier. Everyone deals with it differently. Many plaster their cells with pages of naked girls, which always seemed to me like a teenage boy's take on exposure therapy. There's always an ample supply of porn traded and sold on the gray market. Some guys cop midnight hand jobs from a neighbor, or a furtive beej in the shower. Rape happens. A lucky few get married to their high school sweetheart, or find someone on a prison dating site. Me, I read a lot, and made oil pastel drawings. By my late twenties my libido settled out, and I no longer pined for women.

Rather than sex, I learned that it's the lack of a soft female presence that does the biggest number on most men doing time. Left to our own devices in a brutish echo chamber, we cycle negative, angry, and demented. A good woman (and, if you're gay, a good man, preferably not in prison) could snap us out of much wrongheadedness—such was the case with me, once Lily entered my life.

I have to imagine that women working in prison—as security or civilian staff—often feel awkward and uncomfortable from the sexually charged atmosphere. Ogled and drooled over like a juicy porterhouse under the nose of a starving man, they are ever conscious of not appearing too friendly to inmates in the eyes of their coworkers, and not sending us the wrong message. Maximum-security prison, more than county jail, has its rapists, murderers, and purveyors of domestic violence. Some real hard cases here, psychopaths, schizophrenics, flashers, touchers, and secretors (and then there are the inmates). To be sure, these men inhabited a county jail at one time—but for every one of them, there were a dozen drug possessors, three drunk drivers, a couple of bar fighters, and a car thief. As a group, we're a lot less threatening, I suppose, in county jail.

Still, affairs happen between prisoners and staff—those Lifetime movie plotlines don't invent themselves. I'm aware of two such cases. L, a guy I knew in Prison E's reception, had worked for the librarian, a nice woman who kept me supplied with the classics. Years later, I caught up with him in Prison A. He and the librarian were married—she got fired, and he got flicked to the opposite end of the state. Case closed in the eyes of the Department of Corrections, that great separator of those in love.

A woman from the Department of Health, who spent a couple days a week educating inmates about HIV, had fallen for V, who worked as her assistant. With enough unsupervised time after class, she became pregnant. She quit, someone put the pieces together, and V left that prison via the Box. When I met up with V earlier this year, he and the woman were married, and their daughter was two.

It's stories like these that give guys hope and lead to the much more common ending, the unhappy one. There's the one about the guy who becomes too close to a female staff member—in reality or just in the eyes of staff—and gets removed from a work assignment; if he persists, maybe he gets set up and shipped out of the prison via the Box.

I know of men who have been sent to the Box for an innocuous response to a kind woman's words. Each year, a couple of commissary workers get jammed because a guard thinks they're too friendly with the female commissary employees. Their cells are searched, something is "found," and at the very least, they lose their jobs. At worst, they find themselves in the Box.

In Prison A, commissary is such a well-known trapoff waiting to happen, one can't help but wonder why anyone would want to work there. The deluded possibility of sex behind a pallet of chocolate chip cookies? Perhaps. But, what I've heard from those who work there, in not so many words, is an appreciation of female tenderness as inoculation against an environment that can be cold, boorish, and uncaring on its best day.

Of course, we are not without culpability in these wildly disproportionate retaliations by staff. Eddie recognized a new-jack guard from her days as a stripper, called "Princess." When she walked by his cell, he teased, "There's my Princess." His gate didn't open for breakfast. With most of Eddie's neighbors at chow (i.e., few witnesses), the goon squad paid him a visit, extracted Eddie from the cell, and kicked his fucking teeth in.

Prompted by this, I remembered a scene from county, not eight years earlier than the unfortunate business with Eddie, during which I was on Z-tier, water fighting with two neighbors to find relief from the summer heat. I didn't notice Carrie walking past, making a round, and one errant toss of water soaked half her uniform. Trying not to stare at her nipples—made perky by the cold water—I babbled how sorry I was, that it was an accident. She said not to worry.

If that scene played out here, my faulty aim would earn me a lengthy misbehavior report, and maybe a row of stitches.

Yes, there is certainly a wide gulf in my relationships with female staff between county jail and now. Gone are the nightly talkfests, and McGarnagle's two A.M. back scratches. The difference is so stark, in fact, that it's difficult to believe I once received such treatment.

But, I also don't need the reassurance and attention that I did as a twenty-three-year-old. I've matured, and learned to rely more on myself for a sense of stability. The newspapers let me slip from their pages after I was sentenced, and now, when I want to humanize the murderer, I do so on pages like these.

When I encounter female staff, I look them in the eye, but not too intensely. I am courteous, but brief. In a maximum-security prison, women are an attractive nuisance, even if they are neither attractive nor a nuisance.

Returning PA equipment after a volunteer-recognition dinner years ago, I wound up alone in a darkened chapel with a cute blonde guard. The old instincts stirred: flirt, crack a joke, try to impress her, who knows where it'll lead.

Just as quickly, the will to self-preserve kicked in. I stowed the gear and scrammed posthaste. *Safety first,* I reasoned. *You can always rub one out in the shower later.*

Truth be told, the older, wiser me doesn't even need *that* like I used to.

Gerry Adams wrote that ". . . memories keep us together."[1] He was writing from Long Kesh prison, about a female IRA fighter shot by the Brits. Memories of women hold incarcerated men together (when those memories aren't tearing us apart), and memory itself—the Panavision picture—is what keeps all my broken bits in one wee satchel.

---

1. Gerry Adams, *Cage Eleven*, Sheridan Square, 1993.

SEVEN

UNCHAINED LETTERS

There's a part of all misfit toys that yearns to go back to a time before we became broken, to the days of unconditional love and attention, when our mothers swaddled us in loving arms, cooed, and rubbed our backs. Who can get enough of that?

And on an even deeper level of the subconscious, we pine for the nine months in the womb, the fortress of warm solitude to which—*Truly Tasteless Jokes* aside—we'll never be able to return. For proof one needs only look at how tranquilizing a balmy bath is. Or, a hammock (a good one from Mexico, made of thousands of tiny soft strings)—how it envelops you as you fall into a warm siesta.

Existence is a most lonely venture, no way around it. We're born alone, we die alone. What happens for an entr'acte can be shared with others, but it can never really be experienced by them. We fight that loneliness with religion, sex, drugs, all of the above: an attempt to be part of the collective and lessen the pain of meaninglessness.

We try to connect so as to delude ourselves into believing we're not alone; to stave off the loneliness for a time; to look for answers in others. Maybe it's just good to know that others experience loneliness, too. Maybe these brief connections are the best we have.

We're given an allotment of connections (family and their friends) when we arrive, we're born into these connections, and they increase and decrease as life progresses. Like a Venn diagram, a connection is the shaded area of overlap between two or more spheres of influence. If you want more than your allotted connections, get off your duff and go connect, or be willing to let others connect to you (while doing a better job than I did at avoiding the ever-present Rays and Chuis of the world).

Granted, these connections are artificial: palliatives for womb nostalgia. We live our lives substituting. Cremora for cream. Plastic for paper. Fake for real. Time on the psychiatrist's couch in lieu of actually paying attention to our lives and relationships. The fake, the fugazi, the ersatz. What are porno and phone sex and hookers if not ersatz honey? And what is ersatz honey if not some sweetener drizzled onto an otherwise battle-strewn life?

And what, oh what, is more ersatz than writing?

It was early spring in the early nineties when I got my first pen pal. I was fourteen and the Iraq War Part One had recently begun. My social studies teacher had somehow gotten the names of US servicemen serving in theater, assigned each of us a name, and gave instructions to write. Who knows what I wrote to my soldier. Probably rapid-fire questions: Where you from? What kind of weapon do you use? What's it like over there? Is the desert horrible?

We used the school's address as a return, like it was somehow improper or unsafe to use our own. And for some reason my class was brought en masse to the library, where we were individually given the responses to our letters.

The details are hazy. My class standing on light brown industrial carpeting, near the librarian's desk; the air smelling cleaner, newer than the rest of the school; a fuzzy quiet. I was handed an envelope. White, standard business issue, sloppy handwriting. I was already mildly disappointed, having expected some form of military communiqué: a rugged khaki communication pouch with the letters stenciled on, sullied by desert sand and cargo-plane grease.

Again, the contents are hazy. Army soldier, a private, bored shitless in the desert, from some anonymous burg in America's Heartland. What was remarkable about my soldier's letter was the inclusion of a hastily ripped page from *Penthouse*. I showed it to a few of my male classmates. It caused some commotion and I quickly hid the page back in the envelope, fearing I'd somehow be in trouble for possessing a *Penthouse* page in the holy confines of my high school library.

That this soldier would send a picture of this girl was slightly disturbing. I was no prude, mind you, and had been "using" such images for years. Actually, the page was mild compared with the trove of porn I had secreted away in my bedroom. Hell, I'd lost my virginity by that point. So it wasn't the content that was distressing, it was the context—that this soldier would send me, a high school freshman, the nude pinup. Was he trying to disturb me? Probably not. Most likely, he thought he was doing me a favor—sexually frustrated soldier in the desert, worlds away from American trim, indoctrinated in army-boredom-masturbation-culture, remembering how he was at my age. Regardless, it shattered my hero image. I was expecting to hear from Duke of "G.I. Joe" fame: talk of munitions and fighting bad guys and bravery, not some lonely masturbator whose idea of largesse was parting with Ms. March.

I was that particular type of precocious kid whose precocity was displayed through actions, but whose mind was at grade level. I fucked and drank and drugged because it made me feel older. Appear older. I was, and continue to be, a sheep in wolf's clothing. I was, and continue to be, Holden Caulfield: a self-proclaimed cynic, world-weary fellow traveler, when, in fact, I'm a wounded romantic, a kid who's constantly yearning for meaningful relationships.

I never wrote back to my soldier. Some eighteen years later, when America was winding down Iraq War Part Two, I wondered if my pen pal made it out alive, what he was doing with his life, whether he went back to combat.

Another freshman year, college this time: the midnineties. Blowing five milligram lines of pulverized Ritalin. Strictly as a study aid, I can assure you. Yellow means five milligrams, blue means ten—color-coding for the self-medicating set. Knowing my penchant for losing the plot, doing everything *except* schoolwork, I'd snoot the medicinal lines at my desk, ready to plunge into a meaty text and boring assignment. Quite often, I'd tear through the task like some pharmacological superman, only to realize that it was midnight, my hands were shaking, I had an open bottle of Jolt, and sleep wasn't in the offing.

My room was dark dark, a solitary halogen lighting the desktop, slightly spilling onto my legs. My roommate, Jamal, sleeping in his bed, dreaming of wholesome things. Me on his Mac taking advantage of the Ethernet connection in the room. I would telnet to far-off schools, hubs listed alphabetically on my school's UNIX system. These were the days before the Internet really blossomed. A jittery, conversation-starved wreck, I'd prowl the ether meeting strangers and typing silently like a thief in the night.

I was Fred "Flounder" Dorfman from *Animal House*, meeting strangers, and innocently, boyishly, saying, *So, where do you go to school?* But these weren't dark scary men in a roadside bar listening to Otis, they didn't respond by staring at me like I was about to be beaten into a bloody, collegiate pulp.

These were single-serving pen pals. Conversations scrolling line by line. One to the other. No pressure, no hang-ups. I'd begin by typing something totally banal.

>u of oregon, hows that workin 4 u?
>>cold now. u?
>(New England school). suckz!!!!!!!!!!!!!!!!!!!!!!!!!!!!!!
>>what do u study?
>dunno. started premed, couldnt hack it. psych. then
     philos. fuck knows. u?
>>environmental studies
>cool. so u smoke
>>just did
>nice. im tweekin off 5ml rit & jolt. good pot by u?
>>the best
>feel like sending me some . . .

There's only so much of that one can tolerate. But the experience itself was flight-school cool. I'd imagine a kid like me, sitting in a dark dorm room, whiling away the hours making random contacts enabled by computer terminals. Close your eyes, empathize, drip into the teletype network, come out the other side.

Several years ago, after ignoring a certain pen pal ad countless times, I decided, *Why not.* Nowadays pen pals seem such a relic of the past. An anachronistic throwback to when people actually *wrote* letters—with a pen instead of a keyboard. To the best of my knowledge the pen pal market has dwindled to third world children (*Sponsor a child for a dollar a day, and you get a picture of this starving urchin with a bloated belly in sub-Saharan Africa*); soldiers—American students from

K through 12 are undoubtedly writing to our troops, much as my class and I did; and prisoners.

There are pen pal services and websites that cater to the prison market—for a nominal fee the prisoner can submit a bio that will be listed. (We use these sites third party since our cells don't come equipped with Internet connections.) Technically, we're not allowed to do this. As always, we screwed that up, probably by scamming citizens out of money or making threats or hatching any number of other untoward schemes. And that's why we can't have nice things.

Guys have asked me to correct their bios, or, in a few cases, write them completely. These guys would then ask why I wasn't interested, usually after telling me of their success in finding a wife. My thinking was that anyone responding to a prison pen pal ad had to be a real zero. But since the person asking me why I didn't participate was himself a participant, like my boy Yas, I didn't want to come off sounding elitist. I'd give a line about being super busy with schoolwork. One of these days, I'd lazily add.

One of those days came four years into my sentence, when, as mentioned above, I said *Why not.* The ad appeared in the monthly newsletter from a religious organization which serves Jews in prison and the military. This isn't a dating service, the ad copy huffs, rather a resource for getting Jews together to discuss Jewish things (my words, not theirs). This was actually just what I was in the market for: someone smart with whom to share deep philosophical, geopolitical, and ethical conversations. I imagined my soon-to-be pen pal as an elderly Jewish college professor, someone I would turn into a surrogate grandfather.

Plus, there was the chance that I'd land some ultracool girl, a cute-smart-funny brunette, who was sick of a superficial bar scene and longed for my special brand of humor and thoughtful conversation. We'd end up getting married. She'd be independently wealthy and I'd joke that she was my sugar mommy. We'd have a child named Sam.

For a bio I used what I sent professors when beginning a new correspondence course (finished my bachelor's through the mail): one and a half pages detailing my early background of privilege; how I misspent my youth; the apathetically debauched mess I made of my college years; my descent into opiated madness; jobs I remarkably held while a junkie; a quick segue to my cushy office job in prison and how I'm paid the princely sum of twenty-five cents an hour.

I copy out the following paragraph as written because it is the most descriptive:

> I've painted many a painting, I'm in the process of writing the (not so) Great American Novel and God willing, someday I'll be able to plant a tree. My favorite: color—baby blue; Muppet—Fozzy Bear; musical genre—electronica; Simpson—C. Montgomery Burns; word (today, at least)—panoply. Before being incarcerated I was on the search for the perfect Spanikopita, French toast (so far, any that's made with Challah), Napoleon, gyro, and inside-out tuna and avocado sushi roll. I'm a diehard *Simpsons* fan (I'm talking *true believer*), I have a wicked Peter Pan Complex and I live for good marketing—all the better if it's embedded, tied-in, or in the form of a cross promotion.

I summed up by stating my academic career was second-rate at best, assuring that I've finally grown up, and possess the zeal of the converted. I erased the very last line ("I bring a very positive attitude toward this class and look forward to liaising with you") and replaced it with my Jewish bona fides: Reform Jew who's interested in his Jewishness and certain aspects of spirituality.

Since I was a marketing major (and quite self-involved), I titled the bio: Danner Darcleight: The Autobiographical Infomercial & Shameless Self-Promotion.

This quasi manifesto is what my grandma sent in for me. And then I waited for a response, eventually forgetting about it. My grandma would occasionally inquire whether I'd heard anything and I'd have to tell her I hadn't, feeling every bit the failure.

What did I expect? This website's traffic was probably observant Jews, they didn't want to correspond with some lunatic who had a heroin habit in his past and a pathetically lax attitude toward Judaism.

At mail call, I went through all the superstitious moves: Imagining that I'm not getting a letter; imagining that I *am* getting a letter; silencing the mind, going in with no hopes one way or the other. We inmates swarm around the guard sitting in his cage. Like birds, we hope he'll throw something white our way. More often than not, after giving the guard my cell location, he'd give a quick shuffle to the pile of letters, and mumble *Nah*. I'd enthusiastically offer some mindless rejoinder: "There's always next time" or "Sa-wing and a miss." It went like this for some time until I gave up, stopped expecting a letter.

Two years after placing the ad, I got a response. Mark H. from Arizona, a forty-something cube drone from some faceless state bureaucracy, and a recent convert to Judaism. A crack and crystal meth habit in his past. "Past" as in: he hadn't used recently. "Recently" as in: he didn't see his dealer for a nickel bag on the way to work that morning.

In my first response I asked why he converted: *What, you didn't have enough persecution in your life?*

We began to trade strategies for staying clean from hard drugs, he by sending me printouts from the Rational Recovery website, me by quoting from *Tuesdays with Morrie*, *Man's Search for Meaning*, paraphrasing what I've learned of Buddhism (the parts applicable to those with drug addictions in their past, or those wanting a drug addiction to be in their past).

I loved that he was of the Rational Recovery School. Irrationally, I equate Twelve Steppers with fixed mindedness, stringent rules, Holy Rollers, holier-than-thou-Focus-On-The-Family-shitbirds, Republicans, and Conservatives. Rational Recoverers believe that the drug isn't the problem, something in *you* is the problem; drugs are the smoke that indicates a smoldering fire in the cortex. They also, and this is a big one, don't preach abstinence. Mark H. slipped from time to time, *And that's OK*, but he always came back to the fold.

He sent me a picture of himself. Nondescript, middle-aged, Caucasian. He could've been a grade-school teacher, a postal worker, or a serial killer. Reading *A Clockwork Orange* at the time, I lied that his picture was "proper horrorshow," very cool. Despite explaining why I commented thusly, he "didn't get it." I explained it again and told him to "relax."

Contact with the *world* is scant, so I'm entertained by things that would've bored the living shit out of me in my former life. Like written conversations with Mark H. From the beginning our letters were nothing special. More precisely, the initial excitement of receiving an envelope from someone new quickly faded into the realization that my new pen pal was a drip. The fact that I—an inveterate pack rat, sentimentalizer, saver of letters and mementos—didn't save his letters speaks volumes.

While I can be insightful at times, especially when introspecting, I have moments of complete obtuseness when it comes to pen pals. Some would chalk that up to a lack of empathy, but I'll argue otherwise. It's hard enough reading between the lines when you know someone, near impossible when it's a stranger through the mail. So much of a relationship is built around face time, phone calls that aren't rushed or monitored, observing how one operates amidst other humans and in the open world.

Mark's "roommate," the lack of any talk of a love life—in retrospect, it makes perfect sense. After sending Mark a copy of a rhyming letter I sent to one of my friends in another joint, he wrote, regarding one line about the inordinate amount of jerking off we do in here: "There's a lot of homoeroticism in your writing." An odd reading, I thought, but nothing crazy. Maybe there *was* homoeroticism in my writing. I began to keep an eye out for it.

Then he wrote that a gay friend of his thought I was "cute." I responded that I was flattered. He wrote back and asked if I were gay, that his "gay friend" wanted to know. "No," I replied, "but hold no prejudices toward the lifestyle."

I haven't heard back from Mark H. I've suffered worse losses.

Tempering the blow was the appearance of a new pen pal that coincided with Mark's departure. At mail call one night I was handed a smallish envelope addressed with fuchsia, girl's handwriting. My pulse thumped in the ears, my boxers got warm. Letters are a substitute for sex. Sex is a substitute for love. Briskly walking back to my cell, I pretended not to be overly excited at "meeting" a new girl—a smart, funny, attractive girl, no doubt.

Fuchsia pen in the letter as well. "Hey there whats going on with you?" Normal enough. Her name was Natalie B., thirty-five years old, from the state of Washington, Jewish, "and did some time too." Of course. "I'm a recovering heroin addict." Here we go. "I went to prison twice for heroin." Naturally. "I don't have any recent pics. I'm 5'7, have shoulder length bleached out dreadlocks. I weigh 180 but its all proportioned thank Gd." She also mentioned that she had green eyes and didn't need to wear makeup.

She spoke the language of the incarcerated. "You're programming, probably got some tight bros and money for canteen." This was amazingly empathetic on her part, down to the (pink) letter. She continued. "In womens prison chicks hookup a lot. That makes time go by fast. Infractions galore but it was all worth it. 'Nuff said." She ended with, "Have a nice day, Natalie," which I thought was a nice way to end a first letter.

My response contained questions about the DIY dildoes made in women's prison, and whether, as some news magazine purported, the sex is only as a complement to the mother-daughter role-playing. I sent a drawing or two, complimented her choice of pens. I was on my best behavior, without bringing my A-game—neat penmanship and proper salesmanship—because, let's face it, there was no need to impress, the sale had been made when she chose to write.

Letters are my emissaries out into the world. A note of gratitude, regret, or hopefulness—sometimes in the same letter. A putting forward of my best foot. Licking an envelope sealed, and hoping. Hoping that the mail will be delivered and the message well received. When time begins to accumulate, I begin to second guess. Was I too forward? Rude? Not interesting enough?

Natalie's second letter was sloppier, the ink green, then black. "Cool!" she writes in the first line, "You wrote back." And that was the last mundane thing she offered. Halfway down the first page there's a break, "3 DAYS LATER—" taking up three lines. The writing is messier, now only black ink, "I was all fucked up on Klonopins and did some outrageous shit." Ah, so begins the madness.

"I started using heroin because it was a great self medicator." This was past use, her drug-self creation myth. The words began to dip below the lines, page two. "Anyhoo you want to hear about sex in a womens prison. I knew this girl who was 22 and she was all on my jock etc. I honestly made an effort to not turn her out. We would fuck everywhere. Bathroom stall, shower, my bed, her bed etc. She had never been with a woman but I've had 2 girlfriends. I schooled her and had to put her in check more than once. One time I bit her on her ass with my finger fucking her. The next day she got strip searched (random) and all the guard said was 'Oh you girls.' Everyone liked us, the guards too which comes in handy. I would make dildoes all the time. You take a pencil, wrap it up in maxi-pads into a phallic shape, re-enforce it w/ rubber gloves, wrap it up with whatever you can find. I made these excellent silver ones w/ tinfoil and wrapped it up with a zip-lock from the kitchen. You had to alter the plastic bag so it would look cool. As for Angela and I there wasn't really any gender roles—we were two cute girls together. I don't have a boyfriend as we speak. How many people write you? Do you have a girlfriend on the outs? If you send a pic I PROMISE to send it back along with a pic of myself. Not to worry. I hope to hear from you soon. I like smart people to banter back and forth. Love, Natalie. P.S. I'm sending the most recent pic. I look like shit."

She did. The picture was taken from at least thirty feet away, with Natalie standing on top of a pile of gravel in the parking lot of what looked like a Ramada Inn. But I was working on my shallow nature and tried to not let it affect my correspondence.

We substitute because we lack something. The ingenuity with which she made dildoes was impressive: this is the mothering of inventions. Having exhausted the dildo line of questioning, I closed the matter with a few remarks about how she seems to have made quite a hustle for herself *inside*, what with the dildo-makery and all. I moved on to her thoughts on suicide. Whenever I meet someone who gives the slightest indication of being a suicidal fantasizer, I probe. I try to learn about others in an attempt to know myself, *to heal thyself.*

It seemed to me that the differences between Natalie and me were more a matter of degree than kind. She's slightly more manic, slightly more depressive, slightly more prone to acting out suicidal tendencies. But this is a result of brain chemistry—Natalie's chemicals are slightly more out of whack than mine.

It also dawned on me that in Natalie, I'd plumbed a character depth I'd been searching for in all her predecessors. In realizing this, I learned that one's "depths" are rarely an idyllic ocean trench, but more like the bottom of an abandoned well. While strolling through a forest clearing, we encounter this well, peak over the edge, drop a pebble, and wait for the faint but inevitable splash. Sometimes our flashlight of inquiry is powerful enough and we catch a brief glimpse of a dark, secretive pool. And then there are wells like Natalie whose depths are immeasurable, but by some paradox of nature reveal their secrets to those who are capable of looking. The bottom is partially rocky, there are broken beer bottles, a rat nibbling the wings off a dead bird, and a bad smell. Get past that and there's cool, sparkling water to quench the thirst of any who dare venture (or, so I'd like to think).

Do people like Natalie look to me—the quintessential fuckup—to help stop the downward spiraling in their own lives? In her third, and sloppiest letter Natalie wrote that she's "been to every psych ward in P— County. The first time cut my arm not the wrist. I was going for the big vein. I would have died but my friend. Bill was gonna buy some acid from me. I cut up my foram. It took 54 stitches. I was really fucked up emotionally and physically cuz my boyfriend (whos my EX HUBBY). He played a show and wondering where the hell I was. Unfortunately I was having anal sex with my violent crazy Aryan Brotherhood friend who just got out of the pen. He wanted to kick my boyfriends ass for walking in on us. Nice. Jason was pissed off on Valentines day and I got pregnant around the same time I fucked (illegible name of her Aryan buttfucker). Jason said 'How do I know that I'm the father?' I said 'Jason, we were having Anal Sex.' That is a situation boy let me tell ya."

She goes on to again describe herself to me, using much the same language as in her first letter, this time including "38 DDD bra size and some tats!" Then how she's a quasilicensed hair stylist, yada yada yada.

There was no rhyme or reason to the progression of her letters, just a stream-of-consciousness from a brain drenched in antianxiety medications and who knows what else. She would sometimes lose the plot when transitioning from one page to the next, and begin a completely new narrative midstream. Rarely was a paragraph to be found, instead the content flowed. And flowed. Like I was sitting next to her on the dirty floor of a bus station and we were sharing a stolen pack of cigarettes and a brown bag of Wild Irish Rose.

I wasn't going to learn anything from Natalie except how not to be. But she was an interesting diversion, her letters like a TV show that progressed in serial format. I stayed tuned for the next letter, so I could discover what new world of shit our superhero had found herself in. There were times when I'd cringe during the reading, empathizing despite the detachment.

In the end, however, pen pals inhabit a netherworld somewhere between television artificiality, and friends and family reality. I was never going to meet Natalie, never going to be able to add depth to her character unless she did so for me. Natalie existed in the world, this I understood as fact. True, at times I thought about her, regaled Whit and Yas with secondhand debauchery, but, at some metaphysical level, Natalie only existed when I read her letters. In this way, Natalie was like television: unless one is consuming it, it doesn't exist. And, perhaps more to the point, Natalie the pen pal was a most subjective reality: reading between the lines, extrapolating from letters to form a full person, my mental construct of her likely bore little resemblance to the real-life Natalie.

By the fourth page, Natalie was looped. Her handwriting had taken a marked turn for the worse, scratched-out words dotted the page in much the same way that spots probably appeared in her field of vision as she wrote. "Anyhow when I was 16 I traded some pot for som Xanax. I'm loving those benzos. I get a Klonopin scrip every month. I don't remember Thanksgiving but apparently I traded some of my turkey for a fucking tie dye shirt. The lady lived across the hall. She drank and smoked meth all day. She would hang out at the 'ACME GRUB CAGE' It was right on the ave so I would stop and stay for a few minutes. I usually had an 8-ball habit and I would get it by 4PM I don't work there at night."

That I can get a very vivid picture of these scenes says something about me—and not just that I'm good at visualizing. I've traded drugs for other drugs, I've forgotten holidays. I've had habits, habits with a capital H.

On page five she tells me that she has two sons, but hasn't seen them in seven and a half years, that the father won't let her near the kids. The court granted him custody because she was "an admitted recovering." The loss (of the ex or the kids, or both, it's not exactly clear) hurt Natalie. "I started shooting dope when he left. I was bi-polar schizo-effective with some PTSD thrown in. Then when the kids left I had to be hospitalized for 3 weeks. I was a great mom too."

Natalie's heart is sometimes bigger than her brain, not unlike mine. She wanted to do right, but was too constantly smashed to see the clear picture. If there were some device that allowed people like Natalie and me to see ourselves through the eyes of others, neither of us would use hard drugs, ergo neither would be in prison, ergo we'd never have come into contact.

Page six begins with a message composed—probably after the letter was written, in the going-back-over phase—in the blank area on top of the page: "SORRY THIS IS SO SLOPPY I'M HAVING TROUBLE REMEMBERING THINGS."

In continuation of the pain of the previous page, "It's an ache that never goes away and Heroin makes everything OK." That reads like a sonnet or a verse in some alt-rock song. I prefer to imagine that Natalie composed it herself, cigarette in hand, during a serious dope nod. An acoustic guitar plays in the background while blue smoke twists toward the ceiling.

Page seven. Heroin, jail, ex-husband, aunt, psych ward. The ink becomes shaky purple and even messier toward the end. "I went to get my methadone 4 guys in white were coming for me. The psych ward hospital is next door. I better git this off. Be good. Natalie."

She signed her name a few lines up from the bottom of the page. What followed was the best, most bizarre postscript in the history of letters.

"P.S. I am now reading *Juliette* by the Marquis de Sade. He wrote it in prison for sodomize young boys. I like Voltaire also. I took 5 years of french. Now I'm all remedial now. I read nonfiction, watch A&E, Court TV, PBS, and Discovery Channel. Ever since my kidney failed blah blah (her "blah blah," not mine) I was going thru this trail deal (court-imposed nature hike?). I stayed the nite there. So I wake up, do a fuckin wake up (the bag of dope junkies need to begin their day) and the trails are at the top, and it's a free fall straight down. Well I was there for 20 hours. 70 ft. So they take me in an ambulance and there was a guard there. He ran my name I had a warrant for K— County and one in T—. I told him I just got off probation and happened to have his name and phone (her probation officer's?). I had a fuckin answer about what he wanted to know. Anyhow as soon as I got to hospital I went into a coma. I came out of it 3 days. They called my mom I was dying . . ."

And?! Natalie, you minx, how dare you leave me without closure on that anecdote. Sure, there was no more room on the page, but what's an additional piece of paper amongst friends, amongst *pen pals*?

My response letter went unanswered. What did I do? I must have written something over the line. Asked some question, made some comment that hit a little too close to home. This is me: The Ruiner. I began to fear that she had died— overdose or suicide, six of one, etc.—or was returned to prison. It turned out to be the latter. This I found out some five months later when I received a letter that was *kited, boomeranged*, through many sets of hands before it reached my cell. Natalie got picked up on a drug possession beef, received county time (something under a year), wrote a letter to me, and gave it to her rabbi since prisoners aren't allowed to write to other prisoners. The rabbi gave it to her mom, the mom couldn't find my address and gave it back to the rabbi, the rabbi brought it back to Natalie, Natalie directed the rabbi to pull my address off the pen pal website.

The first line of the last page, easily seen by Natalie's mother and rabbi, read as follows: "I LOVE WATCHING guys jerk off too." I was embarrassed—for her and for me—that the proxies had seen that. Funnier still, my good friend Whit, a one-time biker straight out of central casting, happened upon the letter while sitting on my bed. At times, he very much embodied King Louie, the crazy orangutan from *The Jungle Book*. He read that first line of the last page and laughed, "What have you been telling this girl?" The joke being that "I LOVE WATCHING guys jerk off too" was in response to my confessing that I loved watching my neighbors jerk off.

I wrote back through her mom. Since Natalie would be getting out of jail in a month or so, I wished her a safe return, and told her to write again when she got out.

And so ended my correspondence with Natalie. I figure she got out and got back into a bad scene, had grown tired of substituting sobriety for inebriety, and went back to the real thing. Maybe I'll hear from her again. Maybe not. Maybe I'll drop her a line at one of the addresses she's been known to flop. Maybe not.

Some would look at my less-than-impressive luck with finding and keeping a pen pal and say, Give up, loser. Not me. I maintain my cockeyed optimism when I walk up to the guard at mail call and give him my cell number. I remain open to the idea of the universe sending me someone through the mail. It's not about loneliness per se, but about the desire to connect with someone of substance.

Why not continue with hope—every prisoner's drug of choice? Maybe tomorrow I won't go up to the guard at mail call. I'll sit half lotus on my bed, pretending to be reading. The guard will walk past my cell making his count, double back, and hand me an envelope without speaking. The stationery is college issue, professor Mort Something; he teaches courses in marketing and creative writing. Am I interested in beginning a meaningful and prolonged correspondence? *Am I?!* And his grandson of roughly my age recently died of a heroin overdose. Can I help him to understand the hold that the drug has on some? *Can I?!* I'll read the letter again, slowly, and write comments in the margins. Then, out will come the paper and pen.

Ah, but I shan't be so lucky. I'm reminded of that fact every so often when my grandma asks me if I've "ever heard from" a pen pal from "that organization." A devilish smile curls against the receiver as I think of Natalie's letters. Dildoes, prison shower sex, an Aryan buttfucker, heroin, Klonopin scripts, et-debauched-cetera. All in letters, in ink and paper. "No, Gram. I mean, I had a couple of people write to me in the past, but nothing came of it."

"Oh, that's too bad."

But I'll take the sympathy. I can hear it. It's real.

Invariably, she'll ask, "Have you heard from your brother?" The letters from him don't arrive like they used to, but we speak on the phone about once a week. "He's a sweet guy."

"Yeah," I'll say, "he is."

"Tell me, are you two close?"

"Quite," I say, giving her the abridged version.

EIGHT

THE BROTHERS

I.

The brothers dart around underwater, playing something akin to Gotcha Last. Bubbles effervesce in shafts of light, a skittering trail behind lithe bodies. Their play aimless and trivial, the boys're good swimmers and comfortable in the water. The older one can hold his breath longer, and usually gets his brother last.

Around this pool of sparkling azure, adults sit slathered in sweet-smelling tanning oils, drinking frosty drinks delivered by crisply dressed Mexicans. The boys' parents take the sun and read. A couple of older women—tanned hams in black one-pieces with skirts—laze with boozy insouciance under the quiet shade of a thatched awning. They watch as the brothers get out of the pool, sleek and streaming like seals, water gliding off their tanned little selves.

—They're good boys, one says to the other.

—Yes, acknowledges the other, well behaved, and so handsome.

Walking past, the boys look at their sopping feet, the foot-prints on the stone walkway already beginning to dry. Good looking, smart boys are always noticed, the world an endless set of approving eyes. The older boy is around ten, his brother roughly seven. They stand at the base of a coconut tree, peering at the fruit overhead. The warm breeze gives the palm fronds a tickle and the midday sun pokes through like camera flashes. The boys squint and shield their eyes.

—Look at 'em, Older says to Younger.

—Think we can get one? says Younger.

—Mm, hmm.

—Boys! calls their mother from across the chlorinated pool. The brothers turn their heads.

—Yeah, Ma?

—We're going to have lunch, would you care to join us? The brothers would.

The *hamburguesas* taste and feel different from home, ditto the lettuce and toasted bun, but they devour everything. The brothers drink virgin coladas that their father orders for them *en Español.*

—This is coconut milk, right Ma? says Younger.

She moves a curled strand of dark blondish hair from her brow:—And pineapple juice, sugar, and crushed ice.

As though they have but one hungry mind, the brothers glance at one another. The best ideas are the simplest.

The brothers awake with the earliest of the early birds. They make a good pair. Back home, there is fighting, sure, but no more than normal from brothers three years apart; vying for their parents' affection, subtle like the sweaty pheromones in the air between them. But this morning the brothers get dressed silently—their parents are sleeping in the adjoining villa—and stealthily walk into the cool morning air.

Lush vegetation struggles to reach its green hands onto the walkway. The Yucatán sky comes in patches through the palms. The closest city is an ancient Mayan ruins, pyramids that reach to the heavens. There are still a few remaining stars, white freckles on a leering celestial face.

Older is a tender youth, he needs Younger as a teammate against the harsh eyes of the world. What their parents see as a fine display of sharing is often Older building a coalition one gift at a time. These gifts have taken the form of sharing access to certain toys, showing where their father hides his porn, inviting Younger to use the hiding spot in the silver tree. Older has learned to spend for his brother's affection. The coin of the realm: attention, trust, and indulgence.

Security is here within their quiet bond. They maraud toward the pool. The brothers freeze. A night watchman walks with a low whistle. The brothers jump behind the trunk of a palm tree. A bird screeches and punches through nearby flora—the brothers' hearts lub-a-dub. Bugs make eerie noises. The brothers stand still, sunburnt arms touching, getting cold in the early morning air, listening to the other's breathing; four unblinking eyes, two open mouths. When the coast clears, they continue for the pool.

The coconuts are as they were at noon, hanging like green grapes, rippling from the pool lights. The older brother ducks behind the cabana and returns carrying a long metal pole upon which is plugged a pool-broom. The brothers have a pool at home and know how to handle such gear. They fumble, utter a muffled *shit*. Older uses his shirt to loosen the white coupling, then extends the pole to its full height. Together, they begin jabbing at the coconuts. The pole bends like rubber. The brothers begin to sweat and issue more curses sotto voce at the tall, dumb tree.

—C'mon, implores Older. On this mission they are one—a bond deeper than love and surer than genetics. The shared task and common goal sealing their confederacy.

Younger fixes his jaw and jerks the broom head right into whatever it is that's holding the coconuts so firmly in place. With a satisfying *THWICK*, a coconut breaks from its mooring, like a baby tooth from its red string. The brothers jump out of the way and become still to make sure no grown-ups have heard the crash. Only then do they pick up the large, green coconut and—grinning with triumph—brush off the moist dirt from the fall.

Older quickly returns the pool broom. (These are good boys who leave things as they found them.) Younger cradles the coconut. They smile and nod toward the villa.

Safely inside, they flip on the lights and make for the bathroom, which they figure will be the quietest bet. For the task of opening the coconut—their father did it at home with a hammer and awl—the brothers assemble: three butter knives, two wooden clothes hangers, a corkscrew, a metal shoehorn, and a rock that the older brother had taken as a souvenir on the road to Chichén Itzá (—Look, Ma, it sparkles!). They array the tools on the tan tile floor beside the bathtub. The right tools for the job, as their father would say.

Older wraps the coconut in a plush white hotel towel and twists it tight. The dawn is quiet like alone time. *WHOMP!* he smashes it down on the tiles. The brothers look at each other with eyes wide, then grimace. They stand motionless.

—Think Mom and Dad heard? says Younger.

—I dunno, says Older, jus' wait a second.

There is the hum of air conditioners. Crickets rub their legs.

For more than half an hour they take turns whomping it to the floor, then holding still to make sure no one has heard. Now they poke with the sparkly rock and jab with the corkscrew. When it finally begins to give, they pry with the hanger, shoehorn, and butter knives. They are careful not to cut themselves or each other. The birds outside awake in earnest, calling greetings, and stretching their wings like the brothers do when they wake up. A pair of Spanish voices passes the bathroom's frosted window—the brothers stop and hold their breaths.

The butter knife—the third and final butter knife, the first two having bent—finally punctures the milk womb. A cloudy sweet-smelling trickle of coconut milk splatters the tiles. The brothers smile at each other and exhale. Older wonders what Younger's inner monologue sounds like at this moment, it is probably distinct and very special. He knows Younger looks up to him, that when Younger destroys one of Older's toys, it's because he's hungry for attention. Older has met many of his friends' younger brothers, and none compare. Younger is a swell chap, a good, smart, comfortable presence—though neither boy is big on confiding such sentiments.

—Go get a glass, says Older.

The fruit of their labor doesn't fill up the glass, but the brothers are happy. They have learned the liberties of boys from good homes who stop pleasing adults and embrace the guilty pleasure of acting on their own. Like others on vacation, they break free from the shackles of the quotidian, and nurture their alter egos. In their boyish antics, the brothers become identical twins, communicating by thought. As the sun peeks through the heavy wooden slats, the brothers, damp with sweat, take turns sipping from the glass.

—Good, says Younger.

—Yeah, agrees Older, who momentarily rests an arm on his brother's shoulder.

This is what it is to be completely at ease, to be part of a conversation no one else in the world is a part of. Owing to a slightly anxious cast of mind, Older is forever looking ahead to the end of the good times. To when he'll have to leave the nest and make a success of himself. Their father isn't close with *his* brother. They don't work together, certainly don't play together. Will he and Younger follow the same path? Will they live close but not spend time together? Is their bond to be reduced to a few awkward hours over the holidays? Older fears being alone.

The brothers are tired at breakfast, so notes their father. They explain their coconut adventure, strategically changing details to make the account more parent-friendly. The timeline shifts several hours later to encompass the safe light of morning, there's no mention of butter knives.

Instead of sharing in their triumph, the boys' mother says— But, why? In the face of filial *mishegoss* she reaches for a plate heavy with neatly sliced, multicolored fruit.

II.

The brothers are enjoying their summer together. Older is home from college, in limbo between junior and senior years. He's adrift amidst a sea of classmates who can't wait to graduate and begin their nine-to-five lives. The strain of living up to the world's expectations for him has become too great. He feels himself a fraud. He is not as good, as smart, as virtuous as they think. Not anymore.

Younger is spending his last summer at home. The brothers are popular and their home fills with lubricated party kids when the sun goes down. During these drug-fueled bacchanals, the brothers become less emotionally constipated toward each other. Though there is no verbal exposition, they allow their actions—a loving smile, an approving touch—to speak louder than in the sober light of day. They sigh with satisfaction—that's their conversation.

Older is in the darkened kitchen, eyes on the oven. On Pyrex plates lay clear puddles of liquid Ketamine cooking at three-twenty-five. He has used different flavorings on each of the puddles, hoping to make the gag-inducing postnasal drip less vicious. Brown bottles of McCormack from the pantry: strawberry, lemon, coconut. He flips the oven light off and polices up the scattered pharmaceutical packaging from the kitchen counters.

A couple of weekends ago, during much the same activity, the boys' mother had come down to the kitchen for a late-night glass of iced whatever. A close call. Pot is one thing, alphabetized club drugs another.

Now, noirishly, the older brother's girlfriend sits at the table, lolling her Mentos, transfixed with something from her purse. Older stares at the plates of Special K as the edges begin to crystallize white. When all three plates are cooked properly dry, he dons oven mitts and gingerly removes them.

—Need help? says the girl.

—Just hold this, says the older brother, handing over the bag of detritus. To have the succoring warmth of someone who knows your interior self, without the artificial constraints of filling the space with narrative—this she'll never understand. He hears faint giggling and bong-hit coughing wafting from the basement. Older is eager to get back downstairs to Younger. He wishes he could lock himself in a room of their memories—Older and Younger as children, engaged in imaginative play. The safe space that comes alive when they're alone together.

With a razor, he deftly scrapes the plates, depositing the fine powder into neat squares of tin foil. It is still warm. He sends the girl downstairs, does a final inspection of the kitchen, then quietly makes for the steps.

In the basement, he walks into a giggling, sunburn-freckled cloud of girls and boys—friends of Younger—draped over furniture, on the floor, smoking, smiling, drinking, making out in darkened corners. Electronica plays at a moderate volume, a soundtrack to the night.

Younger looks at the returning Older, —Is good?

Older grins, —Let's find out.

Together, hovering over the shiny surface like their drooling golden retriever over the koi pond, they cut lines on a gilded mirror purloined from a resort earlier in the year. Three downy piles according to flavor, tiny rails cut from each. The mirror gets passed, powder vanishes up tanned beaks and nose-jobbed schnozzes. —Mm, mmm! the kids joke. Each finds his preferred flavor. The heart wants what the heart wants.

The brothers, good hosts that they are, go last. It's the last lines—coconut—that put them over the top. K's a tricky drug to find the dosage on; way too fine a line between loosey-goosey and comatose. Down a dark hole the brothers slide. Each in a comfy chair, their worlds shrink to tiny pinholes of light, then go completely dark. Signals from the extremities become silent. Yet they hear everything. Most of the friends are in K-holes of their own. A girl moans in a corner. *In pharmacological ecstasy or getting fucked?* Older wonders. A bong is knocked to the floor—carpeted, thankfully—and the brothers, despite being turned off from the necks down, know it's a mess they'll have to clean up. Feels like forever, this dark world of the anesthetized mind. Younger hasn't been to these depths often—Older imagines it's a little scary for him. Even in this hole, the brothers manage to comfort each other— Older numbly swivels his chair so their legs are just touching. Before their grandmother died, she often told the boys to be nice to each other, not to bicker. She was an only child.

The dark numb grows stale and both wish for the power of movement. This is why a man should know his measure. Slowly, their limbs begin reporting in. Toes, check. Feet, check. Feeling works its way back up to central processing. The aperture expands out and the dark light of the basement pours in. The brothers look at each other, not steady enough to move.

—Whoa, says Older.

—Uggh, says Younger.

The friends stir to life. Someone reports that they've been tranq'd for only forty minutes.

—Felt like forever, says the brunette with a boner-inducing tank top.

Lighters are flicked, cigs lit, gum unwrapped, eyes dropped. A foggy numb permeates the newbies and frequent fliers alike. A boy and girl dash into the changing room and puke in the trash.

—Welcome to the wonderful world of Ketamine, ladies and germs, Older burbles to the room.

The brothers fix each other in a glance. Nothing need be said, words will only make it worse. Each has seen That Look on the other's face before. *Outside* say their eyes—*to vomit*, gasp their stomachs. They are standing, maneuvering around legs, sneakers, paraphernalia, nightlife accoutrements. They swallow back the sloshing acid yearning to be free. Shepherding Younger, Older slowly slides open the glass door. Feet lope first over the transom, heads follow. He slowly slides the door closed, leaving it ajar. Better to have a few bugs come in, than to have parents hear and be made aware of their presence.

Beyond the brick patio, the pool steams. The surrounding maples form a protective border from the world, their leaves a faint cerulean, lambent from the pool lights, a kinetic electric-blue marble. Older and Younger walk past the pool, Older closer to the edge for Younger's sake. Dodging the yellow patches of dog-shitted lawn, they make their way to the side of the house, the fog of anesthesia still cottony thick. They come to rest on the edge of a steep drop-off, and stand on the railroad-tie retaining wall. Each places a steadying hand in front of him on the smooth, green bamboo. The brothers loop arms around each other's waists, and all is quiet.

Practically in unison, they spray vomit through the bamboo shoots and leaves, plastering the ground below. Between guttural heaving, the brothers regret eating so much steak with their parents that night. Chunks of red, undigested meat flail into their epiglottises like wood chips through their snow blower. A blob of meat catches in Older's mouth, he gags before removing it with a bent finger. —Wheww, the boys pant. Younger isn't done and heaves up another bilious pile. Older rubs Younger's back. Together, they stand. Spent. Breathing. Older notices faint stubble on the side of his younger brother's face and realizes he has begun shaving. Older remembers when he himself first snaked his father's spare Norelco, trying to encourage sideburns like those of the older boys. Somewhere up the block a car alarm chirps. A door shuts, the motor purrs to life, then speeds away.

—Y'awright? says Older.

—Mm, hmm, says Younger.

—Done? says Older.

—Yuch. That's gonna leave a mark, says Younger.

Through the backs of warm T-shirts, the brothers feel each other's lungs working. The boys pant like dogs. On the ground, ten feet below, there is a rustling.

—Dude, did we just puke on a raccoon? says Younger.

—My vision's fucked, says Older. Be pretty funny shit if we did.

—Yeahhh.

Nearby, a bug violently fries to death in the blue, buzzing zapper. A big one, by the sound of it. Stupid bug can't help killing himself.

—She says K makes her horny, Older offhandedly says of his girlfriend. Wanna fuck her?

—Yeah, says Younger, his tone willfully neutral. Sure.

Older slips a vial of K in the cargo pocket of Younger's shorts. There is nothing he won't do for, or give to, Younger. Perhaps that's the problem.

Was introducing Younger to bong hits really the best middle school graduation present? Younger and his boys sure thought so. It was Older who introduced Younger to the drink and drug. When he laid a bump of coke on Younger's hand in a back stairwell at a cousin's bat mitzvah, it was Younger who said—This is fucked up. It was Older who thought: *Better with me than learning from his greenhorn friends.* Older has heart and sometimes heart is enough. But when it's not, Older plays Cool Uncle, the indulger, the intoxicator—hoping to keep the bond alive. Himself an early starter (courtesy of a friend's older brother), Older continuously throws Younger ahead of the learning curve. He's never stopped to ask—himself or Younger—whether this is for the best.

Walking past the pool, they stop for a rest on the chaise longues. Breath flows evenly now, and sweat dries. Gone are the innocent pool parties of youth. They've been taking inebriated dips as of late, leaning against the walls with drink in hand. *Isn't that how Gatsby swam his last?* The brothers fish in pockets and light cigarettes, Marlboro Medium for Older, Light for Younger. The warm smoke tastes like hot vomit, but feels good after the purge. Their silences are never boring or awkward. While unable to articulate this bonhomie, each silently wishes their inner worlds joined at the hip.

—Y'know, says Older, she's inhibitionless.

—Inhibitionless? says Younger.

—In-hi-bi-tion-less.

Someone throws up on a moss-covered corner of patio. Inside, a girl shrieks playfully. The brothers hoist each other up and walk for the door. They are known as guys who *get shit done*. There is a night to breathe life into, an endless summer vibe. There are hours to go before they sleep.

III.

The brothers communicate mostly by phone these days, the mail travels mainly one way. They see each other once or twice a year. The brothers are separated by 150 miles, a forty-foot wall, and a felony-murder conviction. Distance has come to be measured in years.

Younger lives in the city with his wife and golden retriever puppy. They have a nice apartment overlooking a park. He has a high-paying job and a rich social life. There is a baby on the way. Life is good (knock wood).

Older lives in a stony lonesome nestled in the foothills of forgotten countryside. He has a six-by-nine cell overlooking a grassy evacuation yard. He has what passes for a high-paying job in Prison A, making twenty-five cents an hour, his office nowhere near as nice as Younger's. He hasn't swum, played with a dog, or so much as kissed a girl in close to a decade.

Older is different from his peers—more sensitive, quiet. He will never be one of the guys.

It is the late morning on a sunny Friday, the apex of summer. The brothers each beginning a three-day weekend. Younger has just finished his breakfast. Older glugs down his vitamins with a cup of tepid instant coffee. Younger sits on his white leather couch, in his pajamas, cycling through his TiVo menu. He sips an iced cappuccino as the puppy's tail whomps against his legs.

As kids, they reveled in the pleasures of the morning sun and calm, cool air.

Older pulls on khaki shorts and a white polo—both of which Younger bought for him, and are therefore held dear. Slips into his Penguin flips (same patron), walks out of his cell, and stretches his arms to greet the day. He strolls past empty cells, their inhabitants off at work, and makes for the phone booth in the dayroom. Passes the guard sitting in his cage at the front of the company, nursing a cruller, gives him a nod. Only recently has he moved to these relatively posh prison environs. In years past, he'd have to go out to the bustling yard, hoping to get a spot on line for the phone, keeping an eye over his shoulder for danger.

In the stuffy, greasy booth, he dials. Older holds his breath, hoping for Younger to be home; then, hearing his voice, that he'll accept the call. Older finds himself alone, on a limb, not always realizing how much of this burden Younger shares.

—Good morning, says Older, his vestigial tail wagging. Once more that warm, invisible light of brotherhood, bonhomie, and contentment.

—Hey, man, says Younger.

—Is it a good time?

—Eh, I'm going to a ball game in half an hour and I've gotta get dressed. But, we can talk for a few.

And so they do. In this way, the brothers nearly make up for what's lost in physical proximity. They play it safe. Instead of sharing feelings and regrets, the time is spent on matters of entertainment or food. Younger tells Older about what he just made for breakfast: french toast battered with shredded coconut. Older's mouth waters as he prods Younger for details. Younger warns against using a particular type of shredded coconut with a lot of sugar, as it will burn.

Older silently recalls a recent visit during which Younger opined, as in a jocular koan, *One can only have so much coconut.* Older thinks of bringing this up, quoting Younger, but there is no time. There's much left unsaid on these monitored phone calls. Understanding what's important now, and with an acute self-awareness brought by incessant journaling, Older is finally ready to share his inner world with Younger—the fear, the loneliness, the warmth he feels for him. But the time for that is no more, if anything, it makes Younger uncomfortable—perhaps it's too painful for him to read Older's past tense, first-person singular, and so there are compromises made to narrative convention. Older still yearns to visit Younger's inner world, but knows that now it is inaccessible. Instead, Older asks Younger if he remembers their coconut adventure in Chichén Itzá, some twenty years ago.

—Sure, says Younger with a smile felt through the receiver like a dog whistle.

With coconut on the brain, Older asks if Younger remembers the night of coconut-flavored Ketamine, a dozen years ago, puking arm in arm through the bamboo.

—Uh, nooo, says Younger.

The brothers belly chuckle.

(Older doesn't say it's one of his most dearly held memories.)

Younger is focused on the future, on his nascent family, getting his MBA, moving into a bigger place, making the ends meet. There isn't much time for the past.

Older, however, enjoys revisiting his youth, mining it for his writing. Writing that is supposed to help him make sense of the path his life has taken, or, at least bring a happy memory to the fore. These memories are what he has instead of a view or a door or a pool.

The brothers used to dream of one day retiring together to a sunny island in the Caribbean. On a white sand beach, under a jacaranda, the pair would sit outside their red and white scuba shack as the sun peaked through the leaves, and scintillated along the footprint-divoted beach; talking, lounging, all the time in the world like damp sand between their toes. They would take tourists out on their boat, shepherding them down into the warm, clear depths, swimming along reefs teeming with aquatic life. Their skin would be tanned, leathery and they'd be loved by all. When Older imagined this scene, it was just he and Younger, unencumbered, life smoother than beach glass. Their wives were stateside for some plausible reason. Ditto for the kids, who were spawning their own. He and Younger shared a villa where they slept in comfy hammocks, drank rum out of coconuts, smoked fat spliffs, and sheltered itinerant beach dogs.

Younger's dog barks, and he firmly tells her to get down off the couch.

—How is she? says Older. The dog has been having problems with her elbows and is scheduled for an arthroscopy. (She receives better medical care than Older.) This is how it goes—Older asking ingratiating questions as though he were an elderly relative.

—Doing OK, not limping as much, says Younger.

—That's good. Older does the math and realizes that by the time he sees a parole board, Younger's dog, which he's never had a chance to romp with, will be dead.

—Yeah, says Younger. I'll be happy when the surgery's over and she's back home.

—This coming Monday? says Older, knowing that this is as good as it gets. Younger accepting the weekly phone calls, writing biannual letters, schlepping his ass upstate with their grandmother for visits once every eight to twelve months. The connection will only grow weaker as Younger's family-, social-, and work-obligations increase.

—Wednesday. Younger's cell phone chimes momentarily from the nightstand. It's his brother-in-law, confirming with a text that he'll be picking Younger up in a few. —Yo, we can keep talking, but I'm gonna have to put you on speaker.

—That's cool, says Older.

The world of the receiver opens to encompass Younger's footsteps, his humming air conditioner, the faint honking from cabs careening around the streets below, a siren chirping its way through an intersection. Older asks who they're playing, but this is an early model speakerphone, with a unidirectional mic. The words get clipped, and it makes for a jerky, stop-go conversation.

— . . . they playing? says Older to the silence.

— . . . asking who they're playing? says Younger as he hops into one leg of his jeans. His bare feet bounce on the parquet floor, which piques the dog's attention.

— . . . eah, says Older swallowing hard. Who are they playing today?

— . . . illies.

—Phillies, repeats Older, who is practically clueless regarding such matters, and couldn't care less for anything but the sound of Younger's voice: — Should be . . . Should be a good game.

Younger searches for his baseball cap. He riffles drawers, opens closet doors, slides his wife's blouses out of the way, and gets into the angular nooks. Three photos are all Older has as a guide to imagining the apartment. The phone's mic cuts in and out. Younger mumbles interrogatives laced with curses. Over his shoulder, he talks about the box seats he scored, who the starting pitcher is.

Older stands no chance of following the talk. — . . . nd, it's a beautiful day, right?

— . . . otally, says Younger. He finds his cap, and pulls it over his brow. His cell rings again and this time he answers it. —Hey, what's up, man?

Older registers Younger's voice as chipper—different— figures the caller is one of Younger's friends, or a colleague from work.

— . . . going to the game . . . You know it . . . Mm, hmm . . . Right, listen, I'm on the phone with my brother, I'll call you from the car . . . Sure . . . OK, I'm'a letcha go. Bye.

—Sorry, man, Younger says to Older.

—Nah, no problem. (Hearing Younger say *my brother*, Older feels a rush of contented warmth.)

—What were you saying? says Younger as he fills his pockets with the necessities.

—I forget . . . Hey, have you ever heard of *This American Life*?

—What? he says, clicking on a heavy chronograph, wriggling into his kicks.

Older glances down at his watch in the darkened phone booth. Ten minutes left on this half-hour call, but he knows Younger will beg off sooner. With a tightened voice, Younger will say, *Uh, look, I gotta get ready.* Not wanting it to end, he lets Younger devote his time to getting out the door, while he delivers a synopsis of *This American Life* through the speakerphone. Older was recently turned on to the program by a friend from *the world*. It's become one of his new favorite things, which Younger will enjoy as well—a value add, as the brothers say.

— . . . eah, it does sound cool, says Younger. What channel did you say it's on?

— . . . adio. It's NPR. You'd probably prefer to listen to the podcas—

—*ewwp roowp roowp*, comes the sound as the dog's barking overwhelms the speakerphone.

Younger quiets her. —Look, Ky's goin' crazy and my ride's gonna be here any minute.

—Sure, says Older. Thanks for taking the call. Have a great time and wear some sunblock.

—What?

—Have a great time, man. I love you.

—Love you, too, says Younger. Try me on Sunday night.

—I will, says Older. Take care.

—You, too, says Younger.

The speakerphone clips off. Older returns the heavy plastic phone to its cradle. He takes a breath and slides the booth door open. Over convicted felons channel surfing, he sees Younger taking the pooch's smiling golden face in his hands, giving her a kiss, then shutting the door to his apartment. Older extracts himself from the phone booth as Younger pushes the down arrow to summon the elevator. Older looks around the dayroom, a pair of dead-enders stare at televised Judge Something dispensing hyperbole. Younger rides to the lobby in smooth, air-conditioned comfort. Older grabs an essay collection from his cell, returns to the dayroom, and waits for the yard bell.

Snippets of the conversation revolve in his memory, like a tail chased by a dog. He's grateful for those shared minutes each week. Among his elephantine regrets, Older rues the fact that things will never be like they once were with his younger brother. That they can't return to a time when play was simple and life was an azure pool so full of promise there was no need for hope.

Older sees wall upon wall mortared tight with regret. Many of his peers do everything they can to run from their pasts—from creating elaborate falsehoods regarding their origins to chasing bags of dope or tiny joints of dirt weed. But, for Older there is no escape. The only way out is to turn inward, to sit with the memories, both bad and good. The past is dead, long live the past.

When Older gets to the yard, he'll enjoy the same sun as Younger at the ball game, which makes him smile. He is hopeful: the universe will shine again on the brothers, maybe even throw them some coconuts. Their future ain't what it used to be, but the brothers will make do. As they always have.

NINE

EXIT STRATEGIES; OR, WHAT WE TALK ABOUT WHEN WE TALK ABOUT EMERGENCY MEDICINE

Good Old Patrick Flannery, *Paddy Flan*. He was a big brother to me high school senior year, when I volunteered with the fire department. One time, we were first on scene for a car crash involving two girls from my grade. It wasn't bad, they spun off the road and smacked a tree—MVA/car versus tree in ambulance argot. The girls were conscious but shaken. Patty went for the driver's side, reached in, and turned off the ignition. I leaned in the passenger's window. We told our respective victims not to move, that the ambulance would arrive soon. Marni was sitting shotgun. She looked up at me and said there were drugs in the car, begged me to take them as the sirens grew closer. Instinctively, I looked across the occupants and at Patty. He gave the slightest raise of ruddy eyebrows, then an imperceptible nod; it meant: Do what *you* think is best, but I'm OK with you helping them out.

I looked at Marni, held out my hand. "Gimme."

She reached into her purse, unzipped some inner compartment, withdrew two dime bags—one green, one white—that she placed in my hand. I quickly stuffed them into a deep pocket of my turnout coat. Louder sirens. "There's a joint in the ashtray, too." Puppy eyes.

I leaned in over her, grabbed the roach out of the ashtray. A cop was on the scene. I gently eased out of the car. Patty ran interference while I tossed the pungent, half-smoked joint into a row of hedges. He heard me tell the girls that I had taken care of it, and said I did the right thing.

Driving back to the firehouse, Patty asked what they had on them. I took the bags out of my pocket. "Some good weed, it looks like, and some powder, dunno what it is. Maybe coke."

He pulled his truck over, held out his mitt. "Here, gimme the powder." He opened his door, dumped the coke, or whatever it was, down the sewer, then tossed the bag in after it. "That shit'll kill ya."

An hour later, we rolled a ridiculously large joint with a dime bag donated to the department, and smoked ourselves stupid behind the firehouse. After going off to college, I didn't see much of Patty anymore. The last time I met up with him, I was dope sick, and begged for eighty bucks, which I never repaid.

SO GAY. That's what he'd write about the flashback opening. When I first met Chris, he was sitting on the opposite end of a horseshoe of desks, under a fritzing fluorescent, in a classroom that served as meeting space for a creative writing workshop, at night, in prison.

It was a Friday night. I sat by the door, as usual, he by the window. Along with Whit, my long-time writing partner, I'd been in the class since its inception three months earlier. This was Chris's first night. Directly across from each other we sat, cadging glances.

SOOOO GAY, he'd write.

He was youngish, had freckles on smooth white skin, a prominent Adam's apple, wispy brown hair parted near the center, a strand of which hung like an open parenthesis on his forehead. He was equal parts *Little Rascals* Alfalfa and how I imagined Huckleberry Finn when I'd floated down the river with him and Jim a year and a half earlier.

FUCK YOU, DUDE.

In short: Chris was completely out of the norm in a land where most come from seven inner-city neighborhoods downstate.

NO SHIT.

We're hardwired with the ability to recognize cognitive dissonance. Things don't jibe, we look on cockeyed. A story sounds wrong, we tag it nonkosher. Everything about Chris said: Out of place. As in, What's a nice guy like him doing in this shit hole? Thing is, since going away, I've elicited the same response from others. A couple of times a year, I'll get the question, or at least the look: *What's a nice guy——?* So, I was able to tell, with some certainty, that Chris was thinking the same of me. Because Chris was a nice guy, I figured he was in for an incongruous murder, like me.

In the world, we probably wouldn't have given each other a second glance, although we'd come to learn, over time, that we had a decent amount in common. But, inside, as a white kid, I make up less than 10 percent of the prison's population. So, evolutionarily speaking, you see a face somewhat like yours, a vibe somewhat like yours, the reptile brain says: friend, teammate, not a threat. This biological racism often slips over into the real thing—such is the nature of prison, dumping ground for bad attitudes. Cross-pollination affects the enlightened and the ignorant—and this isn't even the West Coast, where race is paramount and gangs run rampant.

These were the early days of the workshop and the group's ground rules were still being established. Who spoke when, what the format would be, and so forth. Jameson—captain, our captain—kept a practiced and subtle hand on the helm, embodying the person-centered approach. Some of us came from a background of lecture halls, Robert's rules of parliamentary procedure, and Socratic methodology—others earned advanced degrees from the school of hard knocks. The professor, Jameson, was (is) a sweetheart, a good egg who volunteers a goodly chunk of his time in driving here and teaching us, the castaways and cutthroats, the fiends and freedom-impaired. All told, there were under ten of us in class that night. A good group, on the whole.

I don't recall the lesson for the evening, or what we had been assigned to read. It was probably something of Hemingway's, because my journal entry reads thus:

> Must make greater attempt at curbing my cursing; while referencing Hemingway's prose in "A Clean, Well-Lighted Place," I managed to say "fuck" at least ten times.

We did an in-class exercise, which Chris and I directed at each other. The workshop pulling double duty, allowing us to bond. I wrote something darkly comic set in an office. He wrote thinly veiled *tranche de vie* of ambulance work. Mine: self-indulgent tripe. His: hyper-detailed piffle, important only to the doer. Trust me, I know from "frivolalia"—having written five such pieces, I was a master of the form. This was a creative writing class's version of badging, establishing one's bona fides and preference set, like conspicuously displaying brand marks (or, as a nonmarketer would say: getting to know someone). Judging by his expression, and he of mine, our pasts overlapped. Again, if Chris were sitting next to me now, he'd lean over and scribble: SO GAY.

In the remaining minutes of class, he approached and we spoke a little. He asked where I'd gone to school. I gave him my brand-name almost-alma mater, then inquired about his. UCLA, a brand name on the opposite coast. Said to him: "That's cool." Chris said it wasn't, that Mexican gang bangers were offered scholarships if they'd "drop their flag"; that they'd attend the school, while remaining loyal to *la familia.*

We deemed each other *simpatico.* (At twenty-five, Chris was younger than my brother, but close enough to get the mirror neurons a-firing.) He locked in a different block, so we wished each other well until the next class, a week or two later. "Be good, be safe," a not uncommon salutation in a place where staying out of trouble isn't easy and keeping safe is never guaranteed.

Chris's writing about his ambulance work brought a good number of memories to the fore. I began using them as fodder for the in-class assignments. Sixty hours of community service was a graduation requirement in my high school. The policy made great sense in a town of obscene wealth, where the almighty dollar was worshipped above all else. Some of my classmates volunteered in a nursing home, others read to the blind, many did nothing, relying on their fathers' secretaries to attest to their volunteerism.

I joined the volunteer fire company. The choice had less to do with serving the community than it did with being able to park where I pleased, rock cool gear, and ignore traffic laws. Each year, a handful of senior boys did the same. Unlike most of them, I had some emergency-medical training, having been a lifeguard and rescue scuba diver. I knew CPR, how to clear an airway, and the sight of blood didn't turn my stomach. With two in-water saves to my credit, I considered myself one cool customer. Signing on as a fire-medic, I'd be able to ride the ambulance and fight fires. It was a wet dream of a community service assignment. While my classmates were changing their oldsters' soiled Depends, I'd be rescuing damsels.

Much to the amusement of my parents, I really got my blue collar on. Literally, I took to wearing a blue, fire department "work shirt" with my name embroidered above the cigarette pocket. Many of the men—fun, hardworking Irishmen and Italians—even accepted me somewhat on the strength of my "passing," and not coming off as the typical pampered high schooler.

The gig came with a badge, a set of dress blues, a pager, and a strobing blue light for my car. I quickly learned that leaving the pager on the countywide band would produce an urgent fire call within a few minutes. It was all I needed to leave wherever I didn't want to be—home, school, my girlfriend's bed. I could get up quickly, say with complete seriousness: "I'm sorry, I gotta go." Better still, they'd completely understand. Sometimes I'd deadpan: *You knew in the beginning, baby, you'd have to share me with the department.*

The work was incredibly rewarding. And it felt good to help people in need, to be a supportive presence during a bad moment that would probably be remembered for the rest of their lives. Of course, I couldn't articulate that. Then it was all adrenaline, now I can see that managing the problems of others allowed me to neglect my own. I was insecure, afraid of making my way in the world, and had a history of depression. From my first ambulance call—an elderly man experiencing insulin shock—I learned how playing Mother Goose was easier than healing thyself. Holding a middle-aged woman's neck in place while the burlier firefighters cut her car apart with loud tools—the concentration entailed in this helped me forget how scared and alone I felt, how clueless I was to myself.

The name tape on my gear wasn't a month old when I responded to my first cardiac call. In the dark, winter night, I skidded to a stop in front of the same temple which saw me bar mitzvahed four years earlier. Hearing the approaching siren, I waited for the "bus" (ambulance) to arrive. It had been snowing.

The five of us walked in as a group, walkies squawking. Stoic is how we rolled, bringing the cold in, and taking the trauma out. Hauling a stretcher and multiple bags of critical care gear, we made our way through the warm lobby and into the reception hall. This was a lavish affair, a couple hundred in attendance. The lights were on, the DJ and his dance troupe milled about awkwardly. Seated at their tables, men and women in eveningwear talked in whispers. Thirteen-year-olds ate. On the parquet floor sprawled a moderately heavy man, bald and middle-aged. His clean white shirt hung opened halfway, and one of the doctors in attendance kneeled beside him, sweating as he did chest compressions. The victim's bow tie draped away from either side of his neck. I was always impressed with actual bow ties (as opposed to clip-ons), a knot I never learned.

We took charge of the scene, securing a perimeter and beginning work on the victim. Our senior paramedic, Evan, delegated responsibilities while he began charging the defibrillator. Evan had a doughy, boyish face, but he was the most shit-together paramedic I'd encountered during my volunteering stint. In the back of a speeding ambulance I'd once watched in awe as Evan set up an IV line and choreographed a ballet of critical care by muttering orders, never bothering to remove the syringe cap from between his lips.

The temple's cavernous hall became quiet, the silence pierced only by the defib's chirping, a walkie's burst of static, and our terse back and forth. While a tech resumed compressions, I established an airway. As is taught in first-aid classes the world over, I took two fingers and raised the man's fleshy chin, further tilting his head back. Then I began bagging. The blue bag—more of a large, rubber football—in my gloved hands forced air into the man's lungs. Unlike during my bar mitzvah, I didn't mind the sea of eyes I felt on me. But I did feel too young, like the grownups in attendance all knew I was inexperienced and had no business performing so critical a task. *What are* you *doing here?* their eyes seemed to be saying.

Time slowed into the rhythmic breaths that I was providing. My eyes met those of a girl, no older than ten, sitting across the dance floor. She wore a white chiffon dress and swung her little legs from the chair.

I'd been to over a hundred of these parties and never witnessed such a tableau. I once walked into a changing room and saw some of my friends' mothers doing lines from their compacts, but that was merely a holdover from the coke-crazy eighties. No death, no blood. No gauze wrappers on the parquet floor.

Looking at this little girl, I understood that this memory would forever stand out amidst the sea of bar and bat mitzvahs she'd attend—more so than the memory glasses made with her friends, filled with soda, salt, tchotchkes, and maraschino cherries. *Whoosh, whoosh*, went the bagged air.

"Clear," called Evan. We stepped back and watched as the gelled paddles met the man's chest, shocking his body upward with a sick, meaty thump. Somewhere, a woman gasped.

Four techs transferred him onto the stretcher and quickly wheeled him out. At some point, I traded the blue bag for a corner of the stretcher.

Hitting the cold air, we made for the ambulance. I struggled to maneuver the stretcher through a curbside channel in the icy snow. Enraged at my feebleness, I kicked at the chunks of dirty ice with my boots. "Relax," one of the techs said to this cool customer. "Guy's not gonna make it."

I slowed my kicking and looked at him.

"Fixed pupils. Here, look. His pupils are large, unresponsive. The brain's dead."

We hoisted him into the ambulance, clicking the stretcher securely in place. I asked if I was to ride along, but was told quietly—for the victim's wife had appeared nearby, waiting for someone to retrieve her car—that there wouldn't be much work done on the ride, that they were merely waiting to get to the hospital so an ER physician could "call it." Calling it meant declaring a time of death, which was something that couldn't be done in the field even by the senior paramedics.

While I couldn't hear it, I'd been to enough of these parties to know that at this very moment the night was winding down, the DJ probably playing "Last Dance" and inviting "the bar mitzvah's family and friends to the dance floor" for one last hurrah.

As the ambulance disappeared with a yelp of sirens, we made for our cars. A guy I'd met a few weeks earlier, Ben, asked if I was OK. I told him I was. No big deal. Ben was a few years older, pre-law at a good school—he had the jaunty, comical air of Doonesbury. A good guy. He asked if that was my first fatality. That was the word he used, fatality. I was accustomed to using it jokingly, during late-night gaming marathons of Mortal Kombat with friends. Apparently, I was the only one holding on to any chance for recovery.

"Where you going now?" Ben asked.

Motioning to the rest of the crew, I said, "I dunno. Where they going?"

"They're going to get drunk."

In the fire company, Ben and I made up the roughly 10 percent Other contingent: the non-blue-collar, the children of privilege out for a few thrills until graduation. "Think we should join them?" I said to Ben.

"Nahhh," he said, and we laughed.

At my house, I liberated a bottle of Scotch from my parents' liquor cabinet. Ben and I drank. "You OK?" he asked again.

"It's weird," I admitted. "One minute this schmuck's probably dancing with his wife, the next he's clutching at his chest."

"You'll get so it becomes routine."

I didn't think death would ever become routine for me, but I didn't challenge him. Instead, we got good and drunk. "Think if the ambulance got there sooner, the guy'd still be alive?" I asked.

"Eh. No way of knowing." He handed me the bottle.

"What was your first fatality like?"

He didn't remember.

"What's the worst you saw on a call?"

Ben thought about it for a moment. "Anything with kids." He was slurring by then. "That and suicides."

Junior year in college, a kid on acid jumped to his death from a freshman dorm room. Dropping off someone later that night, I drove past the scene. It was devoid of activity save a man from the grounds crew who was called to clean it up—his station wagon bore the bumper sticker: SAY NO TO DRUGS. I was baked at the time and wondered who had sold this kid the acid. I hadn't heard there was any around. I'd have to put out some feelers.

At the writing workshop's next meeting, Chris took the seat next to mine by the door. We hadn't seen each other since the last meeting, and I was glad to renew the bond with my new friend. He began whispering to me during Jameson's teaching, which, in such a small room, was louche. And that's how we came to write notes to each other on the edges of our notepads.

I am a writer of notes, a maker of doodles—always have been. In ninth grade earth science, my friend Kodos and I somehow came to believe that our teacher, Mr. K—, fed his wife into a Troy-Bilt wood chipper; it was my task to illustrate such hilarity. But Jameson is cool as fuck, the drawings I did of him were realistic, nice. So Chris and I would crack jokes, on paper, line by sloppy line, about our classmates. Who looks crazy (HOW MANY WOMEN DO YOU THINK HE ATE?), who reads terribly (TUH-TUH-TODAY, TUBBY), whose stories are BORRRRRING. It was incredibly mean stuff, joking about a speech disfluency, like schoolkids, really, but it gave us a tremendous larf. This is when Chris wrote of a classmate's remark to a piece of writing: SO GAY. When he used it again minutes later, I took the jibe not as homophobia, but sophomoric laziness.

WRITING "SO GAY" TWICE IN THE SAME CLASS, I scrawled for him, IS SO GAY. Chris reminded me of those snarky loners in school who declared everyone "poseurs" or "tools." Still, his otherness was attractive. (*No, Chris, not in the gay way.*)

Chris was the kind of guy I would've chilled with in the yard in years past, when I chilled in the yard. In prison, talking often regains its status as art form. Oration, dialogue, listening—important skills around the yard table where time is spent, done, as the seasons pass overhead. You learn, through trial and error, how to tell your story, the story of what a nice guy like you is doing in a place like this. How you learned, in an all-too-personal way, that anyone is capable of anything, and at any time. Anyway, Chris and I didn't have time for that. We had maybe three or four minutes of semiprivate convo after class as we milled about amidst a noisy scrum of felons. The rest of our communication was done through those scrawled notes and in-class assignments.

It was through these short pieces that we learned each had majored in business, and that we both had worked on an ambulance. As far as odds go, the chance of finding someone like that, in here, is like me getting a Pulitzer for this work. When I encounter a fellow traveler, I lower barriers. I share some personal history and goodies. These bonds—however transitory—nourish our better selves.

Chris leaned over and explained that he had dyslexia and recognized words by turning them into shapes. I thought to myself how terrible the condition must be, how rough it'd be for someone like me—a bookish kid who reads and writes almost constantly—to function with such an operating system. Life's like that, though. It teaches you just how resilient you are. As the most adaptable species on the planet, we're capable of horrific shit, but will surprise ourselves with how much we can handle. There's the unreality of the murders I committed, but also the puzzlement that I've survived—and by some metrics, thrived—in prison.

I'm always fascinated to learn of a high-level executive with dyslexia. How it would seem the brain hacks itself, creates some clever neural workaround. There's evidence of survival/adaptation instincts wherever you look. The dog missing a leg doesn't feel bad for himself—he learns balance. The time-starved mother of five can multitask better than any fifteen-year-old riterall tweaker. And when the going gets tough, the dyslexics turn words into shapes.

April, senior year of high school. Late morning on a school day. My tires sliding on wet leaves, I stopped in front of a nice Tudor, several blocks away from the high school. A cop greeted me out front, grateful that he wouldn't have to deal with this thing. I heard the siren approaching in the distance as I walked in the front door.

A middle-aged couple was sitting in the living room. They explained that their daughter was in the bathroom upstairs, having overdosed. On what, they weren't sure. I was the first on scene. The youngish cop looking at me, as if to say, *How do you want to proceed?* On the mantle over the fireplace sat framed pictures of the family from happier times. I recognized a boy one grade below me, and his sister, a sophomore. I told the parents that I was going to try to get her out of the bathroom and we'd take it from there.

Upstairs, I knocked on a thick, white door, and announced myself. I knew her as a nice girl, pretty. A friend of mine had hooked up with her. "L—," I said, "you know me. Let me in." I heard life on the other side of the white door. Above me, in the hallway, a skylight served as a portal to a roiled gray sky. The house smelled clean, crisp. Nonsmokers. The lock clicked and the door slowly opened. In a black sweater, L— looked up at me, her eyes dark recesses of despair. She closed the door behind me, but didn't lock it. Mascara lined her cheeks. I took off my gloves and put a hand on her shoulder, and told her it'll be OK. Rubbing her shoulder with my thumb, I looked around for pill bottles, expecting to see a spilled horn of pharmacological plenty, white somnolent oblongs, or circular, narcotic comestibles.

"L—, whadja take?"

She whimpered and pointed to a bottle of Bayer. It was empty. She'd thrown up some pills that now lay dissolving in the toilet, but there was no way of telling if she'd purged them all. With my fingers on her tiny wrist, I took her pulse, and looked at her pupils; watched her breathing, asked how long ago she'd taken the pills. She wasn't sure, about half an hour ago. I asked if she had ringing in her ears. She did, a sign of aspirin overdose. I heard the ambulance pull to a stop. The front door opened and closed. Voices and walkies filled the foyer. I told L— that the techs would be up in less than a minute. "Let's go downstairs." She pulled in on herself and shook her head. "C'mon, I'll ride with you in the ambulance. This'll work out, I promise." Nothing gave me the authority to make such a promise, but I was seventeen and things always worked out.

I guided L— downstairs and helped her onto the stretcher. To the senior techs I spoke using language that I hoped went over the heads of our victim and her parents.

L—'s parents followed us to the hospital. We drove quickly, but at a speed commensurate with a stable victim. An IV line was set up. While the older techs worked, I leaned in to L— and spoke. I told her that no one in school would ever learn of this and that she could call me anytime she felt like it. She cried softly and thanked me.

Before we left the ER, I made certain her parents knew that I would be discreet, thus eliminating myself from their day's stress equation.

In school, L— and I smiled at each other. It was like that morning never happened. To the best of my knowledge, things for her did end happily ever after.

The first time I remember consciously harming myself was age eleven. I'd lost yet another wrestling match for the junior varsity squad. At home, standing at the mirror, I punched myself in the face. Twice, hard.

I was a skinny kid and had been getting humiliated on the mat the entire season. All the boys in my weight class were sinewy and full of muscle. At eighty pounds, I was soft like bony veal.

I took my soft, yellow blankie, which I had no business still possessing at that age, and twisted it around my neck. My face became warm, then numb. My eyeballs itched. Continued twisting. In the mirror, veins rose on my forehead. Twisting.

I awoke on the floor, nauseated with a bad headache. My mom called repeatedly over the intercom, asking if I wanted to come downstairs for grilled cheese.

May 4, 2007. The third time Chris came to class, and he was bombed. I told him that I'm no square, but he should fix his face, wipe the nod away. He put his pen to my paper and wrote a one-word answer: CANCER.

I felt like the world's biggest asshole. And I became sickeningly sad for my new friend, since cancer is fucking cancer, and prison medical services are fucking atrocious. Leaning to him, I whispered, "Sorry, man."

He wrote: UNDERWENT CHEMO LAST WEEK.

Me: THAT'S CRAZY SHIT.

I HAVE SO MANY CHEMICALS IN THE BLOOD RIGHT NOW. He paused, came back to the page: I'M *SO* FUCKED UP!

I hoped it was the good kind of fucked up, the kind I strove for in college, not the fucked up that people, myself included, termed my life when I was arrested. I didn't have the guts to ask for clarification. RECOVERY?

He shrugged.

REMISSION?

ACTIVE MALIGNANT TUMOR. He underlined it quickly back and forth, letting the ink finally fly off the page— the EKG's flatline.

The most profound response I could offer at the time was: SUCKS. The recreational pharmacologist in me stumbled forth: GET YOURSELF SOME ULTRAMS. GET THEM PRESCRIBED, I MEAN. YOU HAVE TO WRITE A FEW LETTERS. OR HAVE SOMEONE ON THE STREET DO SO (IF YOU CAN). THE PITCH: I HAVE AN ACTIVE MALIGNANT TUMOR! HELP ME MANAGE MY PAIN!

He: EVERY PAIN MED THEY'VE TRIED, I'VE BECOME USED TO AND THEY'VE LOST ANY EFFECT:

MORPHINE HCL
HYDROCODONE
DARVOCET
NOTHING WORKS.

SO . . . TRY ULTRAM. GOOD FER WHAT AILS YA. That's me, the junkie closer, a demented detail man for Big Pharma, joking away the angst. I looked across the classroom at Chris B, who was supposed to have a couple Percocet for me; I'd secreted a joint as trade. But, when he'd walked in, Chris B had shaken his head, wasn't holding. I'd planned on giving him the joint anyway, letting him owe me the pills—he had a drug-trustable face and I like leverage. That was before I found out about Chris.

There was some action going on in the front of the class, Jameson explaining narrative arc on the chalkboard ("Absent that day," I'd later confess).

Being a proponent of medicinal marijuana use, as well as recreational, I dug into my hiding spot (no, not there), and pocketed the joint. I leaned into Chris, affected a stoner: "You cool, man?"

He reacted with confusion, just like the kid who was asked the same in *Dazed and Confused.*

"Do you get high, do you bake?"

He nodded.

Surreptitiously, I slipped the joint into his pocket.

WHAT IS IT THAT I AM CARRYING?

I put pinched fingers to my lips in the international sign for a marijuana cigarette.

He smiled. QTY?

IT'S NOTHING, A STIZZIE. (A stick, a joint.) IT'S GOOD. THROW IT IN A MAKESHIFT PIPE, IT'LL DO.

"Nice," he whispered. "Thanks."

CAN YOU MAKE A PIPE? ARE YOU SKILLED?

DUH!

I asked what meds he was on that night.

LEVETIRACETAM HCL, he wrote on my paper.

I heard Jameson say "dénouement." It was a word I'd encountered and wasn't sure about, so I listened to him describe it as the final outcome of the main dramatic complication. I glanced up to the spot on the page where I'd asked Chris about recovery or remission, hoping for a soft, happy dénouement.

After a time, Chris wrote: DOES HE REMIND YOU OF, SAY, STEPHEN KING?

Never in a million years could the two be confused. If anything, Jameson is a better-looking Dave Eggers. NO. NOT AT ALL. WHADDAYA GOT A BRAIN TUMOR OR SOMETHING?

Chris chuckled softly.

There are things in my past that would make spectacular grist for my essayistic mill, but often I find myself in over my head. Stylistically, my fumferring will indicate that the emotions are too raw to be uncovered—a rotting compost best left for the warm, disinfecting air of spring. There was a piece I wrote about an outing to a particular rave, made poignant because I learn my grandfather has died at the end of the night. His death was near the end of the narrative arc and I spent five thousand words dreading its arrival—procrastinating the sad climax by chocking the piece full of needlessly exhausting details like the times, dosages, and types of the night's drug consumption. (Reader, should you decide to write about a traumatic event, it may prove best to start with it, then talk yourself down with backstory.)

I'll come back to something—dip my toes in the pool of memory—to see if I'm capable of handling it, writing about it without veering into egocentric twaddle or sentimental pap.

Over the years, I recorded a particular memory twice, the first for an exercise using an incident from our past and giving it a story-like shape. Then, per Jameson, for a "sketch of a character in an emotional bind, filling in concrete details along the way, using the third person." The first time I wrote about it (then read it aloud, like we all did), Chris was there. The second time he was not.

"Everyone called it *senioritis*," is how I began, going on to explain that most kids, as soon as they were accepted to university, lost whatever interest they had in playing high schooler. Then how I cut class and lounged in the cozy break room of the firehouse.

I sat alone in the break room, with the TV muted, lazily playing with mini marshmallows, the tasty, bloated flotsam atop a steaming cup of Swiss Miss. In a numb fog, I listened to the mechanical quiet, the sound of a large building at rest. Muted ticking, humming, flushing. The scanners were turned low, always on, reporting often enough to be a friendly white noise.

The 5000 line rang with a loud fire bell. As opposed to the general phone lines for the firehouse, the 5000 line meant business. When it rang, bells went off throughout the vast building. It was eight thirty A.M., I was supposed to be in first period English. When I stepped out of the break room, the dispatcher, Tony, looked past me, for anyone with experience. Tony was a gruff character, I didn't want to piss him off by speaking. He said: "Ambulance call," and gave me the address. He said that no one had called in yet, that I would drive the ambulance. I told him I wasn't checked out on it. He went back into the dispatcher's office and slammed the door. A minute later, he came back out and flung the ambulance keys to me. "You have a license?" I did. "Don't crash into anything, I'm not sending the rescue truck for you."

And before I realized what was happening, I was speeding off from the apron of the firehouse. Tony's voice barked over the cab's speaker: "Hey, kid, you s'posed ta call in or some'in'?"

"Fuck," I muttered and keyed the mic: "Uh, 3-2-6 in service, en route to—" I gave him the address. He repeated my call and clicked off.

Behind the wheel in those days I was a maniac. That was in my car—here was a rolling mass of authority. I'd like to report that I didn't abuse it, but I was seventeen. I'd learned how to operate the lights and sirens from a city paramedic. Every fucking light you want on, he had said. Keep the sirens to a minimum so the civilians don't get used to them. When people are in the way, however, you flutter a blast of chirps and wails that sends them cringing into their headrests.

The center console controlled the fun stuff. I blew through town as cars peeled left and right to make way. Closer to the call, a carload of girls stopped awkwardly in an intersection. The dizzy blonde twist behind the wheel was cutting the same English class. I picked up the mic (almost used her name) and did like the senior techs: fired off two quick chirps, then drawled, "Black BMW, move to your right . . . YOUR OTHER RIGHT."

And I was off again, leaving the girls in a cloud of exhaust. Over the radio, Tony told me that a tech was on scene and I was to meet her inside, third floor apartment, leave the rig idling.

The apartment door was open and I walked in, snapping my nitrile gloves as a greeting. Janice, an off-duty nurse, was hunched over an old woman. "Glad you're here," she said with a warm smile. "Come here, maintain pressure." I spelled Janice on gauze detail. She went into the bathroom to get a med history. The blue-haired woman said nothing, just sat on an ornate settee, occasionally groaning. Blood trickled down her neck, but nothing major. Changing the gauze, I saw that there were two gashes, one that ever so slightly nicked the carotid. There was a long bread knife on the floor. I gently kicked it away, like cops do in movies.

"Let me die," the old woman croaked. Her breath smelled terminal, a green presence in the bright light of morning. I pretended not to have heard. "Why won't you let me die?" I reached into my vest pocket and retrieved more three-by-threes, individually wrapped sterile gauze. At seventeen, thoughts of suicide were nothing new to me, but I was in sober-ambulance mode and wouldn't dream of obliging the woman. Perhaps over glasses of vodka, the old woman and I could parse the merits of nihilism. Interestingly enough, being tasked with preserving someone else's life uncovers one's well-spring of self-preservation.

I called to Janice, asked how she was making out. "Almost done," she said. "Maintain pressure, talk to her." I had no idea what to say to this woman who cut through the waxy flesh of her neck as if it were a challah—*How's it going?* I told her that I admired her Tiffany lamps, for they were truly admirable. She didn't care. I told her how much more radiant the glass was compared with many I'd seen. One asininity followed by the next. She looked at me with rheumy eyes: "Let me die."

What was the right thing to do? I wondered. The moral thing? What if she was trying to exit on her own terms, not on the arbitrary timeline set by a terminal illness? I eased off the gauze. Blood flowed onto the pathetic blue flowers of her housedress. She never took her eyes off mine. Did she realize what I was doing? Was she thanking me? Would this be it, would I leave this call, drink the bottle of Scotch in the trunk of my car, and resolve to finally do it myself? My mind traveled to my bathroom, the set of X-Acto knives I kept under the sink. The old woman sighed. I heard the medicine cabinet close and Janice walked into the room. "How's her pulse?"

"Weak, but steady," I said, reapplying the pressure. The old woman's eyes turned to what, disgust? Sadness? Fuck that—she was the one who called us.

Janice looked over my shoulder: "You need to apply more pressure on the wound. Look at the blood on her dress."

"I know," I said, "I had a tough time swapping the gauze."

Janice drove us to the hospital while I rode in back, taking vitals, my hand on the old woman's throat like a human vise. Again I was alone with her. Once more, she asked that I let her die. I should have remained mute on the subject, but heard myself say something incredibly cheesy, straight out of TV: "Not today." We left her in the ER, where she'd be sutured and referred for a psych consult.

When I was done with my spastic, in-class written recounting of the old woman's suicide attempt, I sat quietly while my peers finished writing or fumbled through books. Sitting next to me, Chris was engrossed in his work. His head looked so normal it was hard to imagine that somewhere beneath his scalp lurked malignant cells, an army of mutants growing larger by the day, playing for keeps. Looking over the class notes from the previous meeting—the night Chris revealed that he had a brain tumor—all the drug names made me thirsty.

Levetiracetam—an anticonvulsant used to treat complex partial seizures. The side effects that interested me were drowsiness, dizziness, and fatigue. At that point in my life, I was still interested in the temporary escape Big Pharma provided.

Even the scary side effects were a respite from prison life. If you're a desperate degenerate, you'll give it a try. Were I a street urchin in South America, you'd recognize me as the dirty scamp with glazed puppy eyes, huffing from a paper bag of toxic glue. Like edible underwear, the novelty of these low-budget chemical vacations usually wears thin after the first dose. But there's only one way to find out. I bought some off Chris. He offered or I requested, I don't remember. But I do have the notes regarding the transaction.

Me: HOW MANY ARE YOU ON?

Chris, way fucked-up, scratched out a column of added dosage numbers: I CAN'T DO MATH.

Me: MATH'S OVERRATED. JUST HOLD UP FINGERS. HOW MANY HITS U ON?

He: HOW DAMAGED DO YOU WANT TO GET?

1. BUZZED
2. IGNITED
3. FUCKED

Everything in moderation I was taught. I circled option two.

He: EFX AT 3500 (Mg.): ATAXIA, BRADYCARDIA, DYSKINESIA. ADVISE IF YOU DON'T UNDERSTAND.

I circled "ataxia," (the loss of ability to coordinate muscular movement) and wrote: WELCOME TO FLAVOR COUNTRY.

Chris got a tremendous kick out of this. He then summed up the high: FEELS LIKE A 12 PK. YOU SEE ME, I'M FUCKED UP. UM, YOU'LL BE TAKIN ½ OF MY DOSE. THIS SHIT IS THE TRUTH, MOTHERFUCKER.

Me: SOUNDS LIKE A PARTY.

He: HOW MANY STAMPS DID YOU—

Stopping his query, I wrote "20." He'd asked for some stamps at the prior meeting after I'd offered "anything you need." When I pressed him, "some" became "Uh, five." I brought twenty—a guilt tax for having a healthy brain. One might be tempted to think that with this drug transaction, I sullied an innocent relationship. The truth is we were both trying to help each other. We transgressed the rules, but adhered to moral imperatives like compassion and friendship. Like Robin Hood, Chris took the shitty meds the state provided and turned them into stamps with which he wrote to his loved ones. I was more than glad to be complicit.

Chris smiled when I handed him the stamps. I'LL BRING MORE (pills) NXT TM.

Growing up, my brother and I had a room separate from our parents when we traveled. No sooner would we get settled in than my dad would knock on our door. My kid brother would be sprawled on the bed, busy scanning the television channels the hotel offered; I would open the door. Told to join him at the door, we'd grumble. Pointing to the emergency exit map, he would say, "This red X, that's where you are. See this red arrow? That's how you both get out in case of emergency."

We'd roll our eyes.

"Boys, look at the map. It's here to help you." His tone calm, but serious.

"OK, Dad," we'd both say, then bolt for the beds and fight for the remote.

As we got older, it became a running joke. "Look, Dad," my brother or I would say while pointing to an emergency exit placard. We'd take turns earnestly reciting: "This is here for you in case of emergency." He would always smile, getting the joke that his two clowns didn't. We had become aware of emergency evacuation routes.

I have little doubt that my brother, to this day, when he closes the door to a hotel room, glances at the placard.

From an early age, I began to look for escape routes in the event of imagined disaster—in crowded restaurants and friends' houses, stadiums, and school cafeterias; later, nightclubs, warehouse raves, and drug spots. Even when I wasn't conscious of it, there was a calculus being performed, a balance between self-destruction and self-preservation. Maneuvering through a dark shooting gallery, on a dangerous mission to hook up with a junkie who would lead me to a dealer, I made mental notes of the couple of bloated corpses I'd have to leap over if things went south and I had to scram. Understand this about me: I always have one eye on the exit. It's served me well in prison. When fights break out near me, I know how to move away quickly, but not so quick as to arouse suspicion. Several years ago, when gas was dropped in the mess hall, I envisioned myself moving through the door before it opened. While most of my peers pawed blindly at their dripping faces and bumped into walls, I hit the fresh air. Anytime I'm in a room, I try to be closest to the door.

Sometimes I wonder how my dad came to teach us the exit-strategy lesson. Was it something my grandfather had taught him? Was there something in his life that made him especially aware of exits, or was it simply good parenting? I can still hear his words: *It's important to be aware of your surroundings.* Never would he have thought I'd be relying on the axiom in prison.

Nor did he know that I consider ending my life an exit strategy. Yet another good lesson I've repurposed, twisted toward a bad end. Maybe I'm so good at adapting, at self-preserving because I work hard at it. And maybe I work on it because I'm wired with a pretty strong will to self-destruct. It is the upside of down.

May 24, 2007. In the upper right corner of my page from that night is Chris's handwriting:

STAGE III METASTASIS
SPREAD TO VENTRICLES OF ♥
SURGERY SCHED, BUT NOT HOPEFUL
WEIGHT=147

The rest of the page contains my scribbling, the one-sided remnants of conversation. This is me, the sentimentalist. I would've fit in just fine with the Victorians and their treasured locks of hair. Are nihilism and nostalgia mutually exclusive?

TOTALLY, JUST ASK SOME NONSENSICAL, NON SEQUITUR QUESTION. That's me, snidely commenting on someone.

Chris, embarrassed to get up and ask for the supplies that Jameson brought in with him, motioned with his chin for me to do so. It was an amusing gesture, like Huck Finn impersonating Don Corleone.

Me: DON'T THINK HE HAS ANY MORE NOTE-PADS. I WILL, HOWEVER, ASK FOR A PEN.

There's some idiotic doodles, then:

Me: DROGAS. ANYTHING DIFFERENT (from Leviteracetam)? ANY YOU CAN SPARE? I DON'T WANT TO LEAVE YOU HURTIN, THO.

Chris's response was written on his page and it escapes me now.

Me: POSITIVE PSYCHOLOGY, SUCKA! DON'T SWEAT IT. I'LL BRING YOU TEN (stamps). COOL? NO MEDS NEEDED AS TRADE.

In my day, I did a lot of ecstasy—somewhere in the neighborhood of 500 hits. I've been away from medical journals for some time, but to my knowledge, there still isn't a longitudinal study on prolonged MDMA use. My gut tells me that the news isn't great. From a very unscientific approach, anything that good has to be very bad for you. Is my souvenir from the rave years holes in the brain? Will my fate mirror Chris's?

How dare I, with healthy gray matter, think of killing myself when my friend is dying of brain cancer? I have a hunch that in his shoes, I'd be trying to worm my way into an efficacy trial, not thinking about aggressive treatment, not a razor.

Home from college freshman year, I made a few ambulance calls in hopes of making my quota and getting off probation. This was a morning call, close to my home. Since joining the department a year earlier, I learned that there was no set time for mayhem. Tragedy made little distinction between the bright light of morning and the cold stillness of night. Often, morning calls meant someone was found dead from the night before. I walked over a lawn frozen with dew. Again, a cop was happy to see me. "In the basement," he said.

The house was silent, furnishings and smells suggested an elderly owner. A clock ticked in the hallway, and a cat brushed against my legs, letting out a *meow*. Gloria, a senior tech, stood in the dim basement.

"Just you?" she said, making zero effort to hide her disappointment.

"Yeah," I said, looking over Gloria's shoulder, at the man with a red rubber-coated wire cinched around his throat, dangling from a water-stained ceiling beam. By eighteen, I'd already encountered death in cars, on the sides of the roads, on serene jogging trails in the woods, in public spaces and tiny rooms. I'd smelled the acrid breakdown of organic material, felt the cold, horrid stillness. I didn't need my eyes to know death was here. The man's tongue lolled past blue chapped lips. The hairs of his nostrils coated stiff with dried snot. Eyes black with petechial hemorrhages. Gloria spoke on the walkie with our dispatcher, who was in contact with the coroner. A step stool lay on the concrete floor, kicked over. Underneath the man's oxfords a puddle had formed.

"Whaddawe do?" I said to Gloria, wanting to take my eyes off the body.

"We wait outside for the coroner."

Away from the stench of evacuated bowels, it felt great to be in the crisp morning air, sucking down a Marb. We were waiting for someone official to arrive and clear the scene, and then we'd be cutting him down. I was powerful hungover, my girlfriend was sleeping in my warm bed, and I wished I hadn't left her. *Fucking moron*, I thought, *just had to respond to this one.*

Clumsily, I questioned my motives for being there that morning, for still volunteering. The obligation ended with graduation from high school. Sure, I'd made interesting friends with gruff, good-hearted men, but that wasn't my *raison d'être*. Was it solely the adolescent adrenaline highs of kicking in a door to a burning house and the intense late-night ambulance work? Again, I totally missed the fact that dealing with some-one else's problems helped me forget my own existential angst, working a suicide quelled, at least temporarily, my desire to become one.

With the cigarette finished, I considered making myself throw up in the bushes on the side of the house. I also thought of going inside and snooping around to make sense of the suicide. Was the old guy given news of an inoperable cancer? Did his wife recently pass? Something with the kids? Maybe the guy just had enough of whatever "it" was.

The coroner arrived and took pictures of the body, and statements from us. He was a pleasant sort and asked me what I was studying in school. Of the four people in the basement, I was the tallest and the youngest, and was thus volunteered to support the body when it was cut down. I was incredulous.

"We're not going to rig some type of harness?"

They looked at me and laughed. I approached the hanging man, my face slightly higher than his braided brown belt. The smell this close made me cringe.

"Just make it quick," I said to Gloria and the coroner. "Tell me when you're ready." I was determined not to spend any more time than necessary hugging the body.

On separate step stools, they climbed near the wire that held the body aloft. "OK," they told me. The coroner pro-duced a linesman's pliers and held it near the wire. With my face inches from the dead man's belly, I tightened my arms beneath his sacrum (the seat). Feeling the foamy, squishy shit, I gagged and tasted bile.

"Ready?" Gloria said from above.

I'd vomit if I spoke, so I grunted the go-ahead. *Pop* went the cable, drop went the body. I held tight as it slumped over my shoulder like a bag of dirt. Literally, dead weight. Everyone rushed over to get it off me.

With the body on the floor, and forms being filled out, the cop told me I might want to take off my coat. I did, and saw bloody drool down the back. The coroner handed me a pink evidence bag into which I stuffed my coat. On my way home, I dropped the bag off at the cleaners and had it charged to the department.

My warm bed was empty. The girl had left a curt note on my nightstand. Apparently, I could just leave her alone for however long I wanted to.

Not an hour before, with death slumped heavily over my shoulder, much of what kept me going was the notion of getting back in bed, hugging something warm and full of life. And that's where my sense making stopped. I was eighteen and didn't realize that on that morning, I'd chosen an ambulance call over staying warm. Death rather than sex.

Workshop, 5.31.07. Again, the right side of my page had notes to Chris. I had given him another joint. He must've asked what kind of green it was. My reply: THE KIND THAT PASSED THRU SOME GUY'S LOWER ABDOMEN.

He likely gave me the finger as a rejoinder.

For class, I slowly began writing about my dark longing. This writing was roundabout—I once spent more than 2,000 words leading up to a piece on suicide, one memory triggering another until I got to the meat. Necessary piffle to be tossed out the window along the road to better writing. Maybe I can bullet point my self-destructive behavior, make a suicidal curriculum vitae, as it were.

- Third grade, on my way to day camp. Standing next to the bus driver, holding on to a safety pole as she drove. She said, "I had a friend who put a gun to his head and slipped and now he's retarded or somethin'. So, if you wanna kill yourself, put the gun in your mouth like this." She removed a meaty paw from the steering wheel, made a gun, stuck it in her mouth, then pulled the imaginary trigger and laughed. I merely stared at her for some time after that, not wanting to seem rude for running back to my seat.

- Elementary school age. There were instances of licking the battery acid that leaked out of a toy. It tasted like an old vegetable.

- At my grandparents' country house I found myself alone in their bedroom while the rest of the family was in the pool downstairs. I unzipped the beige case of my grandfather's .22-rifle and withdrew the weapon. I was around ten years old and wanted to know what it felt like to have the cold gun metal in my mouth—a therapist would later term it morbid curiosity.

- Eleven to twenty-three, self-medicating with all manner of substances, pharmacopeia, and narcotics.

- Choking myself out with my soft, yellow blankie after disgustedly punching myself in the face for continuously losing at seventh-grade wrestling meets.

- Eighth grade, sat on the edge of my bathtub and carved, with an X-Acto, a heart into my arm. In school the next day I showed it to the girl who inspired it, and was saddened by her dismay.

- Fourteen to twenty-three, unprotected sex, often with strangers.

- Fifteen through seventeen, cutting my arms with a razor when I really hated myself and deserved punishment; holding the razor on my _____ artery and watching the hard pulse vibrate the sharp instrument.

- Sixteen and again at camp. On the boat coming back from a rescue-training dive, we discussed techniques for stanching wounds at depth. Becky, an instructor, casually told me: "If you ever want to kill yourself, cut the _____ artery. You'll be dead in under a minute. I have a friend who works in a morgue and that's how they drain bodies." She didn't stress the *you* meaning *me*, it was merely that casual, abstract *you* that makes conversation easy.
- Closing my eyes while driving home drunk from high school house parties, seeing how long my nerve stayed true.
- Nineteen, experimenting with bulimia.
- Twenty-one, began mainlining heroin.
- Twenty-one to twenty-three, made repeated attempts to overdose.

After all these years, the questions remain: Did the bus driver and dive instructor tell me these things because they sensed I'd entertained self-termination since I was just a pup? Were they unburdening to me the way I'd done with my dog? Were they deranged people dealing with their personal demons who sensed a kindred spirit? Or were these merely instances of oversharing—words that would be dismissed and forgotten by anyone who doesn't think about suicide?

What follows here is hyperpresent, my mental pulse as I compose this segment of the piece. Think of it as the Ghost of Suicide Present, an exit strategist's inner monologue.

It is the early evening and I sit in my cell, feeling that I am about to descend to the depths of an ugly depression. This is the calm, introspective moment before I become physically depressed and incapable of writing. Fertile ground for creativity. I'd like to take a snapshot of my brain, as it's reflected in these words.

The cause of my depression is more concrete than usual. I have reason to suspect that my brother, of whom I'm extremely fond, in moving to a new apartment, has abandoned his landline. Since we can't make collect calls to mobile phones, and he's too busy to write letters regularly, my communication with him will nearly vanish. In addition to losing someone very important in my life, I feel like I'm losing a connection to my past, losing a part of myself. The self that existed before I was assigned a number.

When I was in county jail, my family sent a gifted psychiatrist to see me. In describing my attitude toward suicide with her—that it would always be an option for me, that I "ideated" about it several times a month—I would downplay its significance. I assumed that everyone entertained such thoughts. She undeceived me. Not everyone, she said. In fact, it's the rare few who actively think of suicide. We're just not wired to think that way, assume that people with such leanings have drowned themselves out of the gene pool.

I was twenty-three when I was told this. Up until then, I thought it normal to think of ways to take an early way out. These misconceptions were reinforced whenever I read some suicidal musings. Like any reader, I paused at lines that held personal import. Relating to the words of smarter people, who were able to crystallize what for me remained abstract, I would copy the quotes into a notebook. Herman Hesse's *Steppenwolf*, for instance, in which the protagonist, our Steppenwolf, had "days when I calmly wonder, objective and fearless, whether it isn't time to follow the example of Adalbert Stifter and have an accident while shaving."

I never understood the reference, never stumbled across another mention of this Stifter chap. But I don't have to. I am Adalbert Stifter. As coincidence would have it, there are dried spots of blood on my throat and face from my shave earlier. People always tell me: "You're bleeding." And I always respond: "That's how you know you're doing it right."

I'm always surprised by how quickly my depression leads to thoughts of suicide. Cold, methodical planning. Without invitation, visions play like a deranged instruction manual. Close-up of my hands breaking the plastic guard off my Bic razor—I've done this so many times in my mind, that I haven't a doubt I'll perform flawlessly when the time comes. I know where I'll cut. I imagine what it will be like when I'm gone. When I was a kid, this stage of the fantasy was hilariously clichéd: Everyone cries *Why, why?* and mumbles dejectedly, *What a waste*, and they wish I had come to them for help. (Sadly, this was the exact reaction after the murders.) Don DeLillo opined that "Imagining yourself dead is the cheapest, sleaziest, most satisfying form of o." That's me in a nutshell: cheap, sleazy, self-pitying. My "ideating" these days is much more sober. I realize that life is like a finger about to be removed from a bowl of water. The sting of my senseless cut will register as ripples in the water, eventually to be smoothed flat by time.

Yet even as I write these words, I can't make myself believe them. There is a dull ache and tremendous guilt felt by family and friends after a suicide. Rarely is there a good reason. When a teenager kills herself because she feels worthless, her family never recovers. Literally, life will never be the same for them. Best-case scenario, her death registers as an intense longing for an answer. My grandmother, at eighty-eight, still speaks of her cousin's suicide some eighty years ago. The cousin's exit was a roof ledge, and as she left, the family saw her plummet.

Stories like that banish the thought of suicide. It's simply too hurtful to friends and loved ones. Too permanent. And yet, my darkness eventually creeps back.

The blame is to be heaped at my feet alone. I can't even take righteous solace in being a victim. If I weren't in here, if

I hadn't done what I did, I wouldn't have to worry about my kid brother's phone not accepting collect calls. I'd call him (text him, more likely), he'd call me. Simple. But nothing in my life is simple anymore, and thus the suicidal ideation. The exit, should life get too heavy, too dark, should I feel too alone. I wonder if that's not some trick the mind fucks itself with. Again, Hesse: "He gained strength through familiarity with the thought that the emergency exit stood always open, and became curious, too, to taste his suffering to the dregs." And something remarkably similar from Nietzsche:

> The thought of suicide is a great consolation: with the help of it one has got through many a bad night. To think about suicide isn't necessarily to commit suicide. It's to acknowledge the possibility and to acknowledge the precariousness of being alive and to affirm it.

Both of a piece, no? As these men have, I've resorted to dark pondering as an option during a difficult time. For there's little more depressing than having no options. It is to say, *I see the door, and if shit gets too hairy, I can reach for the handle.*

"The easy way out," I've heard said—not on your life, pal. Nothing easy about negating the strongest evolutionary trait, the will to self-preserve. Those who say it's easy have never given it much thought.

With that, my musing has petered itself out. I feel neither better nor worse, and think I may lose myself in a book. I close out this existential metanarrative with a quote from a skilled hand, John Barth, in *The Floating Opera*: "One may go on living because there is no more justification for suicide than for going on living." And let's not forget Dorothy Parker's "Résumé": / *Razors pain you; / Rivers are damp; / Acids stain you; / And drugs cause cramp; / Guns aren't lawful; / Nooses give; / Gas smells awful; / You might as well live.*

My first two months in county jail were spent on suicide watch, one-on-one with Kelly, Carrie, Rachel, and the like. A guard never more than three feet away (even when I showered). Because most of that time was spent in a gown designed to resist tearing (so one couldn't use it as a noose), I dreamed of creative ways to kill myself. Sticking my head in the stainless steel toilet and breathing in water. The guards would be in my cell in less than a minute, though, and could all too easily resuscitate me. I thought of hitting my head against a steel support in the cell, but figured I'd merely knock myself out. Or, standing on my bunk and effecting a swan dive, cracking my neck. I reasoned that with my luck, I'd be left crippled, unable to make further attempts on my life. It finally dawned on me that the bed sheet—the only piece of bedding I was allowed—could be twisted around my neck, tying off on itself. If I positioned myself just right, the guard wouldn't even realize what was going on until I started to gurgle. I tried it out, just to see if it was a viable option. It was. Funny thing: knowing that I could do it stopped all my fantasizing. It was around this time that the good psychiatrist nagged me into keeping a journal. I often credit this chronicling with keeping me alive. Some people go away and find God, I found a pen.

Coinciding with this, the DA, nearing Election Day, declared that the death penalty was on the table for me. It meant that he had a window of time in which to decide whether mine would be a capital case. On one hand, my people were telling me it was just posturing (I've since learned that white people with money almost never get executed—check for yourself). But they continually gave me reports of all the jailhouse snitches—guys who lived near me—who'd concocted my "confessions." I was told to speak to no one about anything deeper than the weather. Aside from the weekly visitors, the only safe space was my journal. On those yellow pages I worked out questions of life and death as one might with a close friend. It's one thing to consider ending your life—quite another to face the possibility that the choice will be made for you. How unnatural and scary to have an expiration date slapped on your packaging, a date toward which you march numbly forward.

Ten months into county jail, a nice black kid was moved near me on the Z-tier. He was my age, twenty-three, his name was R—, and he had also been expelled from college. A nice guy who fucked up. He pulled some ludicrous bank robbery and was in the back of a squad car within the hour. By the next day, the local papers, real dipshit rags that had a field day with me, made it seem R— was John Dillinger. I told him not to get upset, that in a couple of days, they'll find a new criminal to sell ads behind. Not a great feeling reading about oneself in such context, and he took it harder than most. I felt there was more to the story, but maybe he was prone to histrionics. He worried that he wouldn't be able to survive upstate. "Look at me, R—, scrawny white boy, how do you think I'll do?" No, he said, because I was white, I wouldn't be expected to fit in with the majority. He had a point, but at the time, I wondered how he could be so fearful of a place neither of us knew anything about. I decided he must've been a guy who escaped poverty and was called an Uncle Tom any time he visited the old neighborhood. I told him that his intellect would work for him, he'd make it like I'd make it. I was making promises I had no business making; I wonder now how much of this was for myself. He wasn't buying it. "Tell you what," I said, "after lunch, we can continue this." We locked in.

Our gates began to open after lunch, and stopped less than halfway. The electric motor whined and strained. The guard stopped the mechanism and shouted: "Whoever has something stuck in the bars, get it the fuck out!" He tried again, same whine. Madder than shit, he stomped along the tier's outer walkway, looking at our bars. Being a prize pig, I was in the first cell, the closest to the guard's post (nearest the exit, coincidentally). He walked by and I smiled at him like a jackass. About halfway down the tier, he ran back, pulled the emergency-beacon pin on his walkie, and hurried onto the tier. There was grunting and a cell door banged. Guards ran past me. It was scary and exhilarating. Someone was in a bad way. Minutes passed. A nurse walked briskly. A few minutes later, R— was wheeled by my cell. As time slowed, I looked on his gray puffy face, his mouth an explosion of slobber. I knew he was dead and I began to cry. Surprisingly, that evening the rest of us were each taken downstairs for "grief counseling" by an inept social worker. She ended the brief session by making sure I wasn't thinking about suicide. She took my word for it.

I remember sitting in my dark cell, rocking myself on the bed, numb with sadness. R— would've done time, but, even though he was a black man in a system notoriously uncaring for people of color, his armed robbery bid would've been shorter than whatever time I got for murder. I began thinking of R—'s mother, for he had mentioned her. What would the sheriff's department tell her? Would they say they tried their best to save her son? I wanted to find her somehow, to tell her that I was a friend to her son during his last hours. I would've made up some useless lie to alleviate her suffering. But there's nothing you can say to a mother that will ease the pain of burying her child.

Several years later, upstate, ensconced in the routine of Prison A, I met a black kid in his early twenties. I recognized the suicidal depression. After some talk, he made me uneasy. I told him some of my story, some of the guilt I'm dealing with. Then I mentioned R—, who had hung up rather than do the same bid this kid was doing. "There's light at the end of your tunnel," I said. "You're getting out soon. You'll be back on the block, knee deep in pussy while I'm stuck jerking off in B-Block. C'mon, you know I'm right."

I spent the next few days dreading the lock-ins, fearing that our gates would be jammed when they opened. He seemed somewhat better, but determined suicides give few signals. Shortly thereafter he was moved to another block. Part of me worried, but mostly I was grateful that I wouldn't have to see his corpse if shit went south.

I saw the kid a year ago, five years after our encounter, as he waited for his parole board. He didn't recognize me. I knew he'd be hit at that first board, we all are. But I hoped he'd stay alive until he saw the board again two years later. I felt that I had somehow made up for my lack of vigilance with R—.

Midway through junior year in college, a very close friend overdosed and died. This was a Saint Bernard of a human, a friend from back home with whom I'd broken 1,001 nights and consumed countless felonies. Almost immediately, I began to crack. Partied harder, did more drugs, slept a lot less. In the sober gaze of retrospection, this was my self-destructive urge kicking into overdrive.

Alone in my apartment after an extended weekend, I realized that the only things I'd put in my stomach over the preceding seventy-two hours were ecstasy, water, and Starbursts. As the drug fog began to clear, the organism's self-preservation kicked in: *Feed me.*

I returned to my place having taken out an obscene amount of barbecue—savory racks of ribs, smoky sweet pieces of chicken, salty steak fries—which I splayed on the kitchen table, quickly attacking the Styrofoam tray of gooey, glistening spareribs. Still sporting a candy bracelet, I couldn't tear the meat off the bone fast enough. My piggish part in this scene made me giggle, and that's when it happened. I began choking. Not a run of the mill, "Uhp, went down the wrong pipe" choke, but something completely new, a fist rammed down my trachea. My legs kicked out, banging into the table. A bodily red alert: *DYING!!* My fist pounded above the sternum with meaty thumps. I gasped for air and frantically tried to bring up the blockage. My face hot, vision blurry with tears. The canned laughter of a sitcom on the television in the adjacent living room. Sweat sprouting on my brow, sweat steaming my shirt. What went through my head—and we're talking microseconds—is probably what goes through everyone's head in similar situations: *Not like this*. More frantic, I was up and moving, and promptly flung myself over the back of a couch. With a loud, guttural wheeze, I blasted the blue cushions pink with rib meat.

Then I dropped to the carpet in a pile, chest heaving, *my* ribs sore. The sweat cooled as I lay on my back, head tilted so as not to choke on the foul-tasting bile. My mind streamed to age sixteen, on the beach as Becky, our lifeguard instructor, gave instructions for performing the Heimlich on oneself, pantomiming thrusts over the back of a stiff chair. This she delivered as matter-of-factly as her tidbit on the dive boat, about which artery will bleed you dead with the quickness. Following that train of thought, I recalled sitting in bed not a week prior, fondling a razor, becoming mesmerized and sleepy in the lights reflected in the pristine blade. What didn't occur to me then was how unnatural self-destruction is, how it takes planning and tremendous will. Whereas self-preservation is something done naturally, instinctively.

Painfully alone, my only company a stupid television, the adrenaline blast of the event quickly turned to crying. When faced with a final exit, this cool-as-a-cuke exit strategist flailed his arms wild and wide like a cat being put out the door. Between mucous-drenched sobs, I got on with it, and, using a CD case, scraped my vomit off the couch.

Our next workshop meeting was 6.14.07. We were assigned F. Scott Fitzgerald's fantastically appropriate essay "The Crack-Up." Chris gave me an assignment of his own. For a cover to his binder of medical records, he wanted me to make a page with a big EMT logo containing a caduceus, labeled "Medical Information File." Because the printer I have access to isn't color, I volunteered: I CAN MAKE IT HOLLOW AND COLOR BY HAND. Knowing how I work, I probably made the thing and brought it next time for approval before coloring. I also brought for Chris a drawing I made of Clifford the big red dog. Next to Clifford's head was a "Shake (beverage can) Well" insignia. He'd appreciate it.

But, Chris wasn't at the following meeting. Or the one after that. I used up more than a few favors finding out that he'd been taken out to the hospital. The most concrete answer to my question (Is he coming back?) came from a sergeant: "Don't look into it."

It's almost three years since Chris's exit and I still haven't had someone go online and check his status.

After several missed classes, Jameson asked if any of us knew what had become of Chris. He had about fifty pages of yellow paper that Chris had submitted to him and wanted to know if any of us could get it to him. Problem-solving me took it, figuring the pages would be appreciated by his family, like additional memories. It was the same impulse that made me want to reach out to R—'s mom when he hung up in county. I appealed to several staff. The problem was that they're prohibited from having any outside contact with an inmate or his family—at penalty of dismissal. The prohibition applies to outside volunteers, like Jameson, who would be "locked out" of the prison. I finally gave the stack to Sister D—, who could legitimately give it to him when she or a member of the chaplain's staff visited the hospital.

From my journal:

28 Sep 08, Sunday
In Jameson's intro essay to a cluster of our workshop's writing, he writes that one of our class has

died. He must be talking about Chris. I think that everyone has been afraid to tell me, even though I've known it all along.

17 Oct 08, Friday
Encountered Sister D— near her office, asked the status of Chris. "He's passed, right? You can tell me." She looked like she was going to say: *Hold on, lemme check.* But she just split.

Knowing Chris, I can't help imagining his last ambulance ride. Leaving the prison's hospital with an armed guard in tow, Chris would've been handcuffed to the gurney. I believe this scene took place over the summer, so he would've been greeted by the cool interior of the ambulance, and the clean smell of medical-grade disinfectant. No sooner do the doors close, than Chris begins to use terms to badge himself to the techs. Something like: *This lead's loose,* motioning with his chin to one of the heart-rate monitoring lines on his chest. The friendlier tech takes the bait; Chris volunteers his level of training and where he worked. They talk about gear and the rig. They use ambulance argot and the guard feels left out. Chris, handcuffed, itches to get up and study one of the monitors or call the hospital to alert of their arrival or get behind the wheel and work the sirens.

Feeling inept, his mind wanders to the more memorable ambulance calls he worked. The close ones, the lunatic drunks, girls who slipped him a phone number, crumpled car wrecks, gory fatalities. Perhaps he thinks of the stack of papers he handed to Jameson, the assorted tales of his life as a tech, something he titled "Emergency Medicine."

Could he have known this was to be the last siren he'd hear?

Seeing what I've seen in my barely four decades, I realize how lucky one is to be alive, how easily things can take an ugly turn. Come home tired from work and instead of cooking you call a take-out place; one of the kitchen staff didn't wash his hands properly and you retch yourself sore all night; call in sick the next morning and turn on the television, where you catch the news as it breaks: one of your coworkers has just shot up the office before Jackson Pollocking a cubicle with his brains.

There's so much randomness—no need to help it along with a razor. Perhaps that's why Nietzsche, who had his own unenviable physical condition, dabbled in optimism. "He who has a *why* to live for can bear with almost any *how*." Lying on the couch of Viktor Frankl (with *Man's Search for Meaning*, a work that has seen me through dark times), I think of the harm I've caused, which will forever haunt me, and conclude that I have nothing more to expect from life. But Doctor Frankl would reply: "Life is still expecting something from you." Again, Nietzsche: *Was mich nicht umbringt, mach mich starker* ("That which does not kill me, makes me stronger").

After I was sentenced to twenty-five-years-to-life, on what was to be my last meeting with my attorney—a good man and longtime friend of the family—he told me that I'll make it, that I'm a survivor. Like when my father lovingly straightened my tie before an interview, and told me that if I speak clearly, the job is mine, I was fortified by nothing more than a few choice words delivered by someone I trusted. He came to know me as only a criminal defense attorney can, and was capable of such a pronouncement. I *am* going to make it. I *am* a survivor. And off I went to prison, to prove my attorney right.

But doubt inevitably sets in, especially when absolutely no one is around to renew my confidence with such simple, yet palliative encouragement. You see, whoever goes upstate must come down, but not for years, and sometimes not alive. During a dark period a few years later, I revisited my attorney's words and thought: *Sucker, he probably says that to all his clients.* Like a fortune cookie, it could be self-fulfilling. I've vacillated between the two interpretations. And now, years after being told that I'm a survivor, I've come to see that we're all survivors. The people into whose lives I brought suffering—they're survivors, they cope in their own way. I've dealt them a bad hand, and they play it resiliently. Chris could've wallowed in self-pity and, for all I know he had his moments. What he had to undergo I could only guess (and away from the comforts of home and warmth of family). But the Chris I knew met his fate with open eyes and a fine sense of humor.

Thoughts of suicide will always be there, because that's my particular cast of mind. Add to this the fact that after you take lives, you can't expect yours to carry on happily ever after. So burns the hell of my inner being.

There have been times over the years when a guy will want to know, in effect, what my secret is, how I maintain a placid façade in here. They assume I'm getting out next week, so I undeceive them, knocking them into an awkward silence. After a moment, they regain their conversational legs and say either: *I don't know how you do it*; or, *Shit, man, if I was doin' twenny-fi' to life, I'd'a hung up from the jump.*

At one point I would've agreed with them. But here we are, ten years in. The will to adapt, to self-preserve, carries me forward just as it flung me over a couch as I choked on ribs in college. From the safety of your reading nook, you might want to know how I'm going to survive my remaining time behind the wall, what I'll look like emotionally after having gone through the muck and come out on the other side. If I'm still around in fifteen years, I'll tell you. In the meantime, I take the good chances that come my way. Catch a laugh where I can, and seek communion with *simpatico* souls. It's better than the alternative.

No matter how dark it gets in here, tomorrow the sun will rise.

TEN

THE DARKEST EVENING OF THE YEAR

In visions of the dark night
I have dreamed of joy departed;
But a waking dream of Life and Light
Hath left me broken-hearted . . . .

—EDGAR ALLAN POE, "A Dream"

The sunlight is good, but the night is magic, especially when there's bad weather blowing in. Shortly before dusk, I stand with my arms through the bars of my cell: a stock scene in any prison movie. The steam pipes knock and hiss. Over the company walkway, out the steel-latticed window, a terrific ice storm blows the December sky into a murky, swirling maelstrom. High voltage lines, trees, and roads all coated in ice. Power-outage weather. Ours went off a couple of times today, mere hiccups in the grid. Talk has centered on an early lock-in if the guards get sent home before the roads become impassable.

I'm a fan of novelty and kinks in routine. Prison administrators don't share my amusement. In an office in the administration building, administrative staff watch the Weather Channel. They have more than 2,000 inmates in their custody (including yours truly) and serious weather conjures the unimaginable: flash flood drowns us in our cells like rats in a cage (lots of paperwork); tornado knocks down a section of wall, inmates escape, raping and pillaging their way through the surrounding countryside (even more paperwork); power outage enables the inmates to wrest control of the prison. There's nail-biting going on, disaster protocols being studied. Whether the jail is a modern, cinder-blocked monstrosity, or a red-brick retrofitted monolith, there is much the same technology: surveillance cameras, intrafacility communications, motor-driven gates, magnetic lock sensors, equipment panels, electronic sink and toilet controls. So there's a backup generator, and a backup for the backup, and a test of both each week.

Generator power lets me check the local news, parka-clad field reporters on powerless streets while the storm howls through the window. Muffled weatherman voices drift from the cells of my neighbors.

It's dark and gusting by six thirty P.M. when our cell gates whir open. Guys shuffle to the slop sink to wash clothes, to the dayroom to wait for the phone, or merely totter around out of habit. Tremendous storm or not, our routines go on. My neighbor slides out on zories and waters his hearty little plant—as he also does every night, he gives my lovely young geranium a splash. I smile to thank him. At seven, I click a cold metal watch around a warm wrist, gather December's *Wired* magazine, a piece of typing paper scribbled with some notes, a pen, then bumble out of my cell toward the phone in the dayroom. Halfway down the company, I realize I've forgotten to light the Hanukkah candles at sundown.

I like lighting the candles, one of my few yearly concessions to Judaism. Each night that I light the candles I'm a kid again, standing in the dining room with my mom and dad and brother. The prison rabbi—a nice chap, a few years older than me—came by the other night and we lit the candles together. He told me that *technically*, I'm supposed to light them *after* doing the blessing (he made the comparison with the kiddush we say before the ceremonial glass of Manischewitz). But the way we did it at home, and the way I'll continue on this last night, is to attempt to light the last candle as I singsong the last Hebrew word of the blessing.

At the end of the company, a friendly hack sits in his cage, legs propped up, watching a cop drama on USA. "Don't strain yourself," I tell him. He laughs through a great, blue-collar moustache. On third-hand couches in the dayroom, slugs stare at the rare color television. Over low tables, never-ending games of chess in the fierce competition of human pawns.

Neither of the two phones in the dayroom is occupied. This is uncommon, and good. I slide into the booth, sit down, and pull the glass door closed with its accompanying *ah-ah-ah*. I dial my uncle's and a cousin picks up. When a call connects, I dial in my watch's bezel.

Intended for scuba divers and pilots, a bezel is a handy, low-tech contrivance for marking the passage of time. In half an hour, the call will click off whether I want to be saved or not (very, very rarely do I want to be saved) and I like to know how much time I have left.

At about fifteen minutes into my call, I switch from cousin to cousin—two of the rare female voices in my life. I'm warm, content in sharing my time, and again smile inwardly at my good fortune. But a couple of minutes into the call, the lights go out. A minute later they're still not on. I haven't been in this long a blackout since before going away. Rugged watch hands glow green, a pair of stick-figure legs: 7:25.

If rules and regulations are the mortar that holds a prison together, routine is the grease that skids the time. In the nine years I've lived in Prison A, I've awoken every morning at seven o'clock to the ringing bell and the booming instructions of the company officer: "Count! Lights!" Meaning: Stand up, boy-o, turn on your lights. At night, some lights go out, but it's never completely dark. The novelty of actual darkness is unsettling. Routines make the time go by. They align our lives with bells and schedules, framing those we create for ourselves: yoga, journal, jerk off—a routine we can wrap our hands around. Shower after work. Read before bed. Et-routin-ized-cetera.

"Hey," I mumble to her, "the power just went off."

She continues chirping about the sushi place my brother took her to the other night. Outside the booth, I hear the door to the guard's cage close; jangling keys Doppler away in restrained panic. I begin to feel ill at ease, and out of place. The ear to the receiver picks up talk of sake bombs and tempura rolls, but I'm more involved in what's going on outside the protective confines of the phone booth.

A weak emergency light and the violet sky provide the only illumination. Human shadows rove past the windows. Adrift in shark-infested waters, I am in a cage, yet I don't feel safe. My main worry: the guards will return to put us in our cells; I'll miss the orders because I am in the phone booth; they'll find me out, and, in the dark, in a panic, club me about the head and chest with their cocobolo. When I hear my friend Doc's voice, on the freestanding phone next to me, I relax a good deal. If the guards come back, they'll see Doc on the phone, and I'll hear them tell him to lock in.

I'm not holding up my end of the conversation, which doesn't suit my cousin. I repeat to her how out of the norm this is. *Get over it,* her tone says. A phone call can take you out of here while you paint the scene at the other end of the line. But it can also remind you of everything you're missing—the life you used to inhabit. The booth begins to feel claustrophobic. Everyone wants to use the phone. I'm not disappointed when the voice clicks in and announces sixty seconds left. We say our good-byes and make plans to speak again before she leaves for a semester abroad. As a silhouetted Afro bounces by, I shoehorn snippets of generic advice into five seconds, and say "I love you." She says, "I love —" and the phone clicks off.

I slide the door open on its track—*ah, ah, ah*—and extricate myself. "Who's up on the phone?" A shape walks toward me and I move away.

Guys huddle in groups near scant light from outside. Without the distraction of the phone, the senses become acute. I can see enough to recognize a human, but not to make out who's who. I stalk the perimeter of the dayroom, pass the open door to the stairway, and walk toward the windows overlooking the yard. I blink quickly, repeatedly, to adjust to the low light. "Darkness there, and nothing more," to borrow from Poe. (Oh, to host a reading of "The Raven" in the dayroom, just for novelty's sake. We could use purloined lighters to illuminate the page.) I spy a group of guys at a window twenty feet away. By their silhouettes and loud voices, I know which crew this is. They notice me and become unnerved: "Who goes there?" I just laugh, low and ominous. They return to their convo as this Steppenwolf makes for his cell. Along the way, someone brushes by and slips out the stairway door. We give each other a start. Everywhere, guys cluster with backs to the wall, warding off the evil spirits with their nervous palaver. Because they're talking, I can tell who's who, but they can't place the mysterious stranger moving like he has someplace to be. They sotto voce, *Who the fuck was that?* Guys congregate around the two pathetic emergency lights that trifurcate the company.

In my cell, reaching for my lighter, a large white form pops to life with a *BOO!* I experience a quick flood of brain chemicals. Whit, now standing up, asks if someone had told me he was hiding there. I explain that I was in a search mode on account of my lighter, and unless my toilet and sink had conceived a baby, the large object in that nook had to be my friend with a penchant for prankery who often wears white shorts and a T.

Out the window in front of my cell, a pair of muted saffron eyes are aglow where there are supposed to be high-pressure sodium tower lights. It's fittingly ominous for this dark evening, the watchful eyes have gone dim. The most important function of a prison is to keep the nogoodniks in, that wall tower is law-abiding society's last line of defense. It's no place to be without a good set of eyes—the better to shoot us with.

Then I make out the figure of my boy Yas, twenty paces away and approaching quickly. Even at this distance, I know we're on the same mischievous page. You learn to make your own fun in here lest someone make you the object of theirs.

Yas is three years my junior (the same age as my brother), and brings out the kid in me better than Frosted Mini-Wheats. Shortish, boyish despite a beard, tough as nails and quick to giggle. As opposed to the forces in my past that elicited my dark brand of madness, Yas and I are perpetually locked in a game of "Pay you a candy bar to eat that" or "See who can stand on his head longer." He is the good kind of trouble.

As salutation, I flick off a burst from my lighter and give him an amalgamation of lines from *The Karate Kid*: "No mercy. Cobra Kai never die." To which he responds: "Sweep the leg, *Johnnay.*"

By the time we hit the dayroom, our play has evolved into a down-market laser tag—chasing him in the dark, flicking off my lighter like a blast from a toy gun. With the heightened sense of hearing that darkness brings, I pick up guys muttering things about the owner of that strobing Bic: *Fuckin' asshole* and *Retard.* They are just frightened, I reason. For me, this scene is reminiscent of spring dances in middle school; sneaking out of the chaperoned cafeteria and howling with my mates through the oddly darkened halls. Or exploring the industrial side rooms in a warehouse rave. We all need a wild romp-around with life every now and again. My peers, unfortch, are scared miserable, the usual refrain is "I'm in jail, why *should* I be happy?" Their inability to see the light side of a blackout is the darkness in which they live.

But the denizens of the night roam free. We slalom around objects, giggling like mad, scurrying like slippery polecats. At a bend in the railing, Yas jumps up onto it and maneuvers deftly, fluidly, like a martial arts exercise. I almost follow, but visions of my cracked neck keep me on the walk. Instead, I hum Nirvana: *With the lights out / it's less dangerous. / Here we are now / entertain us.* He hops down amidst flashing scintillations in my visual cortex, optical echoes from the stroboscopic litro.

We both partied in the city during the early nineties rave scene and our heads are filled with much the same party anthems. *The drums, the drums the motherfuckin' drums . . .* We dance to the cerebral tune, and then we're off again. As we pass the door to the stairway, I can tell that he wants to go exploring on another floor. Thankfully, the door has been closed and locked since I bumped into someone leaving our floor ten minutes ago (I think Yas is relieved too). A sound bite cues up between my ears, a black revolutionary from the sixties sampled on a breakbeat record from the nineties: . . . *'cause we control the night, an' thass the same shit as ownin' it, an' ain't shit go down in the hood, 'less we say . . .* The rave beat kicks up in my head. A good kind of flashback. We're both ravens, flying happy, free, and wicked, cackling like madasses through the dayroom and companies. "Knock that shit off!" beseech the unhappy masses. Quoth the ravens, "Nevermore, fuckos!"

Those who think of getting even, worry about getting themselves got. The thieves who think about stealing, worry about getting robbed. This is the nature of such negativity, and the reason, *Though I walk through the valley of the shadow of death,* I shall fear no blackout.

"The tower guard's gonna see," Angry Steve hisses. He's right, the tower guard probably does see the flashing, but you know what, we control the night for now, no one sees shit, and the hacks have bigger things to worry about than a strobing lighter.

Yas and I continue to move quick like Wu-Tang Clan lyrics. *Thick like plastah, / bust ya, slash ya, / slit a n'ga back like a dutch mastah . . .* Bob and weave, stick and move, we wind up on his company and come to rest in front of his cell.

A pulse thumps pleasantly in my ears. We cough out a few laughs as the sweat begins to cool.

Out his window I pant. Yas's company looks out onto a 200-yard square divvied up into four yards by two covered walkways—a foreshortened plus sign from this vantage. The view is good tonight. Dark, storybook, *proper horrorshow.* Normally, the vista is akin to the inner courtyard in a lower-income housing project, or an ominous chemical processing facility: the hundreds of windows glow chlorine green like Morse code punched into the dark walls, floor after floor after floor. Tonight, there are no dots of lit windows, little sign of life. A streak of celadon light from the top of a prison building cuts a celestial road in the mist. Against a dark purple sky stand the temporarily worthless banks of stadium lighting. "Those dark lights look scary," I tell Yas. "Like the robots in *The Matrix* that tend the field of human batteries . . . gonna make *us* into batteries."

"Yeah," he says. "Yeah, *wow.*"

I throw a playful chop to his midsection, which he deftly deflects.

Dark homuncular blobs maraud in the yards below. We wonder aloud what brand of madness is going on down there. How are the hooded figures taking advantage of the darkness? Drug dealing out in the open? Settling old vendettas? Rehiding shanks? Copping blowjobs? Ha! How many men have come out of the closet under cover of darkness to canoodle with Cheri? For the most part, they stick to their cliques, invisibly tethered to their metal tables with their backs to the bricks—exactly as I would do.

Yas telegraphs a strike to my neck, which I block clumsily.

I tell him that I'm going to go back around to my crib, to light my candles. "Race ya," he says, then disappears with a peal of laughter.

We catch our breath in front of my cell. I step in and fumble with fitting the white or blue candles into the holders of this chintzy metal menorah. The lighter is put to more responsible use. In lieu of finding my yarmulke, I cover my head with my hand, and, with a few spectators to my back, say the blessing while lighting all the candles. With the full nine burning bright orange, people flutter over like moths to see what's causing this visual commotion. Most of them stand silently, merely enjoying the flickering wicks. The candles throw shadows of my bars and the men onto the wall—blurry background people in a quickly painted crowd scene. Flames dance suggestively in pupils. Jaws slacken, blinking slows. It is a quiet, reflective moment, a solemn communion of shining eyes. The collective memory in our DNA unspooling from eons ago when we were all much more closely related, standing around a fire, grunting approval, staring at the dancing flames. A pagan festival. My cell is an island of luminescence. Like remoras, guys suck up the light—a service I'm glad to provide free of charge. I turn to a group of my friends: "You gentiles have a lotta *chutzpah* soaking up the warm rays from my holy Hanukkah candles." But there is little response as everyone gazes, glassy-eyed.

The silence is broken by the loud closing of a cage door. Four guards have snuck back on the floor and locked themselves in their cage. Calling for us to lock in, they point lights in our eyes—super bright, blue LED key chains. No one, however, wants to give up the newfound freedom just yet. Who willingly leaves a party where autonomy flows from the taps and anonymity is the precious main course? We howl and bay at the moon, just to rattle the hacks in their cage, a role reversal, the blackout tipping the balance of power slightly in our favor. But control is a zero sum game: you either have it or you don't. And *that* is why they have a backup generator.

"Great snakes!" I say to Yas. "Get to the barricade, Valjean,"

"*Tout alors! Tout alors!*" he says, bumping my fist good night.

The guards yell at us to lock in. There are pockets of chanting along the company in response. With the anonymity gifted from darkness, we play it loud like ruffians in the cheap seats: *Fuuuuuuuck youuuuuuu, fuuuuuuuck youuuuuuu.*

There's an old stockbroker's joke that speaks to power roles in a relationship: The buy side says "Fuck you," then hangs up the phone. The sell side hangs up the phone, *then* says "Fuck you." Note that most of us chanters are on the inside of the bars as we curse our worst. Though the power is still out, and the guards are shaky, the balance of power has begun its shift back.

There is a lot of yelling—from their side and ours. The locking mechanisms over our gates emit an awkward thumpy clunking, like sneakers in a drier. Someone a few cells away says with incredulity, "Oh, these muhfuckas expect *us* to lock *ourselves* in?" Raucous laughter. But he's right. There is hooting and howling, giving these guards color for their upcoming ghost stories.

I bang my gate closed, as is being done up and down the company. From the officer's cage each cell's locking mechanism is triggered: metallic thuds roll in and continue past, like piano keys at the low end of the register.

Three guards walk down the company while one stays in the cage to radio it in if things go awry. At each cell the trio repeats their business: two shine lights in the inmate's eyes for cover, one tugs the gate to make sure it's locked. One of the guards, a real menace who works in another block, smirks scornfully at my menorah. Trust that I've been a reliable narrator up until now, trust me now as I lay bare our douche bag's inner monologue: *This asshole isn't really Jewish* and/or *Fuckin' kikes think they're soooo great* and/or *What's this place coming to that he has better lighting than we do down in the lobby?*

No sooner does he think these pleasantries than his two coworkers get to my neighbor's cell and find that the gate slides when pulled. This break in the routine angers their blood. They breathe hard. My neighbor Renzo has the good sense to give them room, and sits, I imagine, on the far side of his cell. The guards' faces are twisted with fear, their eyes dart wild and demented. They repeatedly bang the gate closed until the lock catches, the air thick with tension. I like to think there's a grudging bit of hack gratitude for the light of security the Hanukkah candles provide. *You're welcome,* mean spirits. The mind wanders back to Hebrew school: Hanukkah isn't merely Jewish Christmas, and I can't help casting myself as a modern-day Maccabee and the hacks as Syrian soldiers looking to spoil the fun and darken my light heart.

Minutes later—7:52—our gates are secure and the guards leave the floor. With the candles flickering, and the wind whipping and howling against the windows, I turn to my minute bookshelf that makes up in quality what it lacks in quantity. It's possible to sit at my desk all night springboarding from one title to the next (especially in the anthologies), caught up in the prisoner's version of web surfing. Sitting, the thick volume supported on my crossed legs, with the candles and wind, it isn't hard to imagine Robert Frost in a drafty New England colonial, writing about woods filling up with snow, roads less traveled by, and stone walls. But "The Raven" beckons. From verdant copses to vengeful corpses my fingers walk. The orange flames throw ancient dances on Poe's words. A voice in my head—my inner cinematographer— suggests moving around my cell with the menorah in hand, like a candelabra in a silent horror film; a different voice—the producer—nixes the idea, using words like "unnecessary frivolity" while citing cost-benefit analysis, and closes the matter: "The fire marshal will shit." *Once upon a midnight dreary,* I croak, like James Earl Jones reading the poem on a *Simpsons* Halloween Special, *while I pondered weak and—*

Fuck, nevermore. My shrieking neighbors—led by Chui, who else?—are ruining Poe's macabre romanticism. The loudest guys in here tend to be scared shitless of quiet. If they're not loudly slapping dominoes onto a table, they're loudly cooking. If they're not listening to their loud music, they're listening to their loud TV. That's how they roll, it's their routine. And now that they don't have any of their electric noisemakers, *Why, they sing without trundlers, toot tootlers, and shmendlers.* Harmonious Whoville scene? Think again.

I put on my headphones and try to pull in the radio on my Walkman, but get only static. To silence the hooting which permeates my phones, I press PLAY on the tape. X-Dream's "Future Shock" jumps to life, a progressive trance tape from back before I lived in a cage, the bass line hard and fast like no-nonsense porn. It gets my brain humming at 120 beats per minute, thoughts swirling around. Things I must've socked away while running, to chew on later.

The mind rewinds. No one got on the phone after I was done. Someone said they'd been turned off. That may've been intentional, prison management trying to avoid a thirty-second blurb on the ten o'clock local.

What kind of madness is taking place out in the yards, in the gym, at the night callouts in the school and chapel? (As I'd later learn, if you weren't locked in your cell, the experience was similar: back to the wall, hope for the best; surprisingly there were no cuttings; not surprisingly, there were multiple incidents of petty theft—much of which perpetrated by hacks stuffing what state property they could into their tremendous lunch coolers.) Has everyone been escorted back to their cells by now, is the facility "secure"? Have the roguish guards been torturing the pedophiles in protective custody?

The lights, then excited whooping. Isn't it disappointing when the lights come up in the movie theater and the magic vanishes? It's 8:10 by my watch. I turn my tellie on to elephants walking a long, dusty trail in some arid desert.

At nine thirty I barely make out the guards bellowing a call for a standing count—highly unroutine, but such is tonight. Now jovial, they bounce by, making their count. It's the walk of those who've made it through a nightmare, and can now laugh in the safety of daylight. The counts from the companies get called down to each of the block lobbies throughout the facility. Those tallies are then checked against block population totals, and called in to Command and Control. Satisfied that the rogue guards are present and accounted for, and that the felons are in their cells, the managers give the All Clear, and the prison tucks itself in for the night. Most of the lights go down.

Shucking off clothes before bed, I see that the candles have all burnt down except one. I turn off my lamps and sit staring at the blue flame licking out of the metal barrel. The candle proper is no longer—all that remains is a blackened wick soaked in a sea of molten wax.

A lifetime ago, I liked night dives, enjoyed the brilliantly iridescent schools of Technicolor squid, loved the GloStix that we kept attached as backups for our flashlights. But it was always nice to get back to shore, sit with my friends around a table in a warmly lit hotel lounge, and pen an entry in my diver's logbook, recording the journey below.

My watch now reads a little past eleven. After more excitement than I'm accustomed to in one night, I've tuckered myself out. Flaring up on some asshole's BET-tuned television a few cells away is the latest hourly played Guff Laddy single. I close the anthology and return it to the shelf. ("Leave my loneliness unbroken." I empathize with you, Edgar.) The spuming, choppy waters beneath which I gleefully glided tonight have returned to banal, stagnant normalcy. Nostalgic already, I mutter a few curses, dive under the cool side of my pillow, and descend to the depths of an almost sleep.

Having recently seen the distance-swimmer Diana Nyad on TV, I find myself thinking about her resilience. On each attempt to swim from Cuba to the Florida Keys, this middle-aged woman swam for hours and hours, never getting out of the water, battling cold and hunger and fatigue and every bodily impulse to quit. Because of sharks, electronic shields were used to protect her, but a flareup of asthma, a painful shoulder, and choppy waves cut short her second attempt. Nyad spent another year training, then set off again, only to be stung by box jellyfish and have her skin feel like it was being scalded by boiling oil. Again, she had to be pulled out of the water. More training, improved gear, another attempt. Heartbreaking failures as the years ticked by, but she kept on. Of course she had doubts, but Nyad persisted. Having started again from Cuba on her fifth attempt, after nearly two days of swimming, her coach told her to look at the light on the horizon—it was Florida. Fifteen hours more swimming, Nyad estimated, but fifteen was nothing to her once the end was in sight. When she waded ashore, Nyad later admitted to feeling sad that the journey was over. There are so many admirable and instructive things about her story, but I key on this: no matter how cold or dark it is, or how much pain you're in, or how tired you are, you imagine the lights of the shoreline in your mind's eye, and you keep swimming.

It's not easy battling the inertia of this place, the decades upon decades of routine. The machine will crush your soul if you let it, like the cold depths of the Atlantic can implode a sub. And just as the ocean rubs smooth even the sharpest beach glass, the events of tonight will be forgotten in a week—nothing but a couple of lines buried in official logbooks, an "unusual incident" report stuffed in a heavy filing cabinet. Stabbings, uprisings, natural disasters. They arise and subside. The machine is so powerful that it always gets back to business. The show must grind on.

And grind on it does. The hack sits in his cage, ogling last month's *Guns & Ammo* or staring at the clock, thinking of the parking lot.

The gold-colored menorah sits cold on my desk, glimmering from the guard tower's searchlights. The rabbi will be by tomorrow to take it back until next Hanukkah. Alongside the menorah, a plain white envelope holds salvaged wax stalagmites with which I'll make several candles throughout the year, on birthdays (mine and the boys') and Halloween. The envelope seems to glow in the darkness, a reminder that amidst the gloom, one must kindle one's own light.

ELEVEN

Delusions of Reprieve

A great event in my life, the turning point of my life, now comes into focus and, they want all the details, pertinent and otherwise. Behind their levee of stilted pleasantries and banal conversational make-work, I feel a week's worth of questions about Lily sloshing around.

"All right," I tell the boys, "tonight I'm gonna run it all down. But let's enjoy this meal, pretend it's just any Saturday night."

And with that simple acknowledgment, we regain a sense of the old normalcy. The pall lifted, our clockwork of (incarcerated) domesticity sets itself into motion, like the opening moments of a play. On ossified leather moccasins, Whit slides into his cell—a linebacker's frame meets middle age, rugged and creaky—and returns with his glasses, the better to see his food with. Yas and I share a glance, and smilingly shake our heads at the old boy.

Doc sits opposite me at the square wooden table, Whit and Yas to my left and right. The metal legs of our chairs scrape across the stone floor as we pull them in place. From a large plastic mixing bowl, Yas doles steaming hanks of pasta onto our plates. The bowl is so large that Yas and Doc saw fit to give it a name—so we call it Otto. The turquoise plates—large, sturdy Bakelite—are courtesy of Doc, and they sit in stark contrast to the Rubbermaid containers used by our peers. (Doc, who, after twenty years *inside,* still treats himself to Caswell-Massey, the overpriced soap of blue bloods.)

Whit doctors his pasta with healthy spritzes of artificial lemon and a life-threatening amount of salt. As I reach for the pitcher of ice water, my arm brushes against daffodils luxuriating in a plastic cup vase. Whit cut them from his garden yesterday, their fragrance is soft and sweet and reminds me of home (the smell of daffodils will now forever remind me of this evening). Sipping the cool water, I try to quiet my monkey of a mind and pretend this is just any other fine Saturday evening in May. Out the window, over the prison's wall, atop a distant hill, the arms of wind turbines slowly loop against the backdrop of an electric marmalade sunset. Drink it in, the breeze is warm and alive with sex: springtime, and nature is pollinating.

I map the contours of the surreality: there is shiesty, desperate business taking place all around our table, almost as if we chose to dine on a street corner. Yet, our bond offers a protective barrier of refined contentment against the harsh prison world we inhabit, the marauding, lumpen cutthroats and hustlers we call peers, the collective years the four of us have under our belts (roughly sixty-six years), and the time left before we each see a parole board (don't do a tally now). Silently, I say my version of grace, something once said by the chef Thomas Keller: *When we eat together, when we set out to do so deliberately, life is better, no matter what your circumstances.* Sitting with three close friends, I'm damn fortunate—imprisoned or not—to share the aesthetic pleasures of freshly cut flowers and a good meal that we just finished making in an electric skillet.

Not half an hour ago we stood at a rickety counter bringing life to the ingredients. As I chopped onions and garlic with a can top, Yas put his hand on my shoulder, lightly, lovingly, like a little brother would. He started the fragrant sizzling, while I opened cans of cuttlefish in ink—the label printed in the various languages of merchant seamen, the target demographic—a down-market cousin of squid. Yas emptied the inky-oily contents into the skillet, one of his specialties, an ersatz squid-in-its-ink pasta, of which Doc is quite fond. The hours we spent cooking together over the years, producing extravagant multicourse meals, made all the more extraordinary given the setting—those nights often felt like the posh prison-living scene in *GoodFellas*, but without the tiresome wise-guy bluster.

Tonight we'd have done up something luxe, DIY everything—pitas, baba ghanouj, fried canned beef with an approximation of yogurt dill sauce; or pizza piled ludicrously high with salty meats, various cheeses, fungi, and veg.

But not for me. General Tso's something over pan-fried ramen—because of a mysterious gastrointestinal ailment that befell me six months earlier. With gut pain, headaches, swollen tonsils, and mental fogginess, my body negatively reinforced me until I learned to live without milk, chocolate, cheese, whey, piquant spices, potatoes, tomatoes, vinegar, and more than a pinch of onion, garlic, or citric acid. It hasn't been fun, and I also hate that my condition has affected our festivities. Damn this malady!

In Doc's personal skillet, a solid old Westinghouse given to him by a friendly lieutenant for whom he works, I made a proper focaccia, a square of just-crisp-enough dough, aromatically speckled with garlic and fresh rosemary from the plant growing in front of Doc's cell. The finished product, cut into long fingers, reminds me of the garlicky breadsticks Mrs. Antonucci would feed my brother and me whenever our dad sent us in to pick up the pizza order. Smells like . . . victory. "You know what'd be nice with this?"

My fellow bon vivants look up.

I say, "Fried zucchini flowers from the garden."

Whit puckers his lips and makes gorilla noises of approval.

"Feeling peckish, King Louie? If I'm still here when they blossom in the summer . . ."

An uncomfortable silence takes hold as their eyes go downcast. I've committed a faux pas by departing from the present moment, especially given my earlier exhortation that we pretend this is a normal night. Renzo walks past and we exchange silent hellos. From inside his cell, Chui rapid fires a loud litany of Spanish, breaking Renzo's balls for not cooking tonight since he (Chui) cooked yesterday and shared and yada, yada, yada. That I won't miss. Wink, Thomas, and Boomer mill about in front of the latter's cell—they give us smiles, and some space, recognizing that this is what we're pretending it not to be, a last meal.

And then I see Jimbo walking briskly toward the table, that awkward posture of skinny arms pulled back and close to his torso, a slightly large head. No way he leaves us alone. I tuck into my plate, but it's useless, I sense him hovering near me, looming, zero compunction about interrupting our meal.

"So, uh," he says by way of pardoning his intrusion, in that annoying, Andy Sipowicz-like, Inland North dialect. "I betcha wishin' you never gaht involved with thee-at woman."

Classic Jimbo. Jimmy the Freak. Middle-aged junkie, pill-popping masochist, chronic masturbator with whom I double bunked for six months several years ago, when we both came to honor block, the most comfortable spot in any prison. With him on the top bunk, it was like sleeping underneath a paint shaker. I bailed him out of more scrapes, squared away more of his drug bills than I now care to admit. He taught me that there's no saving a masochist from himself; the more you help, the more it's thrown in your face.

Whit's précis of Jimbo: a complete reprobate. One time, we laughed ourselves sick by likening Jimbo—as he stood in front of us—to Jame Gumb from *Silence of the Lambs*; in particular, the scene in which "Goodbye, Horses" plays in the background while the deranged killer looks at himself in the full-length mirror, dick tucked between his legs, pinching his nipples, asking, *Would you fuck me?* Also, we have a good time with the fact that Jimbo once worked as a ride operator for a carnival—typical, shady carny.

Given our past, it's all the more angering that Jimbo's fishing for gossip, his ass practically dripping for a juicy detail he can share with the friends at work, and, by extension, the guards. "You know, jerkoff," I say, "I've got a jar of peanut butter in my cell that expires in a little over a year. You'll be released by then, right?"

Jimbo coughs out a quick, confused laugh.

"It means that you'll be home then and I'll be fourteen years away from a parole board. It means, who the fuck are you to talk to me about what's right for my future?"

He just stands there, sans rejoinder, stuck on stupid, a demented grin on his face like a dog shitting. Before saying something I'll regret, I put a large forkful of spaghetti in my mouth. That's when I hear Doc say, with a pitch-perfect note of finality, "Thanks for stopping by." Doc stares at Jimbo until the freakazoid walks away, off the company, surely en route to a sympathetic ear, to complain that I acted like a real "ee-asshole."

Doc *went away* in his late forties, and by far has more experience than we do navigating social situations. Over the years, he's described his facility with playing the role of trusted right hand to a powerful, respected mentor, the chief of surgery at a teaching hospital. Now, looking at Yas, he touches fingers to his cheek, then draws them back, unfurling till they're straightened: epicurean jazz-hands miming an explosion of deliciousness. "Gentlemen, this reminds me of a restaurant in Dallas." There was a woman, one of several, with whom Doc trysted during medical conferences around the country. The one in Dallas must not have been anything special, because she receives scant mention each time he's treated us to this anecdote courtesy of pasta-sauce memory trigger. Doc goes on to describe the modern decor of the dining room, the chic atmospherics; linguine cooked perfectly al dente, blackened by squid ink.

For a change, I am not impatient as he relives this bit of his past, my body language doesn't telegraph my annoyance at his repetitive self-indulgence. Instead, I smile, and it's not forced. The magic has been triggered, the light is perfect and dim, we are drowsily ensconced in our bubble of bonhomie, eating, laughing. Taking in the faces of my companions, it feels like a dinner scene in a movie, where the camera pans around the table, and the images play at slightly reduced speed as one of the characters does a voice-over, saying, *That was the last we ever saw of each other,* or, *We didn't know it at the time, but,* or, *This was the night that he ran it all down.* These three men have been like family to me, especially over the past few years, since we all came to live on the same floor, in practically neighboring cells.

Whit, an erudite uncle; he'll crack my back and discuss abstruse social psychology texts. We spend hours together, and I think his mom has adopted me as her own, as if one black sheep in the family wasn't enough. Yas, the same age as my brother—our time together is extra special. I had an eyeball-straining headache once, and as I lay in bed, in my darkened cell, Yas knelt on the floor next to me, pinching the pressure point in the tender muscle of my thumb. We have so many in-jokes and nicknames for each other that I can barely keep track; after recently watching *Revenge of the Nerds,* he's been calling Whit "Ogre" and me "Booger" or "Lewis" or "Skolnick"; since he's monopolized all the good names, I can only call him "Gilbert." Doc and Yas have a father/son connection, whereas for me, Doc's a friend of the family, a trusted and close friend, a polymath whose knowledge base is so broad and deep that I can sound him out on just about anything, and he's always willing to give me his time and attention.

Preparing to lay out my cards, I think about who knows what. Whit's usually my go-to on personal matters, but early on, I detected hostility toward Lily, a jealousy that I was diverting time from him to spend on her. When, for instance, I recently began calling her at three o'clock, breaking away from the boys during our post-work/pre-lock-in get-togethers, Whit began offering quotes in the vein of *Love is irrational.* Doc pretended nothing was amiss, but, aside from our emotional distance, I couldn't confide in him—he works for a lieutenant in the administration building and relationship gossip might be the type of thing he passes on during small talk with his boss, like a chip thrown into the conversational kitty. I don't think he'd consider it betraying my confidence.

It was Yas who surprised me by being a great listener, though I should've known: several evenings of the years, we sat in his cell as he showed me pictures and excerpts of letters from women who'd written in response to a personal he had posted on writeaprisoner.com. He knows what it is to hope against hope. Last week, when I came back from a visit with Lily, Whit and Doc were out in the garden, so Yas and I had the table to ourselves. Without an ounce of jealousy, he asked me all the right questions about my relationship. His joy was infectious and allowed me to relive the warmth of Lily's love, to not feel like I was lording my good fortune (luck doesn't get any dumber) over someone who was desperately trying to find such a partner. "She wants to marry you, you know," Yas said, almost squirming with happiness.

"C'mon," I said. Up until that point, I hadn't even dared to allow myself the possibility of something so fantastic. But since that afternoon with Yas, I have imagined asking Lily to marry me—I could propose in the visit room, using a Funyun as an engagement ring. Though I quickly abandon that line of thinking, shielding myself from a surfeit of hopefulness, because it is good to want something, but the Fates don't allow you to want it too much.

Pushing my chair back, I go to the freezer and return with slushy green chai tea. Pour a round. Not wanting to ruin the moment, we sit in the comfortable silence of a close family. Whit evenly distributes the last of the focaccia. I rip a piece off mine, slowly sop up the sepia-tinted sauce on my plate, and enjoy the remaining morsels. Before it begins to feel awkward, I lay out the facts, all in one package, since I haven't been able to do so all week.

They each know that Lily and I have been writing to each other since late December; that a friend of a friend put her in contact with me hoping I could offer advice on dealing with her fourteen-year-old son who'd recently developed a taste for bong hits; that we've started speaking on the phone, and had several visits. So, that's where I begin, with last Saturday, a timeline I've been able to piece together through various trusted sources.

A guard working the visit room recognized her as a Somebody from the community, and anonymously tipped off a local radio show, which fills the time between furniture-store commercials by reading the police blotter, or viciously gossiping about people from the community, begrudging, and hating. This ostracism elevated to sport plays to the uglier side of small-town dynamics.

On Monday, someone from the show calls the prison and asks them to confirm that Lily was in the visit room. Prison administrators, to their credit, won't confirm or deny anything, but they're pissed at yet another leak by staff, and misdirect their anger onto me.

This I learn on my walk to work Tuesday morning, as a friendly counselor pulls me aside. That afternoon, I call Lily, and give her the heads-up about the radio show calling the prison, and, in the least scary wording possible, tell her that it might get a tad hairy for me here, but since we did nothing wrong, we'd be OK.

In my cell, I compose and type a letter to Warden Sutton, who's been a rabbi to me for several years, and explain the goings on, with the hope that he'll silently still the hands of his deputies, and, best-case scenario, ensure that Lily and I will continue unscathed. No sooner do I finish typing this letter than two guards appear in front of my cell, tell me to step out, then they begin a cell search. I have no drugs or weapons, but, as always, my mouth goes dry with the irrational fear that—for some reason of dark magic—I do have such contraband. Guard A sits at my desk and goes through my papers; Guard B sits on my bed and watches TV. Despite his laziness, it's Guard B who, during a commercial, discovers that day's letter from Lily, still in its envelope, lying on the bed—unread yet by me, the gratification delayer. He brings it to A; they confer, and ten minutes into this highly targeted and precise cell search, call an end to things. I'm shown the confiscated items—letter from Lily, and my letter to the warden—and given a receipt noting when, where, and by whom they were taken. Having read my letter to the warden, Guard A, a friendly, professional sort, agrees with how I'm handling the situation, and says everything will likely work itself out.

Unlike most searches, which leave your cell looking like a team of beavers went to work on your bed, building a dam bristling precariously with your papers, books, clothes, food, and toiletries, there's hardly any mess to clean up after they've gone. Not ten minutes later, Guard B, with whom I've maintained a good rapport for years, returns to my cell to see how I'm holding up; tells me that he was merely accompanying his partner, A, who was sent by "up front"—the administration building—to get any papers to or from Lily, or bearing her name. He's been kept in the dark as to why they searched and it dawns on me that he's actually hoping I'll give up something—not for official use, but to be shared at the bar with his coworkers after their shift.

I'm sitting at my desk reading when the gate whirs closed at eight. P, the company officer, moseys down and asks what I did, says that he got a call to lock me in, that I'm under a seventy-two-hour investigation. Kindly, he volunteers to let me out for a shower, but I tell him I already took one.

Wednesday morning, a guard escorts me down to the administration building, specifically, the office of Mr. Fuhrman, a senior counselor. Aside from his official duties, Fuhrman is part of a somewhat-secretive unit that handles troublesome situations for the facility (those who can, become police detectives, those who can't, play problem-solver in prison).

The troublesome situation is directed to sit in a rickety wooden chair across the desk from Fuhrman. In no uncertain terms, he interrogates me. Hard-core convict I am not, so I imagine he can tell I'm nervous despite my best attempts at playing it calm, cool, and collected. There are two schools of thought going into any interrogation: sometimes they know what's what, and want to see if you'll lie; but more often, they don't know, otherwise they wouldn't need to put your sorry ass in the hot seat. Since I am not a good liar, some version of the truth is my go-to in these situations. Plus, I don't have anything to hide. I answer his questions about when Lily and I started writing, the frequency and modes of our communication, and he notes my answers on a legal pad. From an envelope that is clearly the envelope confiscated from my cell, he withdraws a piece of paper, tosses it across the desk and asks me what it is. It is a receipt from an art supply store; Lily wanted to send me a package and this is what I chose: colored pencils, a set of mini Sharpies, Speedball colored ink (I don't volunteer that I'm hoping to get a tattoo of a bird, the old-school ink sailors got as a talisman for a safe return home), assorted feathers and beads (with which to make a dream catcher for Lily). The total, with shipping, came to just over forty dollars. Yes, I asked her to buy these things for me. No, I've never asked her for money.

Fuhrman puts down his pad, and stares at me for a moment. "You really landed a big one here."

"I'm sorry?"

"Nice try. You start slow, then you'll get more and more out of her. She's gotta be making—what?—six figures?"

"No idea." So crass. His even thinking it says more about him than it does me. He'd never believe me, so it's pointless to mention that, up until that moment, I hadn't once thought about what *she's gotta be making*. I feel not scared now, but dejected bordering on angry, because I see myself through his eyes: some scumbag who's looking to bilk a caring person out of anything he can get away with, and then move on, scorched-earth style.

"Tell me, why're you writing to her?"

In a small voice, I say, "We care a good deal for each other."

"Oh," he laughs. "You're good. I can see what she sees in you." His experience has taught him to disbelieve everything an inmate says; my experience has brought me in contact with peers who do indeed try to scam the living daylights out of unsuspecting citizens. So, he's not pulling his suppositions out of thin air, but he happens to be wrong, my motives are pure, and I'm angry because he's sullying the relationship I have with Lily, something that belongs in equal parts to us both. He's fucking with my partner.

Fuhrman continues his harangue, rehashing old business. There's nothing I can say to dissuade him, so I don't try. When he peters out, I'm dismissed and escorted back to my cell.

That evening a guard delivers a note from Warden Sutton. After he walks away, I read it. *When you read this you will have been interviewed by Mr. Fuhrman, and your keeplock for investigation will be nearing an end.* More importantly, my visitation with Lily "may continue unimpeded," and he's written to her explaining such. My spirits buoyed, I read the sentences again, making sure that the facility won't block my correspondence and visitation. The whole thing is so absurd that I'm transported back to my teens, hoping my parents won't ground me and I can see my girlfriend over the weekend. I parse the warden's memo like a Torah scholar, taking his mention of my interview with Fuhrman to mean that he is indeed guiding the investigation, keeping it from getting ugly. That's enough to allow me a better sleep than the previous night.

Thursday morning, my gate doesn't open. Well, I reason, the warden said my keeplock is *nearing* an end, they're probably just dotting some whatevers and letting me feel the full seventy-two hours of investigation. But, by late morning, alone with my dog's breakfast of worries, pacing my cell because I can't concentrate enough to read, I begin to feel lightheaded. Dawns on me that I haven't been eating. I feel cut off from Lily and am missing her and worrying about her. Cycling with intrusive thoughts, I work into quite a lather, and lie in bed.

The tray delivered at lunch—hot dogs with beans and kraut—is pungent and makes me want to vomit. I give it away.

Keys jangling and loud voices walking from the front of the company propel me out of bed. I splash water on my face, and square myself away, thinking I'm going to be escorted somewhere. But it's only a pair of inmate plumbers, come to unclog the sink in a neighboring cell. They and the civilian maintenance worker stop in front of my cell. We all know each other. They call me a celebrity, say I'm all over the news.

"What the fuck are you talking about?" I croak.

It's only a local rag and that asinine radio show, but it doesn't matter: my name, followed, naturally, by "murderer," has been attached to Lily's. How much grief is that causing her, especially in a small town? How will her kids react? What will happen to her at work?

I spend the rest of the day in a fugue state, acutely nauseated and numb.

Friday morning, my gate opens along with those of my peers. As I pass the control booth, the guard tells me that I've been "cut loose."

At work, I don't even have a chance to unburden to Mr. Bernard, my boss and confidant, before his phone rings. He's told to have me report to Fuhrman's office. I say what I hope isn't my last good-bye to Bernard, and, dry-mouthed, walk to the administration building, where Fuhrman has me wait, just to show me he can. He calls me in, and, as soon as the door is closed, says, "You're outta here, you know that, right?"

That takes the air from me. "I didn't know that." I ask why, and without mentioning the warden's note, say that I thought everything was going back to normal.

Shaking mad, he twice repeats that I'm outta here, then gives me a choice: "The easy way or the hard way."

Me: "What's the hard way?"

"You want the easy way."

I've been in Prison A for nine years, so I know the score. The hard way is I'm put on the wall later in the day and pat frisked, I get punched in the neck, jumped on, then charged with an assault on staff; or while I'm at work, a shank is "found" in my cell.

He tells me that the easy way is to request—in writing on the spot—a transfer to Prison F. How about someplace else? I ask, and he says it's not open for discussion. Picking up a newspaper with a noisy flourish, Fuhrman says he has nothing more to say to me, then makes a show of pretending to read his paper, while I collect my thoughts.

If I don't write what he wants me to write, my odds are 50/50 of making it back to work. Prison F is a dump, five hours away on the opposite end of the state, but it's better than getting set up, sent to the Box for a year, and *then* being sent to Prison F.

With the paper and pen provided, I write that I'd like to be transferred to Prison F.

"Now put your name and number on it. And the date." Fuhrman pulls away the paper, examines it, and stands up. "You'll be eligible for another transfer in two years—don't come back here. Understand?"

All I can produce is a feeble grunt in the affirmative, like a dying animal.

"We're done."

Numb, filled with foreboding, I retrace my route back to work. It doesn't comfort me to know that this fear response is merely a stupid biological echo, a relic from when early humans had to worry about saber-toothed tigers. When I return to the building that houses the vocational programs, a sergeant breaks away from a klatch of guards and sidles up to me. "Come with me," Sergeant Dietz says, casual and non-menacing. I feel my pulse thrumming in my ears, and become hyperfocused on my surroundings. My amygdala is screaming: *Run! Hide!*

The sergeant ushers me into a small, well-lit room and closes the door. We sit facing each other in prearranged school desks, my back to a hallway-facing wall of safety glass. I feel like I'm in a diorama, or a training exercise for law enforcement officers. He's in the tonsured-monk stage of male-pattern baldness; thick, brown goatee: a bizarro-world Homer Simpson, whose gut creeps over the lip of a desk designed for a svelte younger person. "Next week, you'll get the items that were confiscated during your cell search."

"OK," I say.

"You cost her her job. Did you know?"

" . . ."

There's ringing in my ears. *Oh, Lily. I'm so sorry.* She's got mouths to feed. And this jackal is taunting me.

"I don't know what she can possibly see in you." He opens a blue folder and looks at a piece of paper. "Murder. Twenty-five-to-life. They'll never let you go. You think they'll release someone like you?"

For over ten years, it's been instilled in me that prison officials are always right, so I want to plead with him to tell me what indication he's been given that I'll never be released, to share with me what's in his blue folder. Most of all, I'm just flooded with emotions: sadness that I've affected Lily's life, fear that she's decided the cost-benefit on us no longer lines up.

He closes the folder. "You can go."

I walk up the large staircase, emotionally terrified, my bell ringing. No one's ever told me that I'm never getting out. On one level, I know it's just a cruel taunt, the one thing guaranteed to affect even the most battle-hardened convict (which I certainly am not); but there's the overriding dread that he—an authority figure—is right. I begin to wonder why he called me in for that meet and greet. Was there any other reason than just because he could?

When I enter the electronics shop, I quickly walk through the shop proper, not making eye contact with the students, and duck into the office, where it is quiet and still. I move to my desk and I collapse into the comfortable chair, as if it were a therapist's couch, then stare at the screen saver. Because it's my job and it'll distract me, I pull up a database and, in a clicktrance, enter the work orders completed during the two days of my absence.

Mr. Bernard shuts the door behind him, and sits. I swivel to face him, then fill him in. This fine, smart man has been my boss for five years; when I got fired from my last job (the second-in-command found unflattering references I'd made to him in a journal kept on my computer), and the well was poisoned against me, Bernard threw me a major life-line, made me his clerk, and kept me safe from staff reprisal until the heat died down. He's been like a father to me, and some of my fondest memories are set in this office, the two of us talking about paintings and antiques, my making him double over with hysterics after looking at caricatures I drew of Jimbo, who works in the shop.

Like most staff members, Bernard is no fan of Furhman. He picks up the phone when I'm done recounting my week, and calls the warden, who, it turns out has begun his weekend early. The warden's deputy for security returns the call a few minutes later. Bernard asks what the rumpus is, if I'm really being transferred, then lobbies to have me kept here, as a personal favor. And then he goes quiet, just listening. Realizing that I'm staring at him, I return to my computer, and try to do some work.

When he hangs up, Bernard makes a sad chuckle, and says, "Holy shit."

My innards curl on themselves.

The unofficial word from the last word in all matters security: *Your boy* (me) *did nothing wrong . . . except ruin a woman's life.* A copy of Lily's letter to me was sent to her board of directors, who asked her to resign. The local paper has picked up the story—online today, print tomorrow.

So it is true, I did cost Lily her job. I need a minute to fully digest it. "But," I say to Bernard, "what business did they have sending a copy of the letter to her board?"

"It's fucked up," he says.

"Seriously. And *I'm* the one who ruined her life?"

He confirms that I'm being transferred to Prison F, sooner rather than later. My getting transferred is their idea of making the problem (me) go away, and they get to say they're doing it for her sake.

Bernard wheels over in his chair for a tutorial on using the database I created to keep his shop running smoothly. I code a few eleventh-hour additions to make it even more friendly for the next user, the next me. Not knowing if I'll ever see Bernard again, I say my good-byes before leaving work at two. We hug, and I thank him for being so good to me. Damned if we're both not a little teary.

When I get back to the block, I try calling Lily, but there's no answer. We haven't spoken since Tuesday, and I fear that she's gone forever. I call my brother and bring him up to speed; he calls the prison, speaks to the watch commander to make sure I'm safe (i.e., that no weapons mysteriously get found in my cell, and no guards work me over). That's my brother, always the savvy operator.

"And that," I tell the boys, "is that."

They're agog. Yas is especially quiet, and seems on the verge of tears. If he cries, I'll cry, no doubt.

"If I get transferred it'll probably be within the next coupla weeks."

Doc snaps: "Stop saying 'if.'"

Ladies and gentlemen, put your hands together for Captain Bringdown and the Buzzkillers. Whit's wounded expression says I'm not the only one entertaining a delusion of reprieve, some act of Providence that allows Lily to stay in my life, leaves me in Prison A, and keeps together our family of four. I turn to Doc. "You know you're an asshole, right?" Doc was a cardiothoracic surgeon, and he always thinks that gives him the right. Sawbones: one whose idea of help is taking a knife to someone's chest. Now it truly feels like an end of things, the emphasis on last rather than on meal. They get up and start clearing plates, and I announce that I'm going to my cell to make coffee.

I never went in for the coffee filter fashioned out of cloth and wire, more of a cowboy m'self, so I just spoon the rich-smelling grounds into my small, metal hot pot, and pour in cold water from the sink. I've made it strong, as befitting this night. Waiting for the water to boil, I put on my headphones and catch the beginning of a local DJ's Saturday night set of good electronica. From nine to twelve, this radio show has been the soundtrack to many a night, and I know most of the tracks by heart. Out pour the life lessons in monotone from Baz Luhrmann's "Everybody's Free to Wear Sunscreen."

When I turn around, short, cornrowed G is standing in front of my cell. Come in, I say, while hanging the headphones on my wall so we can have some music.

"Tell me it ain't so," he says.

"It's so."

"Damn, man. Coolest white boy in the fuckin' complex. Really think you're outta here?"

"I do."

"Fuck it. This spot ain't about shit anyways."

"Sit," I tell him. "Want an apple juice?"

He drinks from the single-serving container left over from my breakfast feed-up trays during keeplock; fishes in his pocket, then deposits a king's ransom of Starburst onto the bright cover of this week's *New Yorker*. Tropical flavor, the good shit. We exchange smiles, dig in, and toss the balled-up wrappers into the terlet.

G lights a Newport and asks for my ashtray. I tell him I quit two years ago, and offer him the juice cup to flick his ashes into. Going for more candy, he lays the cigarette on top of my locker, the cherry hanging off the ledge, smoke curling toward the ceiling. The coffee begins to boil, so I pull the plug on the hot pot and let it sit. Overpowering the smoke are the rich dark tones of a coffee house.

He says, "Smells fantastic."

"You ain't lying," I say.

We settle into the mellow, a blue miasma taking shape above our heads. Drum 'n' bass sputters percussively out of the headphones. I stand up and remove a multipage rave flyer taped to the wall; the cover is a photo montage of spray-painted street art. Walking around the bed to the dogleg of my cell, I retrieve a fat marker from my desk, and tag the flyer with my nom de graffito: niner.

"For you," I say, handing the flyer to G. "A staying here present."

He thanks me and gets up to leave.

"Stay for coffee?" I say.

"Nah, I'm good. Gonna go see Boomer."

With the fan on, the cell huffs out its smoke. I fumble around with the coffee, pouring it slowly from pitcher to pitcher, gradually eliminating the grounds, until finally transferring it back to the hot pot. I pour myself a Turkish-coffee-sized shot: hot, strong, good.

Next door, hot pot in hand, I stand at the entrance to Renzo's cell as he sits shirtless, pounding away with a large plastic mallet and punch, making holes in the tan hide of a leather purse-to-be. He's engrossed in his work, proceeding with brio and unabashedly humming along with the rock 'n' roll station blaring in his headphones. He turns, and, seeing me, slings the headphones around his neck like a tossed horseshoe. "Come in, my brother. Come in."

"¿Tinta classica?" I say, holding out the coffee, the classic ink, as Renzo sometimes refers to it.

He produces his green plastic mug, I pour him a shot, and we drink together, as if it were a Japanese tea ritual. After a time, Renzo asks if the authorities gave me the ultimatum: break off contact with Lily or leave. He's heard of such things.

No, I tell him. They skipped that stage and forced me to request a transfer.

Renzo works in the law library and is no slouch in these matters: "If you want to stay here, I can help you file an eighty-three. You fight for your lady."

To the best of my knowledge, a 1983 petition challenges an action that abridges one's constitutional or civil rights. The case can be made that Fuhrman, by not adhering to proper procedure, violated my due process rights through coercion. And I could likely get some rhythm on that in court, but it'd be after the fact; or, if I make a big enough stink filing the eighty-three, the transfer order may be canceled, but the victory would be Pyrrhic, and I'd end up leaving here the hard way.

"No," I say. "I don't think that's the move."

"Listen to your heart," Renzo says, thumping his fist twice on a dark, muscled chest. With his accent and Latino machismo, this doesn't come off sounding corny. "Very lucky, my brother. You have a *compañera*."

That's a great way to think of Lily, a companion. "Thank you, Renzo." "You are who you are." This second-person version of Popeye's mantra has been used good-naturedly for years by my Dominican friend.

I step out of Renzo's cell in time to see Ray—*hear* Ray, feel the disturbance in the Force—approaching. In his wake, Dean and Jose sit at a table, likely discussing the assigned reading for Monday's writing workshop. As the apex predator gets within a few cells, he focuses on me and grins: "Another beautiful day in the neighborhood. Just the man I wanted to see."

It occurs to me that the criminally minded are never fully dressed without a smile. He extends his beefy hand and we shake. I follow him into my cell, where he sits on the bed, and lights a hand-rolled cigarette. ("Check this out," Ray says, in a hustler's parenthesis.) "You got two packs?" His eyes like a knife thrust.

"Sorry champ," I say, and partially tune out as he talks of deals and numbers and people who owe. I haven't touched pills in a while, and have no desire to reimmerse myself in that scene.

Ray flicks out his ID card as if it was a straight razor, and deftly squeegees the beads of sweat from his brow and blue-veined pate—thankfully wiping his efforts onto a pant leg rather than shaking it onto the floor. Big smile at yours truly. He gets a kick out of telling me about his business, all the corners he cut, and for old times' sake, I let him. Ray's been cool about my gradual walk away from being his fix-it-up chappie. He's lighting one cigarette off another, high out of his mind, happy that a deal's about to go down that'll keep the withdrawal sweats at bay for almost a week. As if a gear pops into place, he looks at me and asks if it's true that I found a lady friend (he's married to a great woman, long on patience for Ray's excesses).

"It is," I say, and provide a most abbreviated run-through of the business with Fuhrman.

"So, you're getting transferred."

"Looks that way, Ray."

"Hey, it's been real."

"The realest," I say.

Ray is uncharacteristically quiet.

I say, "Ever hear of Boss Tweed?"

He hasn't. I tell him about the Tammany Hall gang of crooked politicians, how one of Tweed's lieutenants would stop at a small church in lower Manhattan on the way to work each morning, and pray only for luck and health, allowing that he could steal the rest.

Not surprisingly, Ray likes this story. Standing, we wish each other luck and health.

"If you see Tommy G.," I say, "tell him to stop by."

"Tommy's on the fuckin' warpath."

Whatever that means, I'm sure it has something to do with his cupidity—pills, gambling, or purloined state food. "Fair enough."

He says, "One last time: Sure you don't want it tonight?"

"Yeah, I'm straight."

Ray nods, makes his exit. I pocket my Walkman, and put in one earbud, like a Secret Service agent—if agents listened to breakbeats while on watch. I return to my crew of platonic conversationalists, and set down the coffee along with a box of graham crackers on a wiped-down table.

As I fill the cups, Whit says, "That smells really good." We dip grahams. I catch Yas looking at me, ditto Whit. Perhaps they're wondering, like me, if our paths will ever again cross.

"I've played Ghost with some of you before, right?"

Yas says we have, but he's fuzzy on the rules. It's the word game my grandma taught me, something we play through the mail; each player says a letter, going toward making a word, but the object is to not be the one who says a letter that makes a word, thus earning yourself a "G," then "h," and so on—like the basketball game, Horse—and the first person to Ghost loses. We do a practice word, going around the table, and Doc's "n" makes "octagon." They get the idea, and we start playing, going around, saying letters, laughing, sipping strong, hot coffee. It's as if the letters cast a spell. Once again, the blanket of contentment settles over us. A benign smile paints Whit's face. Yas and I cant back in our chairs, balancing slightly with our knees propped against the table. *Remember this.*

"Wait a second," I say to Yas. "What word are you making?"

He says, "Bouquet."

"Bouquet," I say, looking at Doc and Whit, "which we're spelling b-o-q-u-e."

The table erupts in laughter.

"So, who gets the letter?" asks Doc.

"I do."

"Why you?" asks Whit, while Yas—technically, the guilty party—remains quiet.

"Eh, because I should've known better. Doc, it's your turn, say a letter."

We resume our game play. It is lovely dim and tranquil, a glassy suspension of reality. We, the sated otters, lounge in a pleasant torpor. But it doesn't last. Doc surreptitiously checks his watch. I get antsy, and sneak a peek at mine: nine thirty. A little more than half an hour before we lock in for the night. I feel like I should be moving around—where, I don't know. On the piece of paper we're using to keep score, I start sketching Doc; but, self-conscious—says he has a horse face— he asks me to stop. The music quiets in my ear, the DJ is speaking. I pay attention hoping for something, the longest shot, a message from Lily, as she did once before. *Nada.*

I tank a couple of rounds, and am the first one to go out with Ghost. Doc's next. It's Yas and Whit, head-to-head, but Whit only has "G-h-o," and after one round, Yas is out. Whit, the big winner, is melancholy, knowing the night is drawing to a close. Doc bids us good evening, and trundles off to his cell. There's a slight hump in his back, a souvenir from years of hunching over a microscope or open chest cavity.

Scootching my chair over, I offer Yas an earbud, which he holds up to his ear. He nods his head along with the blippy, percussive bubbling and glitzy synths of a dubstep track. Whit asks to listen.

"You won't like it," I say.

Whit holds the earbuds astride his noggin, and quickly makes the face of someone who's just encountered a filthy commode. After a few beats, he's had enough. "In every area these days, you've lost the musical talent—scuh-ratching records."

Yas and I burst with peals of laughter—*No way did he just say that.* My eyes watery, I write down Whit's quote. Yas affects a fifties street tough: "Shuddup, old man."

Me: "Yeahhh."

Whit shakes his fist, "You rotten kids."

And we chuckle. On that note, we call it a night. There's sadness on Whit's face. He'll miss me most. Yas has more friends to lean on.

"Breakfast tomorrow," I say. "Spanakopita frittata, or there-abouts. And we'll do mixed grill for dinner."

"Nice," says Whit, wiggling his fingers.

Yas does an intricate kata, his arms a blur, and throws a punch in Whit's airspace, "Pow!" With a "G'night," Yas ske-daddles. He's emotional, too.

I go to my cell, gather a few things, mementos, and bring them to Yas. He's brushing his teeth. Taking a step in, I say, "Hey, dude, just wanted to give you some stuff." He comes over and I hand him a trance tape along with *Searching for the Perfect Beat,* a coffee-table book of rave flyers.

"Wow, man. Thanks." Can't even get cassette tapes any-more; this one, a DJ from back home, is almost ten years old. We hug.

I pull out two Bic lighters, one spent.

"Fuck with Whit one last time?"

"Hell, yeah." Then, he deadpans, "The party. Will begin. In five minutes." Perfect—he sounds like the PA system at a rave.

Sitting on his bed, I break apart the spent lighter, remove the flint and twist the spring around it. "Let's roll."

Yas stands in Whit's doorway while I stay partially out of view, holding the flame to the flint until it glows white hot. "Look at him, Smithers," I say to Yas, "calmly eating candy like a Spaniard." Whit's sitting on his bed, in a darkened cell, watching TV. Yas stands aside; I toss our makeshift firecracker onto Whit's floor, where it comes to life with a hissing shower of sparks. We've gotten him with this before, and as always, Whit's startled, and stares at us like a stunned animal. "You're gonna burn my cell down one of these days."

"Aww, Snowflake," Yas says, referencing an albino gorilla we all saw on PBS.

From the front of the company, in the officer's cage, come the sounds of the heavy, metallic lock-panel being opened.

The guard does this to let us know we've got about a minute to get in our cells. A conditioned response. Another round of good nights, then Yas and I scoot to our cells just in time for the gates to whir closed and shut with a reverberating bang.

After the guards walk, making the final count of their shift, I darken my cell, and throw up the curtains. More caffeine. Rub a cologne tester on my wrists and neck: citrusy, spicy, and clean-smelling. Switch to my good headphones, loud and noise-canceling, with a long cord. *B-boys in the house, turn it up, turn it up, up.* Feels like there's a hummingbird zipping around my overly caffeinated brain. *Sip the nectar, sip the nectar, don't stop till you get enough.* I move to the dogleg of my cell, the music booming in my ears—Santigold's "L.E.S. Artistes"—and dance on the smooth terrazzo floor in my quarter socks, silently bouncing along with the crazy, bulbous punch bag of sound. Four-on-the-mammer-jammin'-floor—just like my rave years—who knew I could enjoy this music without brain-shaking drugs. Such airy, dulcet vocals; I hear a line, "I'm out here by myself," and feel like I'm being spoken to—pattern recognition run amok. The song ends, and I stand, panting.

My cell looks different. I've given away some clothes and baubles and porn; jettisoned piles of clip art that I kept to use in collages, as figure studies, or for reasons unknown; consolidated my papers and chosen the twenty-five books I'm allowed to travel with. My personal effects can use a further winnowing, but not now.

Instead, my mind spins through recent memories, watching the carousel I've just leapt off. Hugging Mr. Bernard—a fine coda if that's the last we see of each other.

Lieutenant Gordon, who made a round this morning and yesterday evening, which he never does; we have a good rapport, so I made nothing of his stopping to shoot the breeze with me, inquiring as to my well-being. Now I realize that he must have been serving as watch commander when my brother called.

During the week, while I was keeplocked and under investigation, a guard who works on the other side of the prison appeared in front of my cell. He startled me, and I just looked at him through the bars—an oatmeal porridge of a person, totally forgettable face. "Just wanted to see who you were," he said, then walked away. Does he live near Lily, or know her somehow?

The last time we spoke, on Tuesday, she was in her office. For fifteen minutes I delayed telling her that things might get a little hairy. She was cool about it, but at the time, there was nothing to worry about other than my nebulous heads-up.

The entire business calls to mind Orwell's *1984*: Winston (me) falls for Julia after she slips him a letter, they have a splendid time together, but eventually get hauled into the Ministry of Love, the really frightening ministry, to be tortured by O'Brien (Fuhrman) in Room 101, the room that contains the worst thing in the world. To my mind, the worst thing would be ending up as they did, alive but dead to each other.

Why couldn't I have read her letter, rather than delaying gratification? I want to know what was in there, what's been shared with the authorities. But more than that, I just wish I had the letter itself, one more thing from Lily, my fount of delight.

I sit at my desk, just as I did this past New Year's Eve when I wrote to her for the first time. After getting my address through a mutual acquaintance, she reached out for advice on dealing with her youngest. There was a tone to her letter that immediately set her apart from most people who write to me—deep empathy in her valuation of my time, the realization that I live a life in here, and do things other than stare all day at the bars of my cell. While most of the world celebrated the arrival of a new year, I sat at my desk writing to Lily, responding to her questions, spooling out narrative, painting scenes of my life *inside*. No drink or drug for me that night, no sweaty bodies, and, aside from the occasional Green

Day song on NBC's New Year's coverage, no loud music—yet, because of my communion with her on the page, I remember the night as more special than practically any other of my thirty-three New Year's—.

The song! "Hold On" by Holy Ghost!—she had this played for me once before. Is this her? I get up and glide with the seductive lyrics. *And hold tight; don't make more plans.* My heart feels like it's going to thump through my chest. *And be still; now move like this. / And hold on; until we kiss.* The hypnotic beat has me dancing with my eyes closed, and through some funky crossed synaptic wire, I'm in a darkened cafeteria, lit bluish with the rotating flecks of a disco ball's light. Unbelievable: the scene is from *Rad*, an eighties BMX movie; at the prom, our protagonist, a mulleted lothario, "dances" to "Send Me an Angel" by doing tricks on his bike, standing on a metal peg while moving a wheel with his other foot. With a shudder, I remember sporting a mullet—I was only eleven or twelve, but that's no excuse.

Blending into "Hold On" are the tones from an electric organ, or some such. Ladytron's "Blue Jeans," my new favorite, which I've been raving about to Lily. This has to be her. Don't jinx it. Get a move on, cut a little rug. Can't make this loud enough. The simple lyrics are sung in a hoarse falsetto, which sounds like little children engaged in a playground game; the accompaniment is robot harmony at its most lush. I'm dancing, sweating, entranced by the trails from my home-made glostix (glow-in-the-dark stickers taped to fat markers). Synesthesia: the colorful song envelops me in swirling translucent bands of vibrant color, juicy like Starbursts. An angelic chorus on ecstasy floats above my head, singing their beautiful melody.

The show's "bumper" plays while Alex, the DJ, speaks over a low bass line, noting what he just played. Then, "That last song was for Danner, from Lily, who says, 'I'll see you Monday. Hang in there, I love you' . . . two exclamation points."

And BOOM goes the dynamite. The chorus to this evening's Song of Happiness, having slowly risen in a shimmering glissando, has suddenly soared skyward with an explosion of bass drums. *Is she not the coolest thing on Earth?* My whole body hums warm. It's as if, in the *world,* we went out on a date, played footsie under the table during dinner, went back to her place, and made love for the first time. I collapse on my bed. Bliss it is on this night to be alive. Couldn't have scripted this better, or more storybook. Like the French fucking Underground operating behind enemy lines, thwarting a Nazi communication blockade with carrier pigeons. *Lily, you rock. Where are you tonight? How are you holding up?*

Just as she reached out and found me in the dark this evening, her first letter pulled me from a depressive episode, a swamp of self-pity. Slowly, letter by letter, I came to focus more on her than on myself—the prescription every egoist needs. It eventually dawned on me that *Finding Nemo* had it right: We survive to fulfill our purpose for others. Maybe my *something special* is being here for Lily. Being her *companero.*

The sweat cools on my forehead, and, after hearing the great lyric, "Come as you are / pay as you go," I lower the volume slightly on Laurie Anderson's "O Superman." There is a wondrous and magical quality to the music of life: harmonious chords reverberating in the fabric of space-time, melodies made by serendipitous pairings, hearts beating together in the space between the notes. This expansive moment—the afterglow of a lovely message from Lily, delivered via the public airwaves—this is the high point of my year. Hell, the high point of the last ten years. That's how long I've maintained this particular delusion of reprieve, that I will find a connection, someone to love me as a partner, extricating me from my personalized loneliness. It goes all the way back to county jail—Rachel, Fawn, Kelly, Melinda, and the other weird crushes. More recent, Natalie, my erstwhile, pill-popping pen pal; random girls from high school who reached out over the years, likely out of morbid curiosity. With all of them I entertained the hope that something would come of it.

Like any quest, there was a low point in my search for connection, which hit its nadir when I referred back to an old map, and wound up drugging with Ray and Tommy G. The wrong people, places and things, as the drug counselors say. Before going *away*—what led to my going *away*—I was searching for connection and love in all the wrong places: drugs, anonymous sex, late nights in loud environs, getting uh-ni-hilated with imperfect strangers. Finally, belatedly, I've come to view that life as played out and tired, more of a young man's game.

Still, there's a side of me that believes I don't deserve to have someone who loves me. It's the same part of me that says Sergeant Dietz is right, I'm never getting out and I'll just ruin Lily's life. The not unimportant difference now is that I'm aware of this self-defeating voice as it arises, and her love is helping me pay less attention to it. Lily's rescuing me from this place, and saving me from myself. So, screw Sergeant Dietz—Lily is smarter and has more pluck than him and me combined, and she'll be the judge of what's good for her.

There's no call for being gloomy. I'm in love with an amazing woman—and beautiful, too. I have friends and family who love me. Tomorrow is another day, as is the day after that. In the morning, I'll make an obscene frittata, big as a doormat, and share it with my friends. Then I'll finish downsizing my property, so it'll all fit in the four duffels I'm given when they tell me to pack up. I still have a peer's work to read and annotate for Monday's writing workshop; must also write a good-bye note to Jameson, explaining all, and thanking him for saving me from the meaninglessness of prison. Hopefully, I won't be transferred Monday—I also want to visit with Lily, and hug her.

Before the roundsman walks, I pull down the curtains. Through the bars, out the window, over the wall and past the hills, twenty miles as the crow flies, is Lily. The mere thought makes me well up with joy. My life has become a *Love is...* cartoon. I see her in everything: songs that play in my head-phones; a meet-cute subplot on *The Simpsons*; the pair of bubbly sparrows who canoodle in front of my cell in the early morning. Love is... the puppy stickers she puts on her letters.

My anxious mind being what it is, I'm afraid of losing her. The powers that be are certainly trying to split us up. I'm also sad for what I'll be leaving: Whit, Yas, and Doc, my surrogate family; Mr. Bernard, a mensch of the first order; my mentor, patron saint of prison writers, Jameson, and the writing workshop that feels like home; the relatively plush environment of honor block. Fortuitously, I took in a televised lecture this afternoon, a psychology professor who used a yin yang to demonstrate that the optimal state for man is to be straddling order and chaos. Too much of either leads one to discontent. Whether my life was too ordered or not ordered enough is beside the point—there's a benefit to embracing chaos. For starters, a transfer will help me put some distance on my bad behavior here, which currently hangs around like a ghost—particularly Odi, the carnival barker and drug monster who kept losing the plot, crewing up with the wrong people, and winding up in dark places like the dirty old man's cell. Instead of getting churned up in the entropy, perhaps it can be used as an engine propelling me forward.

Maybe interrupting my comfortable routine in Prison A will be the best thing for me. Maybe not, time will tell. It may be that what I'm looking at is a world not on the cusp of destruction, but an uncreated one, still in fragments waiting to be pieced together. Shunryu Suzuki wrote that the secret of Zen is contained in these few words: *Not always so.* It feels like I now know what that means, but doubt I'll remember it in the morning.

The phonograph comes to the end of the tune, and the record goes on slightly round and round. As usual, my mind loops back to thoughts of Lily. Just like that, I redirect, and warm myself in the incandescence of her love. There are answers that only time will provide, but as of twenty minutes ago, I know that Lily loves me back, and wants to see me. For now, that's more than enough. The front door to my future yawns wide, aglow with an alchemy fueled by the potential that exists between us. I feel quiveringly alive.

TWELVE

Hard Time; Or, What Doesn't Kill You, Etc.

It's hard to endure the first day of imprisonment wherever it may be spent, Prisons A through F, though going from the *world* to county jail as a twenty-three-year-old was the hardest transition. In comparison to county, getting the lay of Prison F was a cakewalk. Old friends came out of the woodwork and smoothed my landing—I was a known quantity and didn't have to make a name for myself, the word went out that I'm "good people," introductions were made, and various offers of help were extended.

But what really made me feel like I wasn't alone in those first few days were the beautiful memories of Lily, and then reconnecting with her on the phone. Within two weeks her car did indeed make it here, and we sat together in the visit room, our new meeting space.

And so Prison F is where you now find me . . . and leave me. That's right, I know about your escape plan (don't worry, it stays between us). Now is the time for a proper good-bye. They're hard for me, so allow me to spend a little more time with you, and take it back to my early days in Prison F. On an evening like any other, I came upon the following:

Chances are, if you're using a pay phone, things aren't going well.

—Rob Johnson, 27, Lexington, KY

It was in *Esquire*'s "What I've Learned," a feature of the publication's end-of-year edition that offers the pithy wisdom of the crowd. I can't help reading them, hoping for a gem, something that supports or expands my worldview. Naturally, I'm left wanting. The important lessons in life have to be learned, they can't be taught, and they certainly can't be gleaned from glossy pages.

This one, however, gave me pause. It didn't provide advice concerning a boss, offer etiquette on dealing with bartenders, fathers-in-law, or mechanics, nor did it pretend to know what your significant other wants to hear. Those tidbits provide little to no utility for me these days. They don't apply for the same reason that I have no use for gadget reviews and cocktail recipes: I'm out of the market. Crowd-sourced wisdom aside, all politics is local, the pertinent economics is micro, and I use a pay phone.

You see, what I'm most interested in are the tricks learned while mastering the art of living. Viktor Frankl survived Auschwitz firmly believing that "life holds potential meaning under any conditions, even the miserable ones." In contemporary melodramas too numerous to count, the phrase "life or death" has been used to death. That acknowledged, the stakes for me are high. I'm thirty-five years old, confined to a maximum-security prison for at least another twelve-and-a-half years, and, since age eleven, thoughts of suicide have had a knack for showing up when I'm at my darkest. At such times, a sense of life's futility envelops me like a moldy sleeping bag of despair, and I begin to fixate on the fact that death and disappointment are but punch lines to the cosmic joke of one's existence. So, the quest to find meaning under miserable conditions has kept me alive in both spirit and in body. When we can't change our situation, we are challenged to change ourselves—such work comprises the gooey center of wisdom traditions the world over.

As life would have it, when I read what Rob Johnson had learned, I was in my cell, waiting to go to the yard, to brave the whipping cold, a gauntlet of club-happy guards and opportunistic goons for no other reason than that's where the pay phones hang, and Lily would be on the other end of the line. It was a winter evening. An episode of *Law & Order* was ending on a neighbor's TV. The DA strategized with his assistant: . . . *the prospect of doing twenty-five years hard time in Attica might change his tune.* We've all seen this one before—the one where the guy cops out, tune changed, in return for a reduced sentence.

The calm, rational brain isn't well suited to gauging how it will react to a future hardship. This very human condition—what the economist George Loewenstein termed the "hot-cold empathy gap"—is what enables the plea bargains that keep the gears of the criminal justice system running smoothly. (Smoothly, but certainly not fairly: despite what one sees on TV, due process plays no role in the 90 percent of criminal cases which are never tried before a jury; most people charged with crimes forfeit their constitutional rights and plead guilty, ensuring a high rate of wrongful convictions.)

The term "hard time," according to Stephen Cox, in his concise, academic treatise, *The Big House*, was coined by convicts in the late 1800s to convey psychological suffering, "taking your incarceration to heart and really worrying about it." Today, however, it's universally deployed in pop culture as shorthand for any type of incarceration—even the one year "bullet" of county jail time—and has become a caricature, an overly simplified abstraction. Ask anyone who hasn't been kept what they imagine hard time to be and they'll mumble through a vague pastiche of every prison movie and TV program they've consumed. A moonscape of ennui. Their *mise* of the incarcerated *scene*: drab cellblocks; homemade weaponry; brutal guards; a gang-infested population preying on the weak; miserable men scratching hash marks on the walls of their darkened cells, counting off yesterday, today, tomorrow, forever. Or, maybe hard time for them is having no signal on their smartphone. Conversely, the TSA screening procedures much maligned by such people are friendly meet-and-greets compared with what I go through literally once or twice a day.

"Aren't going well," "hard time"—both are well-worn sides of the same subjective coin, wholly dependent upon what your definition of *is* is. So, what does any of it mean?

Twelve-and-a-half years ago, before I could even get to a pay phone in county jail, I had to be booked. While waiting, I was leg-chained to a wall of bars in the jail's inner lobby during shift change. With each passing minute, my body—violently craving a dose of the methadone it had been given during seven days of heroin detox—grew hotter, sweatier, achier. I fought the urge to vomit up the runny nose I'd been snuffling back.

The guards, alerted to my arrival, had a little fun at my expense, slamming a heavy metal gate near to where I was chained, watching me jump involuntarily. The guard assigned to watch me sat in a chair and seemed to amuse himself with a latex glove he'd inflated. (I later learned that this friendly young guard was trying to distract me from the machinations of his gate-slamming coworkers.) To ease my muscles, which, on account of the withdrawal, felt like they wanted to rip themselves in shreds, I lay on the cold floor, comfy as one could be tethered to a wall. There were no windows and, having been relieved of my watch earlier, I had difficulty

convincing myself that the sludge of time was indeed pro-
gressing. As a sergeant walked past, he said to the guard: "Get
him the fuck up." And so I crawled back into the flimsy plastic chair, which now seemed even more uncomfortable. Quietly, so as not to invite attention from the others, I asked the
guard how long it would be before I got put in a cell.

"I dunno," he said, not unkindly.

My eyes, warm and wet for want of methadone, glazed
over and looked on my future: I would spend the rest of my
life chained to that wall.

We tend to deal with grief poorly because we can't fathom
the sadness ever fading, no matter how much time washes
over it. Thus, a corollary to Loewenstein's hot-cold empathy
gap: a brain experiencing hardship cannot picture a return to
serenity.

Chained to that wall—sick and hopeless and consumed
with vague fears—there was no way I could imagine a future
in which I would be standing at a cooking station in Prison
A's honor block, the smell and sizzle of coconut-battered
shrimp accompanying leisurely conversation with Whit, Yas,
and Doc.

Over DIY virgin coladas, slushy from one of the two freez-
ers on the tier, we prepared more than five pounds of shrimp,
courtesy of the appetizer station at Mr. Bernard's wedding the
prior weekend. I fried the shrimp using wooden chopsticks
made for me by a friend in the carpentry shop. Whit slowly
folded the peanut sauce into the cold noodles; there were
even shaved slices of cucumber, grown by us. As was Doc's
habit, he surveyed the comestibles that would be considered
damn good eats at a poolside barbecue, and said, "Maximum-
security prison, gentlemen."

As opposed to believing ourselves to be superior, or more
deserving, we understood that we enjoyed better luck than
our peers, living better than most of our brethren, and often
eating better than the guards. (What we never gave voice to

was how precarious is living well in prison—a guard could have walked by, seen a can top I was using as a cutter, declared it a weapon, and carted me off to the Box before the slushy coladas melted; we'd all witnessed such reversals of fortune.)

And in moments like our evening of coconut-battered shrimp—one good meal out of many—I would silently return to county jail, the beginning of my bid. The fearful uncertainty and privation. While I was learning to survive on ramen, squeeze cheese, and candy bars, a small cadre of inmate workers ("Trustees") were living off bacon cheeseburgers. Over time, I befriended them, and my lot improved.

The truth is, there is no such thing as a standard prison experience, any more than there is a standard college, or war, or marriage experience.

Several months into my stay in county, the possibility of the death penalty looming, I stepped out of my cell in time to retrieve a book being kicked down the tier by a neighbor. It was Viktor Frankl's *Man's Search for Meaning*, a book given to me two years earlier by a therapist for my twenty-first birthday—which I never opened, and likely used as a coaster for my bong. But that afternoon in county I devoured Frankl's account of surviving Auschwitz:

> Another time we saw a group of convicts pass our work site. How obvious the relativity of all suffering appeared to us then? We envied those prisoners their relatively well-regulated, secure and happy life. They surely had regular opportunities to take baths, we thought sadly. They surely had tooth brushes and clothes brushes, mattresses—a separate one for each of them—and monthly mail bringing them news of the whereabouts of their relatives, or at least of whether they were still alive or not. We had lost all that a long time ago.

That was it. By late evening it was as if a switch had been flipped in my brain. How could I pity myself in light of what Frankl and so many others had endured? He would've envied my lot. Hell, the "group of convicts" envied by Frankl would've envied my lot. My glass became half filled. Four months later, the death penalty was taken off the table—I now had it even easier than those in the concentration camps, where the odds of survival were no more than one in twenty-eight.

In the service of improving one's lot, there is practically no end to the comparisons that can be made to harsher situations. Start locally, and expand out. But, even before that, we turn inward.

There's a man I credit with giving me an early push in the right direction. Charlie was a consultant, contracted through my attorney, who visited me almost weekly in county jail for the twelve months between my arrest and sentencing. He'd done thirteen years for robbery and knew a thing or two about a thing or two, but all I saw was a man who was able to leave prison in his late forties and earn a PhD in criminal justice, find paying work, get married, and start a family. In place of the menacing panther tattooed on his muscular forearm, I saw thick Gothic text, spelling out HOPE.

Charlie taught this soft child of privilege how to do a bid. Or, really, in the manner of all great teachers, he taught me to teach myself. "Keep your own counsel," he said. Say little. Watch. Listen. Observe. Read. Write. If I've become something of the amateur anthropologist, it's thanks to Charlie.

I made friends in county, and established a routine of playing cards, drawing, and reading—I was no longer withdrawing from the methadone, was drug free for the first time in almost ten years, and the time began to fly. Then, the shock wore off and the guilt over what I'd done rushed in. I thought some of the darkest thoughts of my life. Yet, I kept on, sometimes merely out of habit. The plea bargaining and sentencing was no picnic—I wouldn't see a parole board until I was almost fifty, twenty-five years later. Moving up to the big leagues,

I was transferred to a state prison reception center. Making good friends—and learning that a prisoner's life is a transitory one, and such friends come and go. Getting sent to Prison A, a hard, scary place far from home. Landing good jobs, moving to the most comfortable block. Having the Fates send Lily to me. Being uprooted from Prison A after a decade of making it my home and sent away from Whit, Yas, and Doc, across the state to Prison F, an even harder, darker place. Getting good jobs, eventually moving to the honor block. Meeting new characters, while staying in touch with Whit and Yas back in Prison A. Good and bad, it's all flux.

Et lux in tenebris lucet. The light shineth in the darkness, and every positive memory can be marshaled into service, replayed during the dark nights of my soul.

Last January was particularly cold, and I hadn't made my move to honor block yet, so I had to go to the yard for the phone. One frigid night I was so happy to be on the phone with Lily that I missed the eight o'clock early go-back, and spent the next two hours standing in single-digit cold. When the yard closed at ten, I had the beginnings of frostbite: my face was a stinging ache and I could not feel my fingers. In a cell without hot water, I managed to take off my outer layers, plug in a hot pot and crouch around it, cocooned in a blanket. As my fingers and toes went from numb to faint tingling to painful pins and needles, I thought back to my last summer in Prison A's honor block, a year and a half earlier.

On a typical weekend afternoon I lay atop a wooden picnic table—stripped down to my shorts—in a small, lush yard between two red brick buildings. Lazing like an otter, I smelled the treated wood of the table as it baked in the sun. My body slowly roasted, sweat dappled my brow. A light fragrance of generic sunblock reminded me of summers past, endless and carefree. Water sluiced out of a spigot as someone watered his patch of vegetable garden. I smelled basil and felt a fine, warm mist of water.

On that cold winter night my fingers finally thawed, and I was slightly stronger for the ordeal. Another module completed in my Survival Training. Surviving hard winters makes a tree grow stronger, the growth rings inside it tighter. The frozen night, the luxuriant summer, and the ups and downs in between—as an economist might say, we tend to find multiple equilibria, different stable points of functioning at each respective level.

That was aided by downward comparisons, of this I have no doubt. There were neighbors with access to the same privileges, yet rather than comparing against those who had it worse, they chose to focus on pettiness and negativity, often seeking out drama, and widening the void of their meaninglessness, digging deeper into a hole rather than treating the bid as an opportunity for growth. I am grateful that I don't share their discontent. More than any outside force, these men make their own time hard.

In the course of a day, I interact with men from harsher blocks in the prison, places I once inhabited. I listen sympathetically to their tales of sneak-thievery, brutal extortion, and malicious guards, silently glad I no longer live there. The proximity, however, ensures I will not forget how quickly I can end up back in a bad block.

Taking the sun one summer afternoon in Prison A's honor block yard, I was wiggling into my sneakers, getting ready to be called inside when fight bells shattered the idyll. Over the three-story cellblock floated stern instructions from the tower guard. Echoing like the PA at a public pool, men in another yard were ordered to break it up, get on the ground, up against the wall. Fights seem to occur more frequently in the spring and summer. It's more than just the heat—when you feel nature blooming and coming alive, it becomes even harder to bear the locked doors keeping you inside, the guards, and being subjected to the will of others.

Inside, twenty minutes later, enjoying a leisurely, cool shower on freshly tanned skin, I took a moment to think about the yard fighters, banged up and bloody, on their way to the Box—but only a moment. There's a certain guilt that comes from living so much better than one's peers. I remember working for a friend's father one summer during college. After spending the weekend at his resort of a beach house, he called me into his office Monday, and asked that I not tell his employees how he lives. Sometimes it's guilt, but often it's about avoiding resentment from those less fortunate.

Even the guys not in Prison A's honor block had it better than some in other prisons throughout the state. Like a state university system, there are good campuses and bad. On one end of the spectrum, there are honor prisons—places reserved for inmates with good luck or political connections, places that host the official tours, where it can be said that everything is done right, and everyone is camera-ready. In the great in-between, there are prisons with harsh guards, but good programs, and vice versa, or maybe it's good for everyone else but not for you, because it's too far from home and your family has difficulty traveling. On the dark end of the spectrum are Box prisons—disciplinary facilities. Do something to get enough Box time (generally, anything over six months), and one can be transferred from a Box in one's prison to a prison that is all Box. The distinction is not academic; a Box prison (sometimes called a control unit, special housing unit, or supermax) is built for people who, according to the administration, can't function in regular prison, and it's run accordingly. Freedom of movement is nil, contact with other humans is kept at a minimum—sometimes for years and years. Your neighbor (and sometimes, cellmate) could be anyone from a chronic pot smoker to the criminally insane. Any talk of the Box invariably leads to throwers, guys who throw bodily fluids and excrement; stories galore of a guy getting "shit down" on his way back from the shower. Just as ex-cons are thrust right back into the world, these Box denizens eventually make their way to general population, often to a prison unofficially designated a catchment facility—such as the place I now call home, Prison F. On these Islands of Lost Boys boredom reigns supreme, but even worse is the notion—entertained by many—that the time is pointless.

To continue the state university analogy, prison systems differ from state to state. Prisons in the Northeast—how ah ya?—tend to be the most humane in the country. The South still has that whole *Cool Hand Luke* thing going for it—chain gangs and swamps and sweatboxes. But for the really draconian, one goes to America's perineum: the southern border states. Texas averages twenty-four executions a year—the highest rate in the modern history of the death penalty.[1] There was a Dickensian scoundrel of a sheriff in Arizona who had inmates living in desert tents and wearing pink boxers; he bragged that it cost more to feed his dog than an inmate in the jail. And California did its daily best to showcase the dark side of American exceptionalism with its unwaveringly applied three-strikes law necessitating any available floor space in prison hallways and gyms be repurposed as overflow quarters. There but for the grace of a few thousand miles go I.

Despite our stratospheric incarceration rate, I'd still rather do time in the United States than elsewhere in the world (save Canada, Sweden, Norway, and a couple other Northern European countries).

I've read of prisons in South America where inmates have access to automatic weapons. The warden cedes control to armed gangs run by strongmen, inmates allow a handpicked guard to come to a certain gate to retrieve dead bodies.

There was a young food vendor on a beach in the Dominican Republic who befriended my brother and me on a family vacation nearly two decades ago—he'd just gotten out of a local jail (for *un poco nada*, something minor, he assured us) where he spent months sharing a cell with dozens of men, and had to "piss and shit in a bucket." Prison time abroad amounting to communal living in some dangerous shit hole

---

1. Mike Sager, *Esquire*, December 2011

for an arbitrary and indeterminate amount of time (see China and every place in the developing world). And if *Midnight Express* is anywhere close to the real thing, a Turkish prison is not the place to cool one's heels.

Though, in an unintentional game of one-upmanship, the US, in its War on Terror, operates so-called black sites, anonymous detention centers in countries where torture is not only standard operating procedure, but elevated to high art. Want to know from hard time? Ask an Iraqi who, for days on end, was made to stand hooded and naked in Abu Ghraib's carnival of depravity. The extrajudicial fiasco that is Guantanamo is no picnic, either. It was there that Noor Muhammed, just one of many men held without charge for years, wrote, in his only letter home, "Please pray for me. I am being held by the Americans."[2]

Around the world and back, this is merely the briefest of overviews of the current state of incarceration. Naturally, things have changed a bit over the years. We've learned to hide our grotesque displays of cruelty, congratulating ourselves on our civilized, camera-friendly society, while sweeping disturbing cases under the American patchwork of razor wire. Dr. Martin Luther King referred to such systemic ugliness as "fraternities of the indifferent." It was relatively recently (early 1970s) that the US prison changed its focus to the punitive retribution from the rehabilitation it had practiced for approximately thirty years; paradoxically, just when policy makers abandoned the idea of correcting behavior, prisons were rebranded as correctional facilities, a euphemism worthy of Orwell. The first half of the 1800s saw something of a renaissance in American punishment: prison reform movements, informed public involvement, social supports, and rehabilitative programs. The founders of this system were men of high purpose—they envisioned prisons as something more than simple warehouses for convicted felons. By comparison,

---

2. Tyler Cabot, "The Prisoners of Guantanamo," *Esquire*, September 2011

when Fyodor Dostoyevsky spent four years (1850 to 1854) as a political prisoner in a military labor camp in Siberia, all the prisoners wore leg-irons, day and night, and had half their heads shaved for quick identification. Sometimes the forehead or cheek was branded to indicate the particular crime committed.

During these years, penologists and social scientists from throughout Europe (most notably, Alexis de Tocqueville) were dispatched across the Atlantic to learn how the United States handled incarceration. Of particular interest were the two cutting-edge models of penological thought: the Auburn style of New York, which stressed penance through work; and, the Pennsylvania System at Eastern State Penitentiary, championed by Quakers who thought the path to salvation lay in solitary Bible reading during waking hours. Silence was enforced whenever an inmate was out of his cell—Auburn prisoners were made to move about in a silent, lock-step shuffle, while men at Eastern were hooded when leaving their cells, and wore felt-bottomed shoes to muffle their footsteps. Regarding his inspection of Eastern in 1842, Charles Dickens wrote: "In its intention, I am well convinced that it is kind, humane, and meant for reformation; but I am persuaded that those who devised this system of Prison Discipline, do not know what they are doing."[3] Isolation, it turned out, was as likely to produce mental illness as remorse. For self-sustaining economic reasons (Auburn's industries actually turned a profit in the early years of existence), most American prisons came to be patterned after Auburn and were as much silent factories as they were prisons. But the real revolution was that both models put prisoners in their own cells. Before then, all was squalid with dangerous communal living. Such dungeons were the fate of debtors, scofflaws, and criminals of all stripes in the salad days of our nation. These early places of incarceration ranged from large, wood-frame houses, to an abandoned

3. "Philadelphia and Its Solitary Prison"

copper mine, which Connecticut repurposed as its state prison in 1790.

Even the premise of incarceration is relatively new. While there were isolated cases of being locked away in a dungeon or tower, or being placed under house arrest, for millennia punishment was doled out publicly, in the streets. Tickets were sometimes sold for these public spectacles. Pillorying, whipping, stoning, hanging, and beheading—these passed for amusing cautionary tales in a time before the *Jerry Springer Show*.

There are men in here with practically nothing besides the clothes on their backs and the overabundance of psychotropic medication coursing through their brains. They too can tell you of hard time. They live off the land, which is to say, the state. If, for whatever reason, they can't eat what the mess hall is serving, they go hungry. Their cells are bare, and they pace or stare at the wall, fighting the intrusive forces of delusion. In the yard they pick up cigarette butts, and bum matches— a base-of-the-Maslow-Pyramid-existence. Yet, they live better than the one-in-fifteen Americans living in extreme poverty or the billion people starving on earth on any given day— they have a roof over their heads, access to potable water and indoor plumbing, receive medical care, eat three hot meals a day, and are paid a few dollars a week with which to buy coffee, cigarettes, snacks, or toiletries.

As David Brooks recognized in *The Social Animal*, the traits that correlate with fulfillment are the ability to understand and inspire people; to read situations and discern underlying patterns; to build trusting relationships; to recognize and correct one's shortcomings; and, to imagine alternate futures.

In other words, it's not the external world that matters so much as our conscious relationship with it; it is with this in mind that I often silently survey my peers and try to suss who's content.

Last week, during lunch in the mess hall, I sat with two acquaintances, Teddy and Benny. Benny gets a kosher tray; it's decent vis-à-vis standard fare, but the fresh veg, tuna, bread, and snack are nothing to write home about. Standard fare for that day's lunch happened to be beef goulash, which bears little resemblance to the version one finds in the world. I concentrated on the apple and water. Teddy, picking through the watery brown slop with his spork, declared: "This shit is straight trash." This was met by our fourth tablemate with the requisite griping about the quality of our menu.

Teddy eyed the contents of Benny's Styrofoam tray. "Damn, Benny, they give you pudding every day?"

"Couple times a week," said Benny.

"Can't remember the last time I had a snack pack . . . they should give them to us, too." He continued on this long-form plea via guilt trip.

Benny picked up his pudding cup with a smile, and asked Teddy if he wanted it.

"Hell, yeah," Teddy said, already reaching. "But, only if you're not gonna eat it."

Benny is in his fifties, from the Dominican Republic, and has been down twenty years. Teddy is a Puerto Rican in his twenties, from the city, and has only been away for two. Both are doing fifty-to-life.

No sooner did Teddy finish, scraping the walls of the pudding cup, than he lost himself in a momentary piece of thinking. "Yo, Benny, how do I get on the kosher diet?"

For Teddy, nothing is ever enough, whereas Benny, you give him an inch, he asks, Are you sure? Can you spare it? Setting aside the manipulative nature Teddy is yet to grow out of, his comments highlight textbook hedonic adaptation; we are very good at habituating to positive things. It comes easily and naturally, one only needs to observe a child who has grown bored of playing with a brand-new toy before its wrapping is even cleaned off the floor. The real work lies in adapting to negative things, learning to change yourself when you can't change your circumstances. Habituation to good things means there exist endless possibilities to be dissatisfied until you get the next new, shiny, sweet-smelling, great-tasting treat. Every wisdom tradition offers advice on keeping this drive in check (Thou shalt not covet thy neighbor's snack pack). By contrast, adapting to negative things increases one's happiness quotient; adapt to a low point, and unless you're a special case, you don't actively seek out a harsher situation.

If I were to inform Teddy that one hundred years ago, not only did prisons not provide pudding cups, but "carrying the baby" (that is, being chained for months to a twenty-five pound iron ball, which one would carry in order to walk) was a common punishment, he might realize how good we have it now. More likely, he'd say he didn't give a fuck.

When I feel sorry for myself, I eventually call to mind a young girl from a documentary film: bald from chemo, she wore a hat to play with her friends, and didn't want special treatment. I have the feeling that merely admiring her courage is in itself a positive coping mechanism; by focusing on her actions, perhaps I will behave likewise. Look for a universal trait amongst those who adapt well, and you will find a lack of self-pity.

Later in the day, I had occasion to speak with Benny, and wanted to know why he gave Teddy his dessert.

"He wanted it more than I did."

The ease and brevity with which Benny answered was reminiscent of Zen parables. And, also the Law of the Jungle: Remain calm and share your bananas. There is a wide gulf between the inner resources of these two men. Teddy—with his unchecked id, frantically dependent on others—is not a happy camper. Benny—thousands of miles from his loved ones—has a quiet contentment about him. He is like Herman Melville's narrator in *Typee* who came to be stranded on an unknown island in the South Pacific, and "determined, therefore, to make the best of a bad bargain, and to bear up manfully against whatever might betide."

What's your secret? I wanted to know. How is it you're so content?

Benny is humble, he didn't see himself as behaving in any special manner. But I persisted, and he told me about his childhood in the Dominican countryside. Benny was the second eldest of eight brothers and sisters; his father owned a country store. They were not poor, but by no means were they well off. For breakfast each morning, the father had the mother cook yucca, even though they could have afforded better. Why can't we have eggs and sausage? Benny and his siblings would complain. The father said that he did it so as to toughen up his kids, so that they would be better equipped to deal with whatever life threw their way.

"Ah, a good lesson," I said. "But, how did you take it at the time?"

Benny smiled. "We called him a cheap prick."

Be that as it may, Benny eventually realized his father's wisdom; he uses it as a Jacob's Ladder out of life's pits of despair and self-pity. As Frankl and survivors throughout history have learned, Benny has recast his predicament into an opportunity for growth. "How we cope," wrote Mihaly Csikszentmihalyi in *Flow* "is both the most important factor in determining what effect stress will have and the most flexible resource, the one most under our personal control."

Once again, the inner decision. Prison is a place where it's easier to believe in despair than happiness, but all that means is we have our work cut out for us.

A few lines from Graham Greene's *The Third Man* have stuck with me, so conducive are they to a positive reframing of my situation: "In Italy for thirty years under the Borgias, they had warfare, terror, murder, and bloodshed—but they produced Michelangelo, Leonardo da Vinci, and the Renaissance. In Switzerland, they had brotherly love, five hundred years of democracy and peace, and what did that produce? The cuckoo clock."

Some years ago, in Prison A, Whit was given the opportunity to begin a garden in an evacuation yard ensconced between two buildings. It was a large grass courtyard, pockmarked with the remnants of gardens past, pathetic affairs gone to seed. With a studied, deliberate approach, he began a proper garden. Whit planted veg, of course—zucchini, bok choy, tomatoes, eggplant, beans, peas, potatoes—berries, and more, and while it certainly added to our nightly meals, the food was beside the point, and often given away to guards or our peers, sometimes in exchange for the damnedest things: seeds brought in from home in a lunch pail; egg shells and coffee grounds for the compost pile; recycled plastic containers for seedlings; bits of twine fashioned into a rickety trellis on which beautiful roses grew. But his real love was the aesthetic, the vast, central flowerbed that stretched easily fifty yards. Over the years of Whit's stewardship, that yard became a lush oasis, verdant and peaceful. Truly, a world apart from the seething madness that is Prison A. Administrators would often stray from official tours to admire his garden. The flowers appeared all season long, blooming like a slow-mo display of fireworks. Yellow, purple, and white crocuses popped up, often through melting snowpack. Sunbursts of daffodils. Vibrant tulips with perfect red petals. Large, sweet-smelling irises, with fuzzy yellow beards and purple curls, enough for van Gogh. Stargazer lilies, positively lusty as they spread wide their creamy limbs, sunburned and freckled toward the center.

I was enlisted as part-time help—weeding, watering, edging a bed, digging out rocks, pushing an old, manual mower. As a boy, my parents tried to get me to do a tenth of the work and I bridled. Now, the labor—albeit hard—was liberating, and I did it gladly, mainly to help my friend whose knees aren't what they once were, but also to return to the work I so hated in my youth, this time behaving properly.

One afternoon in late summer, the angle of the sun and the smell of slightly cool air acted on me like a tranquilizer. I followed Whit and Doc as they toured the beds, using botanical shorthand as my parents would, to comment on this or that plant's progress. We foraged and grazed, chewing on bitter rose hips to cleanse the palate between brightly colored courses of mustardy nasturtium.

More than a few of my peers were of the mind that I was wasting my time out there, tending to flowers when I could've been growing more to eat. But one doesn't live on veg alone. It was the flowers—a raucous, riot of color, delicate and fragrant—that helped transcend a cold, hard existence. And pity on them, I thought, for not appreciating the view.

I came to realize that it's sometimes easier for me to appreciate these niceties because of my past. I grew up in a house that had grass and gardens, inhabited a world where a premium was placed on these things. While I miss it more than someone who never knew this life, I can return to these places in my mind, and appreciate them when I encounter a simulacrum of the past. Whit cultivated his garden, I give the memories as much sunshine as I'm capable of. In fact, I often find myself getting lost in a banal piece of sensory information. A musty smell reminds me of different vacation homes. Sunburns, Noxzema, and a new shower curtain get me floating on a sunbaked pool raft. The cell I inhabited several months ago—over one hundred years old, tiny, with a vaulted concrete ceiling—conjured Spanish dwellings, places I only encountered through Hemingway. While my peers vehemently railed against the cramped quarters, I found it downright cozy. I even reread *Pamplona in July*.

My life is not all coconut shrimp and just-picked nasturtium. These creature comforts are notable for their general absence. Unlike in my past, when all was a never-ending buffet of wish fulfillment, I am grateful.

Some of my peers have nicer clothes than I, more possessions, some make more money, eat better, and have more perks—but I also hear their angry frustration, the attachment to things, the longing. I recognize a facet of my old self, and know that my quality of life is better. The formula—friends, self-sufficiency, and quiet contemplation—is Epicurean. Such is the nature of progress. As Georgia O'Keeffe said: "It is what I have done with where I have been that should be of interest."

And what I have done, after quite a few years, is learn something of resilience. For if, as Gibbon suggests, solitude is the school of genius, then prison—enforced solitude—is the school of resilience. The resiliency of some of my higher-functioning peers is used as a shield against the ravages of prison: their humor (often dark) provides a critical sense of perspective; they know when and how to form attachments to others, so as to be able to give and receive warmth; they create and maintain an inner psychological space that protects against many of the intrusions of abusive others and an uncaring system. Beginning life as a pampered, pleasure-centered creature, I have found my schooling in the very prison experiences that are said (not always incorrectly) to be detrimental to one's character. I have learned that self-control, drive, and a willingness to pay attention are more indispensable than anything else, and with persistent exercise, these traits can lead to numerous admirable characteristics, empathy chief among them. Randy Pausch didn't mean it literally in "The Last Lecture," but it's been the case with me: "Brick walls let us show our dedication." Anyone who transcends a hard environment can talk about walls, barriers, limits beyond which it appears impossible to venture. If lucky, you learn from practice that built into every limit is a space beyond it. Think beyond the whole: there's never a there there.

Beyond survival is adaptation. From there, growth. You may as well ask the cactus how it survives Death Valley. Yes, tough skin and thorns, but also flowers, and an ability to sustain life with precious little nourishment. We become accustomed to everything, and that, perhaps, is the best definition of human beings. American POWs who endured some truly horrific shit in the so-called Hanoi Hilton adapted to misfortune when it became obvious it wouldn't change. They learned to be optimistic realists and strengthened their moral code in the face of inhuman treatment. Like most people who live through what others consider untenable, they downplay their survival (*What choice did I have?*) and talk of those who didn't make it home. Perhaps most remarkable is that, given the choice, many POWs wouldn't eliminate the experience, so transformative an effect did it have on their lives—the experience wasn't good, but it was worthwhile, in that it led to forging meaning and creating identity.

Jorge Luis Borges, writing about his progressive blindness, referred to every misfortune as having "been given for an end."[4] "Those things are given to us to transform, so that we may make from the miserable circumstances of our lives things that are eternal, or aspire to be so." It is this type of transformational thinking that accounts for why the same circumstance could prompt one to write a chapter in his memoir, and his neighbor to leave a suicide note.

The space beyond growth is contentment. One gets there through a systematic realignment of expectations; by learning self-awareness and leaving off the self-pity; and by always being mindful of those who have lived through much worse, and those who are, at this very moment—around the globe and right next door—living a harder existence. Mitigate the downside, and the upside will take care of itself.

Two summers ago, when I first arrived at Prison F, there was a rash of suicides. Seven in total, out of a population of 1,500, over the course of three months. Some blamed the triple-digit temperatures, the air thick and close like a third world favela. Many of my peers riled themselves up if you refused to believe the guards didn't stage these suicides (actually, one or two were suspicious enough to warrant an outside investigation of the guards and supervisory staff working

4. "Blindness"

in the respective housing locations, but the deceased had no family or friends, so no one raised much of a fuss).

During that beastly hot summer, when my peers seemed to be dropping like flies, this place felt like a combat zone. I was numbly standing in the hallway at eight A.M., the temperature already in the high eighties, as forty or so of us were stopped in company formation, waiting to proceed to breakfast. The guards' walkies crackled to life with calls for assistance, a location, the terse back-and-forth of supervisors, then: ". . . better bring the stretcher." The stretcher was produced from an unmarked room, a makeshift parking garage for this conveyor of maladies. With a nurse in tow wheeling an oxygen tank, a guard walked past with the stretcher—an incongruously shiny yellow, up-market Stryker—and nodded to the guard escorting us to chow: "Another one." It was the second suicide in as many days.

Prison F, just like Prison A, has a haunted house that proves too much for some inmates. This dark carnival also features scary rides, games of chance, tests of strength, a freakier show than Prison A. But if there's one attraction that typifies Prison F, it's the motorbike rider inside a spherical cage: smoky and dangerous, you have to keep spinning or gravity will take hold, breaking your neck. Moving fast, tear-assing around, but going nowhere. And loud, too.

In Prison A, I bemoaned the presence of loud neighbors, but was thankful there were actual floors in the cellblock's design. Now, I live on the fourth floor of an open-tiered block, meaning I can toss my pen past the narrow catwalk in front of my cell and it will drop all the way to the flats, the ground floor. Things generally don't fall, however, so much as rise—heat, odors, voices, blaring televisions and radios. My aural landscape is now comprised of about ten men in each direction, times four floors. There is a multiplicity of Chuis, the closest being Chino, on the floor directly beneath mine. While Chui resembled Saddam Hussein, Chino is a Dominican version of Kim Jong-un who sounds like Jabba the Hutt.

He works in the kitchen, so, daily, he recounts to his neighbor all the food he was able to eat or smuggle out. Chino's also a degenerate gambler who shouts along with televised sporting events at a volume that would make Chui wince.

I keep in touch, third party, with Whit and Yas, and we trade humorous anecdotes about Chino and Chui, laughable annoyances in our respective narratives. Yas is still in Prison A, working to get a much-deserved sentence reduction, something that gets him home in his midfifties instead of his seventies. Whit's been transferred to the very desirable Prison J, the best joint in the state—but he'll soon be moving on to Prison K, since he's been accepted into a prestigious master's program offered there. Alas, our éminence grise, Doc, two years from a parole board, was admitted to an outside hospital. Debilitated from cancer, he died in the arms of his loving wife. Rest in peace, old friend. Renzo's where I left him in Prison A, hammering away at his leather work, singing along to classic rock (I can almost hear Chui screaming in the background). I recently got word that Tommy, not wanting to serve out his life sentence, has been trying to overdose on any pills he can get his hands on, and his once-sharp mind has begun to slip away. Ray, now just a couple years away from release, has been transferred to a medium-security prison—I'm sure he's the same Ray as always, and he's coming soon to a town near you. I send holiday cards to my former boss, Mr. Bernard, never neglecting to include a comedic drawing of Jimbo (who's been released). Despite the distance, Jameson's help and friendship has never wavered, and it's mostly thanks to him that you're reading these words. He continues to come into Prison A, keeping alive the writers' workshop. New men have entered the workshop, Yas amongst them—they join Dean, Jose, and Bob P.

Long live my old friends. While I have many acquaintances here, none compare to Whit, Yas, and Doc; the bar was set so high during my last years in Prison A, that I doubt I'll ever again feel such familial bonds with my peers. Especially not here, where the inmate population turns over quickly and is comprised mostly of guys just getting out of the Box. A tough crowd.

No two ways about it, Prison F is a fucking dive. However, it will always occupy a warm corner of my heart. It was here where I finally tossed out the last drug in my bag o' tricks—weed—and have remained sober for over two years. Odi, the drug monster and self-styled Trimalchio, has finally, belatedly, been laid to rest. Not only can I now avoid dealing with scumbag dealers and their attendant drama, but my mental state is considerably more stable. Thoughts of suicide have greatly diminished, depression is less frequent and less severe. I'm still processing the guilt and shame of my senseless crime, and working to forgive myself, but no longer unconsciously punishing myself with self-destructive behavior. I still hate what I've done, along with the pain I've caused, but I've come to not hate myself like I once did, and maybe that's as good as it gets for me, to no longer be at war with myself.

If only my gut got the cease-fire message. After endoscopy, colonoscopy, multiple blood tests, my G.I. condition remains unnamed, though I've gotten better at avoiding foods that trigger my symptoms, and the stomachaches and instances of malaise are less frequent. While I miss pizza and chocolate, etc., I count myself lucky not to have developed a gluten allergy, like my friend Al, who's given rice cakes in the mess hall along with each meal. Plain rice cakes.

I've met up with quite a few men I knew in Prison A, many of whom wound up here the hard way. But, walking laps in the yard one late-summer afternoon, a familiar face in the bleachers prompted a long, unbelieving second look. It was the ghost of Chris, my deceased friend from Prison A's writers' workshop. On the next pass, I walked up into the bleachers—just me and my dark sunglasses—and sat a couple spaces from the ghost. When I got his attention, I asked if he'd done time in Prison A. Pulling off my sunglasses, I asked if he'd recognized me.

"Yeah," he said, squinting into the sun. "What's up, man?"

"Ain't shit," I said. "It's nice to see you. Alive."

Chris told an incredible story: taken by ambulance from Prison A, practically dead, stabilized in a local hospital; transferred to Prison J, which had a unit for inmates with terminal cancer; granted a medical parole with the understanding that he'd be dead inside of a month; not having the courtesy to die within three months, he was ordered to report to Prison E, to be processed back in so as to finish serving his remaining eight years. Chris's girlfriend accompanied him for what can only have been the hardest drive of his life—she was tearful the entire way. He hugged her good-bye and walked in the prison's door a free man. In under a minute he was locked in a bull pen where he waited to be given a new uniform, complete with his old inmate number.

On the plus side, the cancer was in remission and Chris was optimistic about his odds. Having learned my lesson somewhere along the way, I didn't press for details. He was "fucking stoked" to hear that I wrote about him, but was transferred to a medium-security prison before he got to "read that shit."

I was fucking stoked myself to have reconnected with Chris (and learn that he did, after all, receive *Emergency Medicine*, the unfinished manuscript we tried so hard to send to his family years ago).

But what I will remember most fondly about Prison F is the room off the visit room—mauve tiles, tan wallpaper, similar to a highway's newish rest area—where Lily and I were married two years ago by a justice of the peace, a short, friendly woman. My friend David almost made the five-hour drive to be our witness, but it was a winter weekday, and life interrupted (I entered into this marriage, I joked with him, because one ball and chain in my life wasn't sufficient). It would've been cool to have our families there, especially my brother, but prison doesn't work like that—I'm allowed only two visitors at a time. Jersey, with an SS tat on his forearm, who I knew from Prison A, was also getting married that afternoon, so we served as witnesses for each other. As Lily and I said our vows, exchanging wedding rings, I held her hand, afraid that she'd disappear and I'd wake up.

This from the guy who went into the day dismissive of the proceedings—we didn't need a license or some boilerplate ceremony to prove how much we cherished each other—but damned if I didn't get chills as things got under way. Those words that I'd heard countless times in movies and television were now applied to me, they were coming out of my mouth, clumsily. Lily became my wife, my partner, and *compañera* in the eyes of the law. To have and to hold, to hug; to stay up all night with and talk forever. Our crew of two. I was all a-bubble (still am) that this smart, beautiful woman would choose to share her life with me despite my ugly past, the present circumstances, and an uncertain future. After having a Polariod-like picture taken in front of a tromp l'oeil nature scene, we drank Mountain Dew and Vitamin Water in lieu of champagne, then spent the next several hours laughing and talking. It was a year to the day after she first wrote.

There are times when I touch my wedding ring, reassuring myself that Lily isn't a figment of my wildest hopes. It's been quite a ride, this life inside, and now I have twelve-and-a-half years in: halfway to the parole board. Some years ago, my friend Boston (guess where he's from), who had four in on an eight-year sentence, remarked that he felt good at the halfway point, knowing he could do another four years just like he handled his first four. Unlike Boston, who had a determinate sentence, I've got "life" on the back end of mine, so it's up to a parole board to say when I get released, if ever. The prospect of repeatedly being denied parole every two years until either Lily or I is dead is enough to physically depress me. On top of that looming gloom, there will, naturally, be hard times, rough patches for me—events I fear so much, superstition prevents me from even naming them.

Still, a halfway point—though, likely, twelve-and-a-half won't be my halfway point—is an important psychological marker: You've covered this much ground, boy-o, pace yourself, stay strong, and you'll make it home.

For some time, Jameson has gently nudged me toward disclosing my crime, on the grounds that a publisher will likely insist on it. He also thinks it would be good for me—a rite of passage that my actions have set before me. He presumes—correctly, I have to believe—that you will share this curiosity.

Speaking to my grandma over the years, I'd often tell her about a new friend I made, a positive encounter, wanting her to know that her grandson is doing OK. Inevitably, she'd ask what my friend's crime was. I used to get annoyed, and would think to myself, *After all the talk of positive human connection, all she wants to know is what he did.* But I understand her curiosity. I'd often have to tell her, "He's guilty of murder."

The truth is, *I'm* curious about all the crimes of certain peers, mainly the guys who seem out of place. Self-disclosure is easiest for the drug dealers and robbers, hardest for the rapists, and, falling in the middle, are those like me, who committed murder. Sometimes the details are found out in rough outline: a guy gets curious about another or wants ammunition to use against him, so he surreptitiously learns his full name and asks over the phone for someone to consult Google. It's bad form to ask what someone's in for, but because I inspire such cognitive dissonance, guards and peers ask, in effect, what I'm doing here. I'll say, Murder, and they'll want more, yet I won't go much further than that. It's none of their business. Even for those I trust with most everything else, a profound sense of shame and guilt prevents me from confiding in them about my crime. Unlike someone who committed murder, in the course of fending off an attacker, I cannot say I was defending myself. Unlike him, I entertain no self-righteous anger, and readily accept that I must do time.

What I'm about to share with you, I've shared with only a handful of people over the years. I've kept a close circle on this mainly because it has considerable heft, the victims need to be respected, and talking about this is damn hard. Plus, there's the fear that people would stop speaking to me if they knew what I did. So I am entrusting you with my worst, and hoping you'll understand.

Better to just rip the Band-Aid.

I killed my parents, two wonderful people who brought me into the world and loved me.

This is harder for me to write than it is for you to read.

In my mind, where this impossible fact has to be arranged among memories and multiplying regrets, the trouble all began when I experimented with hard drugs in college, or maybe it goes back to previous drug use, my early teens. I was insecure and anxious, and used various substances over the years to quiet the inner turmoil. There were incidental brushes with authority and the law, and I was bailed out of scrapes whose hardest consequences it would've done me well to suffer, but it is the rare parent who allows that to happen. Senior year in college, my path crossed that of a pretty girl, who happened to be an intravenous heroin user. It took little prompting for me to begin sticking a needle in my arm. Within two days I was physically addicted to heroin, and life as I knew it had ended. I became a junkie, a creature that did anything to shoot up every eight hours to avoid getting sick, even if that meant lying to and stealing from loved ones. Attempting to appear functional, I covered up track marks, lied endlessly, and my parents allowed themselves to be deceived, because no one wants to admit that their kid is a junkie.

When it became all too apparent what I was up to—bloody syringes and a blackened spoon found by my mom—they brought me to a psychiatrist for help. The help didn't help. Or rather, I didn't allow it to. The cocktail of meds I was prescribed did nothing to lessen my withdrawal symptoms, and I was violently sick within eight hours. Rather than suffering through detox, I went that evening to cop, cured my sickness like I'd learned to do, and continued the dishonesty that accompanies drug use. I kept up the charade for my parents, while socking away the pills I was supposed to be taking each day. When it came time for a piss test at the end of my supposed seven-day detox, I didn't bother showing up at the doctor's office. Alcoholics talk of hitting bottom— junkies dig a hole to China. It took all of sixteen months to dig myself into that hole, one bag of dope at a time. My parents didn't know what to do, so they started calling inpatient detox centers. The waiting lists were months long. After talking it over amongst themselves, they gave me the option of getting clean or leaving home. I was twenty-three years old, had just crashed out of another job, expended my last favor from every friend months ago, and any money I'd had already went up my veins. Get clean or hit the streets. I said I'd get clean, excused myself to go to the bathroom, and shot up my remaining eight bags.

My parents were smart, capable people, so they thought they could get me sober by themselves by keeping me confined for seven days. Within twenty-four hours, sicker than sick, I tried to run away by grabbing the car keys. Witnessing this mad dash, they shouted to me as I locked myself in their car, saying they'd report it stolen if I drove away. So I went back in, and pleaded with them to take me to an emergency room. Understandably, they thought this was another ploy, and besides, who knew if a hospital would even admit me. They stood firm: get clean or get out. Alone in my room, I fondled a kitchen knife, trying to work up the nerve to kill myself. I couldn't imagine a future in which I got clean, but I could see no way to continue living like this. How long I sat there I do not know, but eventually a powerful longing took over.

I envisioned shooting up again, maybe overdosing, hopefully overdosing, but at least getting high again. Just one more time. That was what I latched on to. I unearthed the pills that

I was supposed to have taken to help withdraw, swallowed all two handfuls of them, then washed it down with half a bottle of Scotch. I wanted to go to sleep and wake up days later, sober.

Sometime later I awoke. Was it the same day? It was dark outside, and I couldn't feel anything. Vision blurry, arms and legs tingling, head hollowed out. Nauseated. Dizzy. The room spun and telescoped and throbbed. I was apart from time. Seemingly from above, I watched myself leave the room. Floating.

When I came to, I was barreling down a road, oncoming headlights honking past. I skidded to a stop on the side of the road, opened the door, and threw up.

How does one know what he did without knowing what he did? It's like looking back on another person, or remembering a movie. It's still surreal now. How could I have done it?

Years later, having my grandma ask me that question, and knowing just how much my actions have affected, and continue to affect, the entire family—you don't know what sorrow and regret are. The best I can come up with is that there is no sense to be made of the senseless, and that's just as unsatisfying to my family and me as it probably is to you. If you haven't been addicted to heroin, you'll never know the hold that drug has. But most addicts don't kill their parents. What was I thinking? I wasn't. I was reacting, a dope-sick animal in a confined space, getting sweatier and more desperate by the second, frantically searching for an exit. It was a recipe for tragedy.

That's not an excuse, it's just my terrible reality. I am accountable. I am responsible, but absent heroin, I'd still have my parents. This is how powerful a demon that drug is.

More than one person has ruefully asked what my parents were thinking. I have to believe that they didn't fully know what they were up against, but they loved me more than anything, and they wanted to help. They pitted the power of love against the power of heroin. In that moment, heroin won. They didn't volunteer for this sacrifice, so I work every day to prove worthy of it, to demonstrate that their love was stronger than my addiction after all.

When Lily reached out to me for advice on her son, it reinforced for me how a parent will do anything for her child to be safe. Getting clean has allowed me to receive love from my family. They are truly great people. I've had their support despite what I did, and they continue to love me. The way I get through every day is to imagine that my parents are watching me, and I behave in a manner that makes them proud. Even in these horrid places I work to be the person they raised me to be. I'd like to think that I've developed the skills they knew were in me all along. This tragedy has been my catalyst for change. My mom and dad wanted me to get clean, be safe, healthy, and make use of my potential. I honor those wishes.

That's what I lost sight of in the past, when I was seeking connection in all the wrong places. I lost an unconditional support system because of my actions, so I've had to work to establish those connections, I've had to learn to trust others, and, even harder, to trust myself. This is why family support and the connections I've made in here are so valuable. Never again will I take that love for granted. I'm the guy who ends every phone call with an "I love you." With my family I mourn the loss of my parents, but it is, of course, a painfully complicated grief, since I am the cause of that loss. Self-loathing accompanies my grief, as other strong feelings attach to theirs.

What's kept me from killing myself is the same thing that's kept me from using heroin again: it would be a slap in the face of my parents' memory. You would've liked them. My mom was talented and smart and creative, and though I bridled at her grammar lessons, I am now grateful for them.

I always admired my dad for how smoothly he navigated the world, and for helping me be a person others like spending time with. And for his thoughtfulness. I will never forgive myself for what I did to them, the family, and myself. But what I can do is live each day as if I am living it for them.

If I get out, I will have spent more time in prison than I've spent as a free man. So I fold the worst thing I ever did into the narrative of who I hope to be. I seek meaning in this tragedy, knowing that I'll never truly find it. I will continue to cry for my parents and the loss felt by my family. I will continue to cry silently at the chain of events that led to me, and no one else, taking my parents' lives.

Por favor perdoname. Me hacen falta, y los amore siempre. I love you, Mom. I love you, Dad. I miss you terribly and hope we meet again.

Six years ago, I was kicked out of Prison A's honor block after a pipe (which tested positive for cannabinoid residue) was found in my cell. It was a friend's, but that's not to say I didn't also help accumulate its residue. While my disciplinary hearing was ongoing, I was kept in honor block, but confined to my cell.

My peers stopped by, offering trite palliatives, fishing for gossip, taking a vulture-like interest in personal items I wouldn't be bringing with me when I moved out of the block. I felt like the living dead. But not everyone made me feel worse. A big lift came from Bishme, a guy I'd never particularly cared for.

On the way to the slop sink to wash his clothes one quiet morning, he stopped in front of my cell, set down his plastic laundry bucket, and asked how I was doing. His tone was more genuine than those of some of my close friends. This was someone who'd been kicked out of honor block before, and knew what it was like going back to population—the lack of privileges, louder living quarters, rougher neighbors. I told him that I really wasn't looking forward to being kicked out, and hoped that, somehow, I'd be able to stay (we maintain our delusion of reprieve even as the gas canisters hiss into the chamber). He didn't call me foolish for entertaining such hope, but neither did he encourage it, as did most of my friends behind their sad masks. What Bishme did was tell me a story.

He'd met a nice woman through a pen-pal service, and the two had developed a very warm relationship—letters, calls, visits. Suddenly, he wasn't alone, and there was love waiting for him at mail call. After more than a year together, they decided to marry. He worked in prison industry and busted his ass hauling scrap metal for eighteen bucks a week; saving for months, he sent his fiancée 200 dollars, and had her pick out a pair of wedding rings. They filled out the requisite paper work with the Department, and waited as their application for a marriage license worked its way through the proper channels.

On the day they were to be given the license, she visited with Bishme until a correction counselor stopped over and had her join him in an office adjoining the visit room. In the office, he went through Bishme's rap sheet, per procedure, to make sure the fiancée knew the truth. Veering from established policy, he attempted to dissuade her from marrying a convicted felon. She was aghast. Finally, Bishme was brought in, the couple signed on their respective lines, and a marriage date was set for the end of the month—a justice of the peace would officiate at a ceremony in the very same office. They returned to their table in the visit room and celebrated with cranberry juice and vending-machine sandwiches. With the process nearly complete—the upcoming ceremony but a formality—the couple was happy.

In front of my cell, Bishme luxuriated in that memory for a moment, reliving sensory details: his soon-to-be wife's auburn hair, lustrous in the early afternoon light; her perfume, soft and sweet smelling; their knees touching under the table.

It was the last time he saw her. Bishme would later learn—indirectly, through an inmate who was mopping a floor when it happened, and from her, in a letter—that, leaving the visit, she was accosted by several guards wanting to know why she (a white woman) would marry Bishme (an incarcerated black Muslim). Obstructing the exit, they asked if she knew he had raped and killed a woman (she didn't, because he hadn't). Of course he didn't tell you about it, they said, and he'll deny it if you ask him—got off on a technicality, so the records are sealed, but we have access to them. One of the guards named where she works, and asked what her coworkers would think if they found out she was married to a convict. These guards worked in the visit room, after all, and had a copy of her driver's license. One asked if her neighbors knew she spent afternoons in Prison A's visit room, surely there were good men to pick from in her home town, better guys than a convict-black-Muslim-rapist. In the moment, I imagine she felt herself imprisoned, and powerless against the reach of an omniscient monolith. Crying, she nudged past the guards and quickly walked out the front gate.

It's beside the point to ponder their motives, whether they were acting with demented altruism, hoping to "save" this woman from marrying a prisoner, or just hoping to crush Bishme. If you were to ask, "What gives you the right?" they'd smother your naïveté with their self-righteousness.

In her letter, she explained it all to Bishme, apologized, returned the money he gave her for their wedding bands, and promised to keep in touch. And then dropped off the face of the earth.

"Damn, man," I said to Bishme, through the bars of my cell. "That's a kick in the soft stuff. I'm sorry." I thought: how silly of me to sweat getting kicked out of honor block in light of his having a loving companion ripped from him.

"I got over it," he said. "Here's what you gotta under-stand: when the judge banged his gavel and gave me seventy-five-to-life—that was my worst. What more can they do to me?" In effect, he was saying that the floor on his suffering was set so low, there's no place to go but up. His expectations were realigned.

"Thank you," I said, with utmost sincerity, for it was just the perspective I needed.

"You'll be all right," Bishme said, then picked up the plastic bucket, and walked away to wash his clothes.

It was with a grain of Bishme's salt that I took Rob Johnson's thoughts on using a pay phone. Shortly after reading his line, I found myself outdoors on a winter night, one of twenty men standing at a bank of phones on icy blacktop, in a yard peopled with hundreds of felons. An old Chinese man occupied the phone to my right, a boisterous Ukrainian was on my left, both speaking in their native tongues. I counted myself fortunate for having someone who'd accept my calls, as opposed to guys I know who have been cut off from contact with the outside world for decades. Compared to them, things *are* going well for me, and the pay phone has something to do with it.

In the year since that scene played out, I have maneuvered my way into Prison F's honor block. Now, each night I use a phone indoors, where it is warm and relatively safe. Looking back on my nights spent in the cold yard, I think, *Things are going well*. But, I'm not immune to hedonic adaptation: the novelty of a warm phone booth wore off after a month or so. And therein lies the practice. The daily renewal of gratitude that comes from looking at those who don't have it as good, who have to stand in the rain to use the phone.

As to the time—hard or easy—it's what you make of it. Just like anyplace else on earth, the human experience is a complex and relative thing. Pleasure can often lead to pain, and everyone is in a prison of some kind. They only own you if they own your mind. Freedom comes from within. We should strive to emulate an imaginary golden retriever named Sisyphus, chasing a bright-blue ball up a never-ending hill—retaining faith that we'll prevail in the end, *while* confronting the harsh facts of our current reality—keeping somewhat of a smile on our faces, and wagging our tails. Bitter today—better tomorrow. Don't take life too personally. Meaning is where you make it, and life is absurd. The most we can hope for is the inner strength to make the best of the bad bargains that inevitably come our way. If something is done by one person, it can be done by others. It's not the worst thing to have a little hardship in our lives, the better to learn these important lessons.

The prescription is simple, the practice isn't. You get your mind where it needs to be by thinking about what you think about. You do whatever it takes. You keep going.

ACKNOWLEDGMENTS

The road to published work is dotted with an untold number of serendipitous encounters and gatekeepers. This is doubly true for prison writers. The prison walls keep us in. They also keep the public out. So it is with monumental thanks to the following people that my work has found an audience.

I am forever indebted to Jameson, founder of the workshop in which I grew up as a writer: mentor, tireless advocate, and friend. He taught me craft, provided great literature, and opened my eyes to the great tradition of prison writers. Had our paths not crossed, it's likely I would still be writing short fiction populated by robots and golden retrievers.

Martin and Judith Shepard at The Permanent Press are uncommonly decent people. They began as my publishers and editors, and quickly became caring friends.

Through it all, my family has never given up on me. Words cannot express my gratitude, so I let my actions speak for me. My brother and cousin J have been particularly supportive, whether facilitating a connection, giving balanced feedback, or posting my work on the Interwebz. Maxine, my fairy godmother, always provides encouragement. My grandma, who passed away in 2014, was an early reader of drafts, an impeccable grammarian, and she would've gotten a real kick out of seeing this in print. I miss her dearly.

My friends *inside* have been like family, helping me persevere and helping me write—motivational coaches, close readers, providers of material. Alex, Alexio, Angelo, Ant, Beef, Benny, BG, Bob, Boston, Chris, Dag, David, Dean, Doc, Eric, Francois the K, Geri, Gerry, Glocks, Herman, J-Rock, Jason, Jay, Jake, Johnny 50, Jon, Jose, Kells, Kenny, Larry, Leno, Lo, Luke, Marty, Mete, Mike G, Mike R., Murph, Nick, Paris, Paul, Peter, Petros, Phil, Ray, Renzo, Richie, Rucc, Saleh, San Jose Jay, Sean, Sheldon, Sherif, Spanky, Tony, Valiente, Whit, Yas, and Zen. They are so much more than the sum of their rap sheets.

My friends in the world show me love, even if it doesn't always arrive at mail call. They are well read, and offer sound advice. Abbey, Amy, David, Janet, Karen, Kodos, Macha, and Raina.

There have been volunteers—people who drive great distances, and subject themselves to tedious intake procedures to spend time with inmates—whose empathy I've had the pleasure of basking in. Five years' worth of Saturday mornings were spent with Alan, eating challah, saying a few blessings over grape juice, and discussing global politics. Every Friday night these days, my theatre-group family reinforces for me that there's great fun to be had without drugs, while providing the space to act like my natural freakazoid self.

Certain prison staffers have been kind to me over the years, and I thank them by not going into detail, other than to say that they treated me like a person, not a number, and that made all the difference. Messrs. D, F, L, L, M, N; Mss. B, F, M, R; Rabbis K and M.

Big picture, all of us in here are grateful for those advocating for a better criminal justice system: the prison litigators, the outside reformers, CURE, Vera Institute, The Marshall Project, The New Press, Prison Legal News, and The Sentencing Project, to name just a few.

I am thankful to you, the type of reader who reads acknowledgments. You and me both, we stay in our seats to watch the credits roll.

And a special thank you goes to my lovely wife, Lily, who is still too good to be true. In addition to rescuing me from the unending loneliness of prison, she remains my wise counsel, a wellspring of thoughtful feedback and positivity, the data entry ninja, digital archivist, blogging proxy, social media wrangler, e-mailer, etc., etc. Some couples fight over bills, our squabbles concern formatting in a Word document or her scanner's OCR capabilities. She sacrifices a great deal to be with me. Without equivocation, I am a better person because of her love, and I look forward to writing more chapters about our life together.